PREFACE

Having lived on O`ahu and Maui for almost twenty years as an African American woman, I have witnessed, the constant search for identity, understanding, and the unending search for what it means to be Black in Hawai`i and to live in a space on the earth often referred to as Paradise.

I am no stranger to islands, having been raised on the biggest island of all, New York City. Thus, it's no surprise that I would arrive on the shores of Hawai`i, take up residency, and make my own contributions. I have long held the belief that the world is my laboratory and I, a scientist, can create in a world of endless possibilities.

African Americans in Hawai`i: A Search for Identity provides new information and perspectives on a neglected part of Hawai`i's history. Some of the greatest individuals who have walked these islands during their life time and have contributed and expanded a sense of awareness, diversity, and enrichment to the local communities, extolling values, and raising consciousness, have been black men and women.

I am deeply indebted to those black historians who have paved the way prior to my arrival, and to those who will continue the work after my departure. There are two individuals who have influenced me greatly in the compiling of this book.

First, there is my She/Hero, Kathryn Waddell Takara, PhD. Having met Dr. Takara for the very first time in Spring 2009, I aim to forge an indelible lasting professional relationship. Reading through her voluminous writings, I realized that it was Dr. Takara, whose study, work and research laid the foundation for this book. For without her pioneering work, there might be little, if any, documentation on African Americans in Hawai`i. Dr. Takara hails as the first black educator of Black Studies at the University of Hawai`i, blazing trails and new beginnings for students in their own search. Dr. Takara guided the young minds of her students through interdisciplinary studies and ethnic studies by developing and teaching these instrumental classes on campus. Dr. Takara's research is seen throughout this book and her voice bears witness to the contributions, injustices, and progress made in Hawai`i by African Americans. Dr. Takara's unveiling of the long history of African Americans in Hawai`i, is one of her lifetime goals, to which I pray that someone will continue to document and write the story of our people long after the story ends in this book.

Next, there is Miles M. Jackson, PhD., Professor Emeritus and former Dean of the School of Library Science and Technology at the University of Hawai`i. Dr. Jackson began his search and study of African Americans in Hawai`i after his arrival in Hawai`i. In the past decade, Dr. Jackson has published two books on blacks in Hawai`i, and co-produced a documentary film on blacks in Hawai`i that includes scholars, oral historians and a wide range of contemporary residents. Dr. Jackson contacted me as a performance poet for inclusion into his film, which inspired me to write, research, and photograph blacks in Hawai`i, and document the story. I am honored to have met and conferred with him. To Dr. Takara and Dr. Jackson, I publicly thank you.

For years African Americans have been searching for their place in her/history, a place in which they can continue uninterrupted, to nourish, to nurture, and to grow. Many African Americans are seeking to unfold spiritually, to release their inner imprisoned splendor, and to express their magnificent unique creativity. What a disservice to justice, to have their history and assets marginalized and withheld from society, dating from the birth cradle of the motherland, Africa, to present. The extraordinary contributions of blacks to world civilizations have been ignored and/or lost.

Let the reader examine this book with a genuine eye, and peer into the lives of African Americans in Hawai`i, learning how they have adapted and adjusted to coping, and thriving with life in Hawai`i, leading healthy prosperous lives, and contributing to a society of mixed doctrines and races to survive. After all, survival as a culture is what is important.

Let the reader take a brief overview of some of the values of the Hawaiian culture to better understand how and why many African Americans have felt so comfortable. Hawai`i is renowned for its hospitality. Unconditional aloha, trust, and friendship to all people and the spirit of sharing were fundamental to the early Hawaiian philosophy and way of life.

It is the connection of Hawaii's language and concepts that creates relationships between the people and the environment. The philosophy of Hawai`i is revealed in a few key words. *Aloha* in its' intimacy welcomes the receiver (from the giver) into one's personal space. It is the compassion, love, and forgiveness. Aloha is Hawaii's gift to the world. It is a universal force that transcends race, color, or creed. Aloha is a way of life. *Alaka`i* is about a person's willingness to assume the responsibilities of leadership, while *H`anohano* is to conduct oneself with distinction, honor, and dignity. It describes a regal bearing that one earns through acts of distinction. *Ho`omau* speaks to perseverance and endurance, to be unceasing and committed to achieving a goal or completing a difficult task.

Ho`ohiki* s about keeping one's promises. It is the equivalent of a pledge or oath and a serious commitment to doing what one says one is going to do. *Po`okela means to strive for excellence, to excel, to surpass, to set one's sights to the highest level of achievement.

Ko`kua* is the act of being helpful, to provide relief by assisting others. To lend support whereby one assumes the same sense of responsibility as the receiver of the assistance toward completing a task or activity. *Ku`pono is about uncompromising honesty, to be fair and just in one's relationships, to always seek the just and decent path in one's dealings and decisions. *Lo`kahi* means unity, to be expressed with harmony. *Laulima* is the condition of cooperation that causes everyone to work together toward a common goal, without attention to rank or position, so that one person's success is everyone's success.

And, there are other values, such as: *Malama*, to care for, and to offer support. *Ohana* means family, a deep rooted connection to all, knowing that every living thing is family. *Honua Pono* means living in an expanded relationship with our beloved Mother Earth, the environment, the plants and animals. Honua-earth, pono-truth means we are earth and earth is us.

From these common values in the heart of everyone who remembers, a culture flourished in these islands, a culture that is familiar in African American and African communities. The spirit of the values will guide the canoe. It is the hope and anticipation of this writer that African Americans, in their search for identity, will find before them, inside them, expressed beautifully on the shores of life, in Hawai`i, the blessings of Unity, wholeness, and power, because they persevered and achieved much. Their beautiful color of blackness shines under the rich Hawaiian rainbow.

Historian Legrand H. Clegg, Esq. discusses his research on black migration in an article dated, 1992. In it he speculated on the African origins of the original, indigenous people of Hawaii, but that has yet to be further researched. Clegg writes that, "most anthropologists, paleontologists and archaeologists around the world generally believe that human beings evolved on the continent of Africa, from 3 to 5 million years ago, and that they eventually migrated from Africa into Europe, across Asia, the Pacific Islands and finally to the Americas. In time, these Black settlers developed very advanced societies that sent navigators to explore and settle various islands of the Pacific Ocean. They reached such places as Melanesia, New Guinea, Fiji, New Hebrides, New Zealand, the Society Islands, Tahiti, Easter Island and thousands more."

The ancient land of Hawai`i was much like an African society. It was a series of islands ruled by strong-willed chiefs or kings who believed that they had descended from gods.

No written records of the islands were maintained, so a court genealogist, similar to the African *griot*, recited names, family histories, battles and past glories of a proud people and their royal leaders.

If ever there was a paradise on earth, the Hawaiians appear to have had it. Blessed by a glorious climate, the people basked in the sun and swam in clear water. The people shared their harvest so that no one was without food, and everyone found shelter in the marvelous huts built mainly from the leaves of palm and *hala* trees. "The people worked, swam, sang and danced, isolated from most of the scourges of the rest of the world," writes Maxine Mrantz in *Hawaiian Monarchy, The Romantic Years.* "But that was soon to be changed. The 'Garden' would be discovered. "Gone would be the sunny static days of peace and order. Disease, decadence and cultural shock were to take a terrible toll of the Hawaiian people, decreasing their numbers alarmingly."

Captain James Cook was the first white man to reach Hawai`i. He visited the islands in January of 1778, traded with the natives and was well treated. Through the years, the Hawaiians suffered greatly after contact. Their numbers decimated by diseases, their land taken, and the monarchy overthrown. The last native ruler of Hawai`i was the celebrated Queen Lili`uokalani. Following the queen's ascension to the throne on January 29, 1891, a Chicago newspaper woman, Mary H. Krout, described Lili`uokalani as "strong and resolute. The features were strong and irregular. The complexion quite dark, the hair streaked with gray, and she had the large dark eyes of her race."

The queen was a brilliant writer, poet and composer who worked tirelessly for the welfare of her people. While she sought to strengthen the monarchy and to literally return "Hawai`i to the Hawaiians," the queen was years too late, and died on November 11, 1917, at the age of 79 under house arrest.

American businessmen and missionaries now had strongholds in every corner of Hawaiian culture and were redoubling their efforts to overthrow the monarchy and to place Hawai`i under a provisional protectorate. By the last part of 1892, these plans were carried out and the U.S. Marines were placed around the royal palace.

The queen stood steadfastly against the U.S. forces but finally, on January 17, 1893, she yielded under protest, as was recorded in the "Pacific Commercial Advisor" of January 18th:

"I, LILIUOKALANI, by the Grace of God and under the Constitution of The Hawaiian Kingdom, Queen, do hereby solemnly protest against any and all acts done against myself and the Constitutional Government of the Hawaiian Kingdom by certain persons claiming to have established a Provisional Government of and for this Kingdom.

Now to avoid any collision of armed forces, and perhaps the loss of life, I do under this protest and impelled by said force yield my authority until such time as the Government of the United States shall upon the facts being presented to it undo the action of its representative and reinstate me in the authority which I claim as the Constitutional Sovereign of the Hawaiian Islands."

In 1900 Hawai`i became a territory of the United States and a state by 1959. From King Kamehameha to Queen Lili`uokalani, most Hawaiian rulers were very dark-skinned and had Negroid features. The destruction of this people and their culture and the forceful annexation of their land were tragedies of staggering proportions, and a sad chapter in the history of the United States.

As we move through the chapters of this historic documentation, we begin to feel the invitations conferred upon us, by the spirits of the elders, who seem to be welcoming us into a diverse, yet all embracing spirituality, respecting our humanness.

Ayin M. Adams, PhD.

FOREWORD

Thanks to the foresight of Dr. Ayin M. Adams, PhD., and organizations like the African Americans on Maui Association, and Arts Education For Children Group, the history of African Americans in Hawai`i will not be easily forgotten. With Adams' book entitled *African Americans in Hawai`i: A Search for Identity*, this history will live on, inspiring posterity.

When our Board of Directors for the African American Heritage Society of Long Beach decided to research, the history of Blacks in Long Beach, California, we knew it would be an historic achievement. For too long, this history had been hidden, and lost to our generation. We wanted to document and preserve the early history of African Americans in Long Beach, so that future generations would know their history.

We also wanted to highlight the many citizens who made significant contributions to our city, and tell their stories. Many generations of African Americans have grown up not knowing their history and heritage. As a result, they spend years searching for their identities. Our group published the long-awaited, *"The Heritage of African Americans in Long Beach: Over 100 Years"* in 2007. This book highlights the history and heritage of African Americans in the City of Long Beach. This history has now been documented and preserved for future generations.

The historic *African American National Biography (AANB),* was published by Oxford University Press in February, (Black History Month) 2008. The eight volume set was edited by, Henry Louis Gates, Jr., and Evelyn Brooks Higginbotham. This collection is considered to be the largest publication of biographical and historical recovery in the history of African American studies. The AANB contains the biographies of over 4,000 African Americans, some of them are world famous, and others are not as well known. These books are now in schools and libraries throughout the world. Gates and Higginbotham are still accepting biographies, and hope to collect an additional 2,000, or more within the coming years.

The biographies of President Barack Obama, Betsey Stockton, and Frank Marshall Davis are featured in the AANB series. *African Americans in Hawai`i: A Search for Identity*, has also included their biographies. *Barack Obama* was born in Honolulu, Hawai`i on August 4, 1961. As an African American, he would eventually break barriers in numerous areas. Obama would become the first African American President of the Harvard law review in its 104 year history. On February 10, 2007, Obama announced that he was running for President of the United States. Obama was inaugurated as the 44th President of the United States of America on January 20, 2009. He is the first African American elected to the highest office in our Nation.

Betsey Stockton was born in Princeton, New Jersey in 1798, and was once a slave. Stockton went on to become a missionary, nurse, and educator. In 1822, she traveled with other Missionaries to Hawai`i. Stockton eventually helped establish a school at the Mission in Lahaina, Maui, and also became the Superintendent. Stockton's school became the model for Hampton Institute in Virginia.

Frank Marshall Davis was born in 1905. He was a journalist, labor activist, poet, and expatriate. He lived in Hawai`i for almost forty years. Davis became well known for his writing for the *Honolulu Record*, and he was very outspoken on many controversial issues.

With the publication of *African Americans in Hawai`i: A Search For Identity,* Dr. Adams is paving the way for others to record their neglected history. The reader will find in this book detailed information about the 19th

Century history of early African Americans in Hawai`i, 20th and 21st Century Pioneers who have paved the way for Dr. Adams, and a brief history of cultural and community events.

Cultural and community history events included in the book are contributions to Hawai`i by the Buffalo Soldiers, Black Soldiers during the bombing of Pearl Harbor, Black History Month, Juneteenth Celebration, and the Dr. Martin Luther King Jr. March. Also covered in some detail is information about various social organizations, education, and previous racial/social problems in the military and the community. This book reveals a great deal of the history and heritage of African Americans in Hawai`i that has been overlooked for too many years.

A very important feature of this book are the biographies of many of the African American pioneers of Hawai`i with a focus on their accomplishments. Their biographies give detailed information about their lives, and reveal the tremendous effect that the individuals had on the development of Hawai`i. Some of these pioneers are still living, and contributing to society. They have also been instrumental in helping with the documentation of this book.

The extensive bibliography and credits listed will prove very helpful to anyone wanting to learn more about the culture, the history and heritage of African Americans in Hawai`i. Family historians and genealogists will be happy to find a book like this, because it contains such detailed information and history about outstanding black families in the Islands.

Dr. Adams has done an excellent job of compiling and outlining the history and heritage of African Americans in Hawai`i. This book needs to be in schools and libraries throughout the world. Hopefully, it will serve as an inspiration for others who are interested in researching, documenting, and preserving the history of African Americans in their communities.

Aaron L. Day and Indira Hale Tucker

INTRODUCTION

The urgency to recover the neglected and/or ignored history of blacks in Hawai`i is becoming more apparent with each passing day. Since the election of Barack Obama, the first African American President of the United States, more local and national attention is being focused on Hawai`i black history and the experiences and identity issues of blacks in Hawai`i where Obama passed a formative time of his youth. The ideas and personal philosophy of Barack Obama were undoubtedly influenced by his socialization and education in the Hawaiian Islands and certainly his democratic approach to politics and his beliefs in diversity, unity, and community (ohana) were surely in part formulated by his multi-racial family and life in a multi cultural Hawai`i.

Ayin Adams, PhD. is one of a growing number of scholars and writers who understand the importance of this new historicism and the necessity of publishing African American history in Hawai`i. A long time resident of Hawai`i herself who has worked closely with the local community, Adams explores some of the dilemmas of identity and conflict in a place where Blacks are only 3.5% of the population and presents the unknown successes and triumphs of some special black residents, accompanied by photos. Unfortunately, the local media and education system have ignored, controlled, and/or marginalized blacks in local history. Thus images and perceptions of blacks in Hawai`i have been controlled or omitted, intentionally or by default or ignorance, thereby preserving the dominant American status, culture, and control of power and assimilation. Historically, identity and status in America, Hawai`i, and the world have been based on the privilege of skin color for too long.

Fortunately, at the beginning of the 21st Century, Americans have reached a new plateau exemplified by the election of President Obama. Now we have an emerging New People of mixed races and cultures, a growing population of young people, immigrants, and others full of tolerance and a hopeful optimism, a belief in unity, equality, environmental and social justice, health care reform, and a better understanding and acceptance of otherness. No longer is the world bent on sailing toward whiteness as the only model of success.

The contents of this book are straight and unforgettable. Through reading these selected essays and interviews that validate Hawaii's African Americans' contributions and the historical issues, the reader will also discover issues of identity and pain, resulting from the derogatory images of blacks in western art, literature, and the media that have permeated the local psyche and eroded a positive self image and respect for blacks.

The reader of this book will be left with fresh new images of and respect for blacks in Hawai`i, after learning of their 19th century migrations, leadership roles, successes and contributions to the whaling industry, medicine, business, education, science, civil service, the arts, social work, the military, and politics. The reader will learn that some blacks, before Oprah and other celebrities who have bought homes in the islands, have lived large and often very successful lives and often gone unrecognized in the lush and verdant beauty of the Hawaiian Islands.

In this book, Adams presents selective histories of black residents in the Islands, she presents interviews of some outstanding black residents who talk story, politics and ethics, chewing the water, sharing their experiences of life in the Islands. She presents significant cultural and community organizations and events demonstrating how the small African American community, especially on O`ahu and Maui, works together to perpetuate values and to build a strong community and exemplify their civic responsibilities.

Adams recognizes the power of words to represent and unveil history. She includes essays documenting migrations of blacks to Hawai`i in the 1800s and the histories of those black men who left slavery, families, and/or communities behind. Their initial acceptance into a generous and welcoming local Hawaiian community, their contributions to the small and evolving cultural and business worlds are extolled. Some chapters reveal the increasing alienation and exclusion of blacks and Hawaiians in the growing immigrant community, leading to the current paucity of blacks in the islands compared with other immigrant groups, including Caucasians, Asians, Southeast Asians and Europeans, given their relatively strong representation and successes amongst the foreigners in the early 1800s.

Black contributions to the military in the Pacific theater, island politics, education, sports, medicine and culture are highlighted. The struggle of blacks to navigate between race and culture, ethnicity and history, is energized their enduring spiritual tradition, gallons of patience and buckets of hope. As blacks slowly emerge from a storm of stereotypes, unseen sharks of prejudice still lurk just below the surface of respectability and fair play in the form of glass ceilings, preferential hiring patterns, poverty and homelessness, absence in the media, invisibility in advertisements and tourism, and lingering images that stereotype, demonize, or otherwise make blacks look different and inferior.

Unfortunately, the role of blacks in world civilization and history is almost unknown in the islands, and in the past, youth, especially those with dark skins, have had few positive role models to inspire them to strive for success. With the recent election of President Obama, it is hoped that there will soon be a more balanced teaching of black history in the Department of Education and higher education in Hawai`i, including mythology of ancient dark skinned African gods and goddesses, like Osiris, Isis, Nefertiti, the Queen of Sheba, the early African architects and astronomers, the black Magi, the ancient African universities and history of medicine and surgery, the mathematicians who envisioned the Pyramids, the black Madonnas and Saints, the countless agriculturalists, environmentalists, musicians, actors, healers, dancers, and the genius of black inventors, scientists, and artists. If for no other reason than the future unity of our country is at risk, the values of continuity and connectedness seem important goals to cleave to.

There is medicine in memory. For the past 40 years, blacks have begun to research and write their own history in Hawai`i, debunking the myths and stereotypes, opening doors of opportunities and promoting racial harmonies to displace the feelings of exclusion and marginalization. The absence of aloha accorded the average black resident/immigrant contrasts strong with the aloha shone many others. The lack of inclusion leads to negative behavior and a disproportionate representation in the penal system.

Adams extols the role and value of the keepers of history and culture and understands how they can bring dignity and respect to a group and to individuals. She includes the voices of local black writers, organizers, activists, and the black national anthem, Lift Every Voice and Sing, to show the power of collective effort, the inspiration in music, and the magic of working together for a common aim. She does not accept the mantle of mind control and social and economic violence against blacks. Instead she sees a psychology of spiritual redemption in the study of black history in Hawai`i as the genius, talent, and history of African Americans in Hawai`i is recognized and celebrated like the many other ethnic groups in the Islands; the bonds of fear, mistrust, and color prejudice have no place in these gentle islands and can be released in sharing and learning, history, culture and communication.

Finally Adams shares the speeches of President Barack Obama in an effort to situate and dignify blacks in Hawai`i and their significant and often overlooked and forgotten roles in the values basic to democracy on the national stage. Obama's speeches contain themes of "we not me," freedom, equality and justice under the law, values of citizenship, service, community, family, the sacred environment, spirituality, compassion, health care reform, the end of poverty and homelessness, the development of a progressive, practical and empowering educational system.

In the 21ˢᵗ century, Hawai`i stands first in line in intercultural communication, understanding, and respect for other and different cultures and ethnic groups. Blacks, as a group, must join the circle of aloha and enlightenment by sharing our contributions to local, national and international histories and earning the respect of others. Beyond education, love is the bond that heals and social interaction, intermarriage and mixed race children all help to strengthen trust between groups and keep the soul fires burning. Miscegenation has not been an issue in the islands, although housing, and segregated facilities for the military did promote unsavory racial relations in the past. Today people and groups navigate between the liquid mirror of race and culture to accept each other, to compromise and find mutual interests, to respect our humanity.

Finally, it is important to remember what African Americans have brought and continue to bring to the Hawai`i community. African Americans have brought service, research and inventiveness to the inhabitants. They have shared their gifts of compassion and passion, laughter and song, rhythms and dance, intensity and creativity and of course, the values of family and community. Through their experiences, they have contributed to the history and politics, forging a better understanding of democracy and justice. They have shared in the spirit of nature, beauty, and humility. African Americans have helped to make the islands a better place to live.

Dr. Kathryn Waddell Takara

ACKNOWLEDGMENTS

I am grateful to Spirit. I am grateful for knowing. I am grateful for the Oneness that I share with the Divine Light and the Divine Spirit. I am grateful that I exist this day in the heart of God. I am grateful for all that I have ever been and all that I shall be, so that I may integrate the fullness of the Divine Light into my journey and touch all those whose paths interconnect with mine.

I acknowledge my parents for fulfilling the promise of bringing me into this world. I acknowledge nature that waited patiently for my discovery of her. When I reflect back on my childhood of writing, each original poem neatly written in pencil on colored construction paper, I give thanks for the writing Spirit guides who nurtured my thoughts and quieted my mind, so that the Divine Flow made its presence felt and manifested itself in my life, which is indeed miraculous.

Next, there are those souls whose own light lit my desire and filled me with the unerring possibility that "I must outdo everything I've ever done in the past." As a metaphysical student of Truth, always seeking, always uncovering and recovering a sense of conscious awareness and newness, a challenge was born to create an avenue where I am catapulted into a new dimension. I then decided to create a photo book of pictures of African Americans living and thriving in Hawai`i.

This idea to create a coffee table photo book took shape and began to grow. I acknowledge the hand of God present, and I allow my hand to be placed into the ever expanding all knowing hands of God, to which this book grew by leaps and bounds, culminating in this historic document of African Americans in Hawai`i, including other islands and early histories told orally and written by the historians who came before me. I then knew that I needed to allow the process to unfold very lovingly with the help, contributions, and editing skills of Kathryn Waddell Takara.

With endearing hands, lending their strength, courage, commitment to research, fortitude, and gratitude to this project are, Kathryn Waddell Takara, Aaron L. Day, Indira Hale Tucker, Helene Hale, Miles Jackson, Bryant Neal, John Stan Rippy, Sodengi Mills, Sandra Shawhan, Frieda Groffy, Z'ma Wyatt, Alalani Hill, Karunesh Kumar Agrawal, Arid Chappell, Claire Gibo, Shirlee Teabo, Shirley Davenport, Linn Conyers and many others, here and over there. You are all present with me and your presence is here and now. I salute you all and say, Thank you.

I dedicate this book to the way, the will, and the work of my ancestors, and to my parents, Robert L. Adams and Virginia Glover Adams.

CONTENTS

Preface	Ayin M. Adams, PhD.	iii
Foreword	Aaron L. Day and Indira Hale Tucker	vii
Introduction	Kathryn Waddell Takara, PhD.	ix
Acknowledgments		xii
Contents		xiii
Section I	***Black History in Hawai`i***	1
Chapter 1	The Story Behind: Lift Ev'ry Voice and Sing	2
Chapter 2	African Americans In Hawai`i/Part I	4
Chapter 3	African Americans In Hawai`i/Part II	9
Chapter 4	African Americans In Hawai`i/Part III	12
Chapter 5	African Americans In Hawai`i/Part IV	15
Chapter 6	Betsey Stockton	18
Chapter 7	Nolle Smith/Iwalani Mottl	22
Section II	***Pioneering S/Heroes of the 20th & 21st Century***	31
Chapter 8	Helene Hilyer Hale	32
Chapter 9	Frank Marshall Davis	44
Chapter 10	Kathryn Waddell Takara, PhD.	61
Chapter 11	Miles M. Jackson, PhD.	75
Section III	***President Barack H. Obama***	77
Chapter 12	44th President of the United States	78
Chapter 13	Barack Obama Early Beginnings in Hawai`i	79
Chapter 14	2004 Democratic National Convention Keynote Address	81
Chapter 15	Official Announcement of Candidacy for President of The United States	85
Chapter 16	A More Perfect Union	90
Chapter 17	The American Promise	98

Chapter 18	President-Elect Victory Speech	106
Chapter 19	Inaugural Address	111
Section IV	**_Contemporary Hawai`i_**	141
Chapter 20	Who's Who In Hawai`i	142
Chapter 21	Building The Stone of Hope	172
Chapter 22	Cultural and Community Events:	176
	• Dr. Martin Luther King Jr. March	176
	• Black History Month	184
	• Juneteenth Celebration	186
	• Kwanzaa	187
	• Third Sunday Group at Kamehameha III Park	188
	Contributors	194
	Appendix I	200
	Appendix II	201
	Appendix III	202
	Bibliography	204
	Index	208
	About The Author	215

Section I
Black History in Hawai`i

Chapter 1

The Story Behind: Lift Ev'ry Voice and Sing

Chapter 1 takes a look at the Black National Anthem, "Lift Every Voice and Sing," by two brothers, James and John Johnson. The meaning of this song conveys a sense of hope and unity despite hardship. Although there was no slavery in Hawai`i, readers will see that the long history of African Americans in Hawai`i includes issues of race that have appeared since the 19th century. At President Barack Obama's inaugural ceremony in Jan. 2009, the Rev. Dr. Joseph E. Lowery began his benediction by quoting from the third verse of Life Every Voice and Sing, *"out from the gloomy past, till now we stand at last, where the white gleam of our bright star is cast...,"* highlighting its continuing significance in the community.

On February 12, 1900, the Stanton Public School Chorus performed a new song honoring President Lincoln's birthday during celebrations in Jacksonville, Florida. With lyrics written by Stanton's principal, James Weldon Johnson, and a melody by his brother Rosamond, *"Left Every Voice and Sing"* was an immediate hit.

The Johnson brothers were born in Jacksonville. James Weldon Johnson earned a B.A. degree, summa cum laude, from Atlanta University in 1894, and a law degree from Columbia University. He was admitted to the Florida Bar in 1897. At age twenty-eight, he was the principal at Stanton, a Black public school for grades 1 through 10.

John Rosamond Johnson, who composed the stirring melody for the poem, was educated at Atlanta University and the New England Conservatory of Music. He also studied piano, organ, and voice in Europe. In 1900, he was a choir director for a large Baptist Church in Jacksonville, and a composer and arranger as well.

In this song poem, James W. Johnson wanted to recapture the spirit of hope and rejoicing that African Americans felt after Emancipation in 1865. He felt that if slavery had been banished, then racial injustice could also be overcome, provided individuals stepped forward to take action. Drawing on the powerful imagery of Black spirituals, he challenged everyone to fight for freedom and dignity for ALL Americans.

The Johnson brothers forgot about the song when they went to New York City to develop their successful careers. While Rosamond continued his career in music, James Weldon became a lawyer, diplomat, author, national Executive Director of the NAACP, and professor of literature.

Meanwhile as early as 1900 black organizations steadily began to adopt the song for their own inspiration until *"Lift Every Voice and Sing"* became known as the Negro National Anthem, and today it is still recognized as the Black National Anthem.

Freedom is *NEVER* free. It must be won, maintained, and enlarged through *struggle by each generation...* and can easily be lost when apathy and despair prevail. From the beginning of the 20th century to the new millennium, *"Lift Every Voice and Sing"* summons all of us to rise and *"March on 'till Victory is Won."*

The 100th anniversary of this song was celebrated in 2000. We honor its longevity, the historical context of its origin, and the continuing relevance of its challenging message.

Lift Ev'ry Voice and Sing
James Weldon and J. Rosamond Johnson

Lift ev'ry voice and sing, till earth and heaven ring,

Ring with the harmonies of liberty;

Let our rejoicing rise high as the list'ning skies:

Let it resound loud as the rolling sea.

Sing a song full of the faith that the dark past has taught us;

Sing a song full of the hope that the present has brought us:

Facing the rising sun of our new day begun,

Let us march on, till victory is won.

Stony the road we trod, bitter the chastening rod,

Felt in the days when hope unborn had died;

Yet with a steady beat, have not our weary feet

Come to the place for which our fathers sighed?

We have come over a way that with tears has been watered;

We have come, treading our path through the blood of the slaughtered.

Out from the gloomy past, till now we stand at last

Where the white gleam of our bright star is cast.

God of our weary years, God of our silent tears,

Thou who has brought us thus far on the way;

Thou who has by Thy might, led us into the light,

Keep us forever in the path, we pray.

Lest our feet stray from the places, our God, where we met Thee;

Lest our hearts drunk with the wine of the world, we forget Thee:

Shadowed beneath Thy hand may we forever stand,

True to our God, true to our native land.

Chapter 2

African Americans In Hawai`i

Part I

One of the early researchers in Hawaii's black history is former University of Hawai`i ethnic studies and interdisciplinary studies professor and academic scholar, Dr. Kathryn Waddell Takara. In chapters 2-5, Dr. Takara's research and oral histories document the migration and early arrival of African Americans in Hawai`i. She writes of their roles and relationships, and the developing racism against the Hawaiians. She documents the prominent roles of early black settlers in business, music, and later politics.

The earliest settlers of African ancestry arrived in Hawai`i well before the missionaries' 1820 arrival. Until Hawai`i became a territory in 1898, many of these black immigrants were active in the community as advisors, entrepreneurs and musicians. At least one black man, called Black Jack or Mr. Keaka`ele`ele, was already living on O'ahu when Kamehameha I conquered the island in 1796. He helped to build a store house for Queen Ka`ahumanu in Lahaina, and made his living in the maritime industry.

Black Joe was a long time resident on O'ahu, a trader, a good friend of Gov. Boki, and sail master for King Kamehameha II. He was a peace maker helping to resolve many misunderstandings and also served as an advisor and interpreter for the King. He died in 1828.

In 1810-1811, there came to the island of O`ahu an ex-slave, Anthony D. Allen, from Schenectady, New York. He married a Hawaiian girl, acquired land and livestock, and became one of the most prosperous foreign residents on O`ahu during the next quarter of the century. When the first American missionaries arrived in 1820, he prepared a feast of welcome for them, and continued his aid by supplying them with vegetables, goats' milk, and fruit. He opened a farm on the plains toward Waikiki, ran a small boarding house for seaman, and sold his goat's milk in town. He is credited for building one of the first schools for commoners in the islands and the first carriage road to Manoa Valley.

He was so respected by the Hawaiian royalty that they gave him land to hold and pass on to his descendants. The land is the present site of the Washington Intermediate School near King and Kalakaua. His son was an excellent *paniolo* (cowboy). Allen died in 1835. He was well respected among the missionaries and they all attended his funeral.

The whaling ships arrived in various parts of the islands between 1820-1880. On these ships were descendants of black Portuguese men from the Cape Verde Islands off the Coast of West Africa, blacks from the Caribbean and slaves and free blacks from the Northeast of the United States. Some seamen stayed, married, and became residents and worked as musicians, tailors, cooks, barbers and sailors.

It must be remembered that a number of African American men became entrepreneurs and active in early Hawaiian business matters, a paradox of opportunities given the extreme racial climates of oppression and slavery in the states. William the Baker was the King's cook and sold his place in 1833. Joseph Bedford, known as "Joe Dollar" had a boarding house from 1826 for almost twenty years. Spencer Rhodes operated a barber shop in 1838. Fredrick E. Binns had his barber shop by 1845 and Charles Nicholson, an African American tailor, was designing and sewing from 1840 through 1861. Another barber shop was owned by William Johnson in 1863.

When King Kamehameha III formed his Royal Hawaiian band in 1835, he hired two African Americans who had previously worked on the ships and had great musical talent to lead it. They were America Shattuck and David Curtis. Because of their outstanding musical talent, they later moved on to higher positions in California. David Curtis's daughter later returned to the islands. She and her husband did well in ranching and she became a writer of history. In 1845, the Royal Hawaiian Band was led by African Americans, George W. Wyatt and Charles Johnson, and later came under the direction of Henry Berger.

Betsy Stockton, an intelligent and dignified ex-slave of the President of Princeton University, who had studied extensively using his library, attended evening classes at Princeton Theological Seminary. She accompanied the Charles Stuart family with the second group of missionaries to arrive in Hawai`i aboard the ship *Thames* in 1823 from New Haven, Connecticut. She quickly learned the Hawaiian language and was one of the founders of the Lahainaluna School on Maui, probably the first school for commoners, where she spent two years as a teacher of English, Latin, History and Algebra (1823 -25), before her untimely return to the East Coast due to the illness of Mrs. Stuart. She is well remembered for her high moral and religious character and for helping to heal the sick while on Maui.

Because of the great slavery debate in the United States and the fact that many of the plantation owners were from or familiar with the slave system in the south, Blacks were intentionally excluded from the proposed lists of immigrant groups sought in the 1850's and after to provide contract labor to the Kingdom of Hawai`i. Many local missionaries and abolitionists opposed contract labor. At one point, U.S. Secretary of State Blaine urged the importation of Blacks and not Asians to help replenish the dwindling Hawaiian population, only to meet resistance and aversion to Negro immigrants until after Hawai`i became a Territory in 1900.

Although individual African Americans were accepted into the local community, mass immigration was discouraged by legal restraint as early as 1882 when sugar planters wanted to import large numbers of blacks to relieve their labor shortage. Moreover, again in 1913, there were strenuous efforts to keep the 25th Negro Infantry Regiment from being stationed in Hawai`i. Yet black soldier came and remained for several years without creating friction and soon made a favorable impression on the locals. Unfortunately, there were later some prominent African American immigrants who never wanted to be affiliated with the darker races and silently blended into the local community denying their African American heritage.

In the late nineteenth century, Booker T. Washington, the famous educator from Tuskegee Institute in Alabama, was to come to Hawai`i to investigate the possibilities of African American plantation workers being used to supplement the growing Japanese, Chinese, Filipinos and Portuguese workers many of whom were dissatisfied. Unable to come, he sent a representative, and to his surprise and discovery, he learned that the working conditions were in many ways worse than in the South at that time. However, by 1901, the first group of about two hundred African American laborers was brought here by the Hawaiian Sugar Planters' Association recruited from Louisiana and Alabama to join the other Oriental plantation workers on the islands of Maui and Hawai`i.

The prospect of bringing experienced plantation laborers and their families from the South to Hawai`i was welcomed by many plantation owners. Not only would this mean additional farm hands to work on the plantations, but it also meant African American women could provide personal and household chores to the white wives of plantation owners. The first group arrived in the islands in January 1901 and by June 1901 several hundred had been recruited for the plantations on Maui.

They were offered $26.00 per month, free housing and firewood and roundtrip transportation if they fulfilled their three year contracts. Unfortunately, the several hundred African Americans who went to Maui to work were very soon disappointed because of the harshness of working and living conditions on the plantations, and many fled to Honolulu, or were amalgamated into the local community, or returned home to the south.

The Puerto Ricans who came to Hawai`i around 1901 were in the main also of Negro, Indian, and Spanish descent, although in the census they were listed as Caucasian until 1940, probably due to the Spanish part of their heritage.

In 1907, another small group of twenty-five to thirty families came to Maui recruited from Tennessee, Mississippi, and Alabama, including the Crockett family and Mr. Maple, a chemist. The Maple School on Maui is named for the family.

It is difficult to know what the day to day life was in the islands during the early 1800's because there were few records or journals kept to record them with the exception of the ship captains' logs. It is said that often times the Captain would find a stowaway aboard after they left port in the United States and there was nothing they could do except make that person work his passage aboard. Some returned from their place of origin, but others jumped ship and disappeared among the natives. Some proved their worth and others did not.

Carlotta Stewart, Principal, with her faculty at
Hanamaula School in 1931. Ms. Stewart is fourth from right (rear).
(Moorland-Spingarn Collection, Howard University)

T. McCants Stewart
(Moorland-Spingarn Collection, Howard University)

Dr. William
Lineas Maples

Dr. Maples worked as
attending physician for
Hawaii Commerical and
Sugar Company from
1901 to 1931.
Men of Hawaii, 1917

The "25th Infantry" on parade, passing Iolani Palace, in 1915
(U.S. Army Museum of Hawai`i)

Betsy Stockton
arrived in Hawai`i in 1823
(Hawaiian Mission Children's Society)

The "25th Infantry" Baseball Team" in 1916
(U.S. Army Museum of Hawai`i)

Judge William F. Crockett,
arrived in *Hawai`i* in 1901 from Alabama.
(*Star Bulletin*, 1917)

Descendants of William F. Crockett (1860-1943)
are African American, Chinese and Caucasian.
(*Honolulu Advertiser*)

Letter to Booker T. Washington from William F. Crockett

Montgomery Ala. May 11th, 1900

My dear sir: I came down town early this morning, hoping to see
You before you left the city, as I desired to extend to you my sincere
thanks and congratulations for the noble work done, and assistance
give by reason of your presence in the gallery among your people
at a time when their dearest interests were being violently assailed.
Indeed it was a great help in those trying moments for one to feel
that you were not only there by your sympathies, but really there in
person, not on the platform but side by side with those to whom
you have given the best years of your life. I have heard not a few
express themselves, as having been stimulated by your presence in
those moments when all hope seemed to have been buried beneath
popular sentiment.

You were to them what the presence of a general is to his men in
was no place where you could have been more eloquent, and
powerful than where you were. Side by side with your own people.
the lesson you taught me that comes to us from the life and teaching
of a Master, the one of all that is most difficult to emulate. A life
That can silently bear such great hardships as you must have borne
During the past three days will some day be claimed as the heritage
Of the ages.

Wishing you sufficient length of days to see the highest and best
Results of your work, I remain

Yours truly,

W.F. Crockett

TLS   Con. 168 BTW Papers   DLC.

1 W.F. Crockett was a black lawyer who was born in Virginia in 1859. In about 1903
(1901) he moved to Hawaii, where he was District Attorney on the island of Maui.

Chapter 3

African Americans in Hawai`i

Part II

To understand how the African American was introduced to the Hawaiian Islands, we must remember that the islands were a melting pot, where many ethnic cultures freely intermixed with one another. The time line of contact can probably be traced back to early migrations from Africa, if one tries to understand the peopling of the world from early Africa.

While Europeans had always known about Africa, they hadn't known much about the people and cultures, and their desire to make money, when money was much needed, made Africa interesting with her many resources. Long after early contact with Egypt, Ethiopia and Sudan, the first real substantial relationships Europeans forged with Africans were after the industrial revolution in trade, probably with the Islamic civilizations in North Africa. These two groups had sporadic but undefined contact all through the European Middle Ages. In the fifteenth century, the major Islamic civilizations were beginning to decline in power, but not their impressiveness. The Europeans were amazed by what they saw, especially in the Sudanese empire.

Initially evidence suggests that Europeans were not interested in adapting African culture nor were the Africans interested in theirs. All the contemporary facts suggest that many Europeans saw the Africans as equal partners in civilization, government, and commerce. The Africans, it seems, also believed this. During this heady period, at the start of the cultural exchange in the 16th Century between the two hemispheres, Africans regularly came to Europe to study Western culture. In 1518, for example, Henry of the Congo, traveled to the Vatican and became the first bishop of the Congo. All of this would change however as the two hemispheres were headed for a collision. After the industrial revolution, and during the colonial period, the modern history of Europe and Africa became overwhelmingly saturated with Europeans forcibly deporting Africans into European states. Equally Europeans forced political, social, religious, and economic practices on Africans during the colonial period and afterwards.

The tragedy that broke this initial historical pattern of respect and equality was slavery, and slavery, in a great irony of history, was driven by the discovery of a new world in the west. Initially, the European slave trade was small. Rather, Islamic traders of North and West Africa had a booming traffic in black slavery as they marched slaves across the Sahara to the regions of the east. Surprisingly, though, slavery was not racially based in most of human history, racial slavery, that is, slavery, that was predicated on race as a way of separating and dehumanizing slave from free, was a creation of the seventeenth century. Some form of slavery has been a constant throughout most of human history.

Throughout most of human history, slaves were drawn from conquered populations and defeated armies, and many slaves were simply sold (or sold themselves) into slavery by the rulers or their families. These people were slaves by virtue of being slaves; there were no racial, ethnic, or physical markers of slavery or subsistence servitude. Such was the situation that the Europeans encountered and traded in. When the Portuguese forged contacts with the Islamic civilizations and traders of North Africa, they diverted much of this trade to Europe, including the Muslin traffic in black slaves. The Portuguese, however, were not satisfied with the trade with North Africa and pushed down the western coast of the African continent.

In 1414, a group of Portuguese sailors exploring in West Africa discovered a village of black natives and, to make some money, attacked them and kidnapped as many as they could. As a result the European traffic in black slaves began. By 1800, the Portuguese were importing thousands of Africans per year into Portugal to work as indentured servants. This traffic, however, was far different from the character of the later slave trade. Technically, the Africans were not slaves; they were indentured servants. After a period of service, they were freed. It was not possible to be born a slave in Portugal. The children of indentured servants were free.

This would be the case throughout the 16th Century. Slavery was not racially based. The Africans kidnapped by the Portuguese were baptized, many were educated, and they all integrated into the lower classes of Portuguese society. Africans and Europeans intermarried, and to this day, many Portuguese are of mixed blood. Thus, one can assume that the migration into the Sandwich Islands, was begun by the European Portuguese who were sea going, and the early intermarriage of Europeans to the Sandwich Island natives was the result of their direct contact with these European sailors. This happened with the Polynesians as well.

It is said that in Captain Cook's expeditions, his ships' crews for three voyages carried servants. It is well known that Sir Joseph Banks and Thomas Richmond each had two black Portuguese servants whom they acquired from the Cape Verde Islands off the West African Coast, while on the ship, *Endeavor.* If these men had servants, one wonders if other ships carried servants as well.

Here again, one may surmise that the Polynesians, who were early settlers in the Sandwich Islands, intermarried with this mixed race, Portuguese people some of whom were surely of African descent. This can be said to mark the earliest immigration of blacks to Hawai`i. As there are no written records, we can only take this as a logical theory.

As the Hawaiian Islands grew, so did the number of ships that visited the islands for water and supplies. Many were whaling ships from the European countries, North America, and various other vessels going to trade in Asia. Whaling ships came for supplies and water. Also the crews needed their rest and recreation and to bide time for ship repairs. They could only hunt and catch whales certain times of the year. The islands with their mild temperatures and relatively calm waters were an easy place to hunt whales and to gather the much needed oil and whale bone that was used in trade.

Crews of trading ships from various nations brought the early black immigrants who were run away slaves from the Americas, and sailors from the Caribbean, Spanish and English ships. Many black seamen were navigators, blacksmiths, sail makers, musicians, barbers, cooks, and cabin boy apprentices. These cabin boy apprentices were knowledgeable, and learned to read, write, and speak English well as they had been taken aboard the ships to be able to learn everything about the practices of the maritime industry.

It is estimated by some that 70% of the ships' crew were of the black race, because they were cheap labor and quick to learn. They also signed up eagerly to escape the watchful eye of slave kidnappers from Southern plantations. Some of these sailors took Hawaiian wives and others left children with Hawaiian women whom they did not marry.

When put into Hawaiian ports, the ships that carried African sailors sometimes had crew members who would jump ship. Being of African descent these sailors easily blended into the rest of the dark-skinned Hawaiian society and sometimes they were AWOL (absent without leave). Sometimes they were found and were forced to return to their ships, but oft times they were not found. So these positions had to be filled. These jobs most of the time were filled with native Hawaiians. What could be better for the Hawaiian than to be trained onboard ship, and many learned and became experienced in western ways, culture, language, ship building, machinery and western methods of navigation, especially during the time when ships made port.

It is said that the chiefs (*Ali`i*) of the early days were of the Polynesian race and that some had intermarried with non Hawaiians. Here again are traces of the beginnings of the mixed race peoples of Hawai`i.

Not surprising, today one can look at the early art works of the islanders, and see many similarities in design, theme, and mythology between African and Polynesian cultures. Again there is remarkable evidence of early contact that must be studied more thoroughly. The reader must remember in this study, that when using the term African American, the term "African" refers to where they originally came from, and the term, "American" is used when blacks became American by being on American soil. This is commonly misunderstood when one discusses the African Diaspora in the islands. One could correctly use the term Euro-Africans, Portuguese Africans, or Polynesian Africans, to describe early black residents in Hawai`i which makes the blending of the cultures especially unique in the Hawaiian Islands. So many people mixed with Hawaiian cultures and heritages make for a blended racial and cultural inheritance. These people mixing of diverse settlers contributed to the unique Hawaiian history of a mixed race people, which today few other places in the world can claim.

Chapter 4

African Americans In Hawai`i

Part III

Just before and after the annexation in 1898, several African Americans from the United States participated in education, politics, and medicine and made the islands their home. One of these was T. McCants Stewart, a black attorney, who was in the cabinet of King Kalakaua and helped in drafting the Organic Act of the new territory of Hawai`i. On several occasions he also aided Hawaiians in regaining their lost properties. In 1892, Hawai`i had enacted the Chinese Exclusionary Law to prevent Chinese from coming to the islands. Stewart was violently against the act.

His daughter, Carlotta Stewart Lai, was just 18, when she graduated from the Punahou School. After her marriage to Mr. Yum Kim Lai who was from a well known Chinese family, she became a teacher. He died suddenly in 1935 in Hong Kong. Eventually, Carlotta Stewart Lai she became a principal at Kauai's Hanamaulu School. She is buried in the O`ahu Cemetery.

William F. Crockett, another Attorney, came to Hawai`i in 1901 from Alabama. He later became district magistrate of Wailuku, Maui, then a judge, and finally a territorial senator. His arrival brought him from Alabama as an attorney for black workers at the Sprecklesville Plantation on Maui. His wife, Annie Crockett, was a teacher at Wailuku Elementary School. Her hobby was flowers, and she developed numerous marvelous hybrids of the hibiscus flower. The hibiscus yellow is Hawai`i's State Flower. Annie Crockett died at the old age of 94. Their son, Wendell Frank Crockett, graduated from the University of Michigan Law School and returned to Maui to practice law, which was interrupted by his military service in World War I. In 1926, Wendell married Myrtle Lau, also a teacher, who became mother of their three children. Wendell became deputy county attorney of Maui in 1919.

Another early black pioneer to Hawai`i was William Lineas Maples, a physician and musician. Maples was born in Sevierville, Tennessee, on March 31, 1869, the son of Edward Maples and Martha Jane Runions. He graduated in the first class of the segregated high school in Knoxville in 1888. Showing a talent for science, oratory, and music, he received the Dodson medal upon graduation.

Maples taught school for one year in Austin, Tennessee and then entered medical school at Howard University in Washington, D.C. in 1889. He received an M.D. degree in 1893 and returned to Knoxville to establish his medical practice. The Spanish-American War in 1898 interrupted that practice and he joined the U.S. Army's medical unit of the all black Third Regiment of the North Carolina Volunteers. He ended his service a year later and returned to Knoxville to resume his practice.

In 1900, agents for the Hawai`i Commercial and Sugar Company (HC&S Co.) on Maui traveled through Tennessee and Alabama looking for workers for Hawai`i's plantations. They also sought a Physician to staff the hospital that would serve the contract workers.

Dr. Maples was recruited as the anesthetist for the HC&S hospital. This hospital was to serve 200 African American workers who were to be employed from the southern states. His older brother, Samuel, a lawyer, also accepted a position as a representative of the black contract laborers recruited for the HC&S plantations.

Prior to leaving Knoxville, Maples married Miss Sadie Williams who accompanied him on the voyage to Hawai`i. He was assigned to the hospital in Puunene, Hawai`i, and for the first two years lived in plantation housing provided to the medical staff. William and Sadie Maples had not planned on staying in Hawai`i for more than two contracts, or six years, but he increasingly found the work professionally satisfying. The hospital had installed a new operating room comparable to any found in a small, modern hospital in Tennessee, which was an incentive to stay in the islands.

William and Sadie Maples had two daughters, Gladys and Elizabeth, and the family became active in the community, especially after they purchased a house in the town of Wailuku in 1905. Recognizing the need for a first class drug store in Wailuku, he opened Maples Drug Store in April 1905. The drug store closed after a few years as Maples' responsibilities at the hospital mounted because HC&S employed more African Americans. Dr. William Maples was also known locally for his interest in music. In 1911 he became the manager of the Navarro Orchestra in Wailuku, which provided popular contemporary music for the Maui public. He also wrote the Puunene school song in 1931.

Dr. Maples, the first African American university trained physician to practice in Hawai`i, remained on Maui working for the Hawai`i Commercial and Sugar Company until his retirement in 1931. He died in Wailuku, Maui, in 1943 at the age of 73. Maples Elementary School is named for the family.

James Oliver Mitchell was born in Koloa, Kauai in 1893. He was a teacher for 46 years on O`ahu, and Maui. He became a Principal, Coach, and finally Athletic Director at Farrington High School in Kalihi on O`ahu. He earned the respect of the students and parents as well, and his athletic talents went a long way to help and inspire others. His fellow teachers thought highly of him for his integrity and thoroughness.

(Left) George Wellington, retired principal bassist with the
Honolulu Symphony and music teacher, with his late wife, Taeko,
and two of their children. Wellington came to Hawai`i in 1956 with
his family after completing his graduate studies. (Right) The
Wellington children (1-r, Haruko, Yuriko, George, Jr., and Nobuo)

Honorable Judge Wendell F. Crockett

Chapter 5

African Americans In Hawai`i

Part IV

Dr. Takara has written that before the annexation of Hawai`i to the United States in 1894, the earlier African Americans did not face the same problems that the African Americans did in the Jim Crow United States. They blended into the society of the Sandwich Islands (Hawai`i). They lived under contract and freedom. Even though some lived with poor wages, they had freedom to live in the Islands where they could provide for themselves and for their families, and sometimes prosper. It was not until the development of the plantation economy, annexation, and the military presence that they started to feel the effects of prejudice.

In 1917, during World War I, over 200 African Americans were stationed in Hawai`i. They were of the 25th Infantry Unit, called Buffalo Soldiers. They were stationed there because of the shameful history of racial incidents on the mainland USA from White officers, personnel, and civilians. Military commanders felt that these black soldiers would blend into the already mixed race people and alleviate some of the racial problems. And in fact, black soldiers were generally complimented and commended for their peaceful and honorable service in Hawai`i.

As for African American civilians, in 1911, a distinguished African American by the name of Charles Cottrill was supported by President William Taft to become a tax collector for the Hawaiian Territory (This today, is called the Internal Revenue Service). Cottrill brought his wife and son with him. His son attended Punahou School. Cotrill socialized with top business executives associated with Hawai`i's top five corporations who were often the descendents of the first missionaries who came to Hawai`i in 1821. Cottrill left the Hawaiian Islands in 1915 when President Wilson transferred him to Ohio, where he continued his career.

Once more in 1941, at the outbreak of World War II, there was another movement, to exclude black military personnel from Hawai`i, including, but not limited to the City and County government of Honolulu; The Honolulu Chamber of Commerce, the central council of Hawaiian organizations, and several unions also tried to discourage the War department from sending a labor battalion of 600 African Americans to unload ships. Yet with the bombing of Pearl Harbor, several thousand African American men and some women came to help the war effort serving as soldiers and defense workers. During this period, there was much friction between Caucasians and African American soldiers stationed in Hawai`i which manifested in fights, racial slurs and near riots.

During this time, the Army, Navy, and Marine corps generally maintained separate (segregated) living quarters. Only at Schofield Barracks could men live, work, and play together without friction.

Unfortunately, as the military established itself in the 1940's and more tourists began to arrive, the local population learned indirectly, often through rumor and hearsay, more about African Americans and their inferior status on the Mainland. The consequence was the subtle adoption by many locals of attitudes and stereotypes from the economically dominant and socially acceptable whites.

Moreover, the media perpetuated the latent anti-black sentiment of the mainland press by reprinting stories which presented the African American in negative stereotypes, identifying him/her by race whenever a crime was committed, and pointed labeling. Likewise, news and reports from the Mainland of lynchings and riots were sensationalized in contrast to the relative racial harmony in the islands.

Fortunately, these often latent anti-black feelings brought by many mainland Caucasians did not develop into the crystallized prejudice often found in the U.S., but they have nevertheless manifested in some local attitudes in the form of aversion to blacks in varying degrees.

For example, during the 1940's and 1950's, for some Japanese, "on the spot" after the attack on Pearl Harbor, it was deemed "indiscreet" to be too friendly with African Americans, and it was known that the FBI opposed an affinity between them and the suspected recalcitrant Black group. Other instances of this aversion to African Americans were patterns of discrimination in hiring, refusal of service at some restaurants, barber shops and taverns, reluctance to rent housing units, sell leasehold or fee property to them, and the denial of cordiality generally given by the average local person to a white person. There was also the ostracism of women who dared to date African American men. However, this was no different than what was being experienced by most blacks in cities across the United States, especially within the areas where military personnel was stationed. Even in Hawai`i, the African American soldier, sailor, marine, civilian, war worker, or nurse was expected to have their place in the back of the bus, or in special sections places in restaurants. There were several blocks of housing within Pearl Harbor for the black civilian workers and special places of business within the area.

Doris "Dorie" Miller enlisted in the Navy in 1939 and was made a mess attendant in the United States " Jim Crow" Navy. Miller was eventually promoted to Cook, Third Class and assigned to the USS West Virginia stationed in Hawai`i. Miller was aboard the *West Virginia* on December 7, 1941, when it was subjected to a surprise attack by Japan.

During the attack, Miller secured an unattended anti-aircraft gun and began firing at Japanese war planes. Miller shot down at least one Japanese Aircraft before he ran out of ammunition and was ordered to abandon ship. Although Miller's courage under fire was initially overlooked, the black press seized his story and pressured the Navy to recognize him. On May 27, 1942, Admiral Chester W. Nimitz awarded Miller the Navy Cross.

During the spring of 1943, Miller was assigned to the *Liscome Bay* and was still serving as a messenger on the warship, despite his previous heroism, when the carrier was sunk in the Gilbert Islands in 1943. In addition to the Navy Cross, Miller received the Purple Heart, The American Defense Service Medal-- Fleet Clasp, The Asiatic-Pacific Campaign Medal, and the World War II Victory Medal. In 1973, the Knox-class frigate USS MILLER was named for Doris "Dorie" Miller.

After the war, conditions became less strained when most African Americans returned to the mainland. Those who remained and those who arrived subsequently most often blended into the local community since there was no defined black neighborhood or community, after the military got rid of CH2-CH3 (segregated housing areas). Many became active business persons, government employees and a few have had successful careers in education, law, politics, and as entertainers and athletes.

Recently, Oscar Award winning actor Cuba Gooding, Jr. portrayed Dorie Miller in the 2001 movie "Pearl Harbor," and in 1991 the Alpha Kappa Alpha sorority dedicated a bronze commemorative plaque of Miller to the Miller Family Park located on the U.S. Naval Base, Pearl Harbor.

MESS ATTENDANT DECORATED FOR PEARL HARBOR HEROISM

Doris Miller, colored mess attendant first class, who distinguished himself, during the Japanese attack on Pearl Harbor, today was awarded the Navy cross by President Roosevelt.
He was cited "for his distinguished devotion to duty, extraordinary courage and disregard for his personal safety during the attack."
On April 1 Secretary of the Navy Knox commended Miller and he has since received an advance in rating. Secretary Knox commendation described Miller's brave action as follows: "While at the side of his captain on the bridge, Miller, despite enemy strafing and bombing and in the face of a serious fire, assisted in moving his Captain, who had been mortally wounded, to a place of greater safety, and later manned and operated a machine-gun until ordered to leave the bridge." Miller, a resident of Waco, Tex., enlisted as a mess attendant third class at Dallas on September 16, 1933

Chapter 6

Betsey Stockton

Dr. Kathryn Waddell Takara, in her pioneer research, pays homage to Betsey Stockton, a former slave, who arrived in Hawai`i on the second ship of missionaries in 1823, where she taught Princess Nahi`ena`ena as well as commoners how to read and write. Stockton also established a school in Lahaina, Maui which was the first school for common people and represents the educational component of African Americans' presence and service to the community and to the Hawaiians.

Born in Princeton, N.J. in 1798, as a slave of the Robert Stockton family, Betsey Stockton, was given to his daughter, who later married the Rev. Dr. Ashbel Green, president of the College of Princeton. Rev. Green had an extensive library and allowed his sons to educate Stockton. They spent many hours with her, discovering she had a fine mind and an intense desire to learn. Under their tutelage, she learned to read and write, and once those skills were mastered, she went on to study mathematics and science. Whenever she had the opportunity, she would read from Rev. Green's large classical collection, including such works as Caesar's *Commentaries*. Stockton was publicly baptized in the Witherspoon Street Presbyterian Church in Princeton in the winter of 1817-1818, and given her freedom shortly thereafter.

Upon hearing that Rev. Charles Samuel Stewart of Cooperstown, N.Y., who was about to be married, had applied for service with the Sandwich Island Mission, she "voluntarily and unsolicited sought admission to his family as a humble friend and assistant missionary". Rev. Stewart wrote to the American Board of Commissioners for Foreign Missions (ABCFM) asking permission for Stockton to join him should he be accepted as part of the company.

His request to Jeremiah Evarts, corresponding secretary and clerk of the "prudential" committee of the ABCFM, included letters of recommendation for Stockton from Rev. Green and Dr. Michael Osborn of the Theological Seminary at Princeton, whose Sabbath School she had mastered. In his letter to the ABCFM, Dr. Osborn wrote, "She has a larger acquaintance with sacred history and geography and the Scriptures than almost any ordinary person, young or old, I have ever known." (By *ordinary person*, you will understand me to mean such as are not clergymen or candidates for the ministry).

On April 27, 1823, Sabbath Sunday, a black woman named Betsey Stockton, once a slave, who became a missionary nurse and educator, stood at the rail of the brig *Thames* as it rounded the southeast end of the island of O'ahu under the light of a midnight full moon. She had finally realized her lifelong ambition of spreading the word of the Lord as a missionary, and the Sandwich Islands (now the Hawaiian Islands), would be the scene of her work for her God.

The wild beauty of the promontories forming the headlands of the islands spread before her. By sunrise, the whole south side of O'ahu had come into view, ochre hills rising gently from the coastal plains, changing abruptly to the soaring, green ridges of the rugged Ko`olau mountain range.

The *Thames* casts anchor a half-mile offshore from the harbor of the sprawling, dusty village of Honolulu. Several of the male missionaries and Capt. Reuben Clasby, master of the *Thames,* were lowered into a waiting longboat and rowed ashore through the narrow break in the reef. They were greeted at the dock by King Liholiho's wife, Queen Kamamalu, accompanied by John Coffin Jones, the American consul, who then escorted them to his home.

Since the head of the mission, Rev. Hiram Bingham, was away, the young mission printer Elisha Loomis welcomed the new missionaries to Hawai'i. Two days later, after the *Thames* had been towed into port by 108 men in two rows of boats, the remainder of the company came ashore.

At that time, the majority of the tall-masted ships which crowded Honolulu Harbor were American. Dockhands kept loading and unloading the lighters which piled between boats and docks. Curious Hawaiians paddled out in outrigger canoes and climbed aboard the *Thames*.

The color of Stockton's skin and her turban and clothes intrigued them, for there were few black American women in the Islands. Betsey Stockton was not bothered by their curiosity and looked forward to doing God's work in this exotic land. She smiled at the Hawaiians as they crowded around her.

In spite of Stockton's education and training as a teacher, her position and duties with the missionary company were ambiguous. It was the intent of the ABCFM that Stockton not be used as a domestic in any other missionary household except the Stewart's, and that she perform her duties as a missionary teacher.

To make sure her special status was clear to all involved, an agreement was drawn up before leaving the U.S. One of its major clauses was that Stockton was to be treated "neither as an equal nor a servant, but a humble Christian Friend." The Stewarts and Stockton both had the option of terminating the agreement, either mutually or individually. About a month before they left New Haven, Connecticut, the agreement was signed on Oct. 24, 1822, by Rev. Green, Rev. Stewart and Stockton. Betsey Stockton sailed with the Stewarts from New Haven on Nov. 20, 1822 for the Kingdom of Hawai`i on the *Thames*. The voyage around Cape Horn was long and stormy, but the members of Hawai`i's second missionary company arrived safely at Honolulu after a passage of 158 days.

After the arrival of the new missionary reinforcements, the brethren debated at length as to where the new mission stations should be established, and the final decisions were not made until October of that year. However, Queen Keopuolani, the King's mother, who was moving her permanent residence to Lahaina, urged the missionaries to establish a station there as quickly as possible.

One month later, the Stewart family, their son, Charles, Betsey Stockton, the Rev. William Richards and his wife, Elisha Loomis and a young Hawaiian man, William Kamo'oula, who had been educated at the Mission school in Cornwall, Connecticut., left for Lahaina, Maui on the King's brig *Cleopatra's* Barge, captained by Prime Minister Kalanimoku and accompanied by Queen Keopuolani.

The voyage of 70 miles lasted four days. The decision to start a mission station at Lahaina had been made so precipitously that there were no provisions for housing the new arrivals. Mr. Butler of Lahaina invited the group to use one of the houses on his luxurious plantation grounds.

The missionaries were thankful that they were called upon to do God's work on the verdant island of Maui, instead of the barren plains of Honolulu. Queen Keopuolani gave the missionaries property on the beach, and with help from the local Native Hawaiians, two Hawaiian houses and a church were soon constructed.

A few days after their arrival in Lahaina, Stockton's nursing skills were put to use as she helped save two Hawaiian children, one from the croup and the other from a nasty cut.

The facility with which she learned the Hawaiian language and the wonderful rapport she established with the Hawaiian people in her daily contacts as she walked along the dusty roads of Lahaina, or visited them in their homes, always wearing her turban, helped Stockton befriend the Hawaiians, and later teach the Hawaiian women sewing, childcare, and housekeeping.

Stockton's dream of opening a school for the common people, the *maka'ainana,* was initially thwarted by the chiefs. Rev. Stewart made an entry in his journal on June 2, 1823, noting that while schools for the Hawaiian chiefs and a few of their particular favorites had commenced, the rulers opposed the instruction of the common people in reading and writing, stating, "If the palapala (learning) is good, we wish to possess it first ourselves; if it is bad, we do not intend our subjects to know the evil of it."

The chiefs finally decided that the *palapala* had merit. In his entry for Aug. 9, 1824, Rev. Stewart wrote, "For some time the chiefs had decided to extend instruction in reading and writing to the whole population and have only been waiting for books and an increase in the number of qualified native teachers in order to put the resolution, as far as practical, into effect." The Stewarts and Stockton traveled to O'ahu while preparations for the new school were finalized.

Meanwhile, when the *maka'ainana* heard of this, they immediately applied for instruction. The first school ever devoted entirely to teaching the common people in Hawai'i was established at the mission station in Lahaina in September 1824, with Stockton as superintendent. The small initial enrollment quickly grew, and her school gained a reputation of producing well disciplined, well-instructed students. Though she had to travel thousands of miles to do it, Stockton's abilities as a professional teacher were finally recognized.

Meanwhile, Levi Chamberlain, the missionary's business agent headquartered on O'ahu, had befriended Stockton right from the initial arrival. In her letters to him, she expressed a great desire to see the spectacular Pali (cliffs) at the head of Nu'uanu Valley, where Kamehameha the Great had defeated the armies of Kai'ana and Kalanikupule in the final battle for O'ahu. Chamberlain granted her wish and invited her to see the battlefield. On Friday, July 23, 1824, Chamberlain led her on the seven mile walk to the head of the valley.

When they reached the precipice, the strong, swirling winds buffeted Stockton her about, making it difficult for her to keep her balance. She laughed aloud in sheer delight. A thousand vertical feet below her lay the widely cultivated and thickly inhabited plains of Kailua, whose lush greenness contrasted strongly with the white waves of the surf on the reefs of Kane'ohe Bay and the blue-green of the ocean beyond. It was an experience she would forever treasure.

After a stay in Honolulu of a little over three months, Stockton and the Stewarts returned to Lahaina on the new brig *Kamehameha.* Stockton later wrote to Chamberlain thanking him for his kindness to her. On these faraway tropical islands, she had discovered more freedom than she had yet before known, and it was reflected in her letters. She wrote, "You may be surprised when I tell you that I have spoken more freely to you on the subject of religion than to any other person since I left America."

But Stockton's time in Hawai'i was to be brought to an end by an unexpected turn of events. Mrs. Stewart had fallen into ill health, and her condition worsened until eventually, in 1825, the whole family-including Stockton-was forced to leave the Sandwich Islands and return to Cooperstown. Although Stockton wanted to remain in Hawai'i and continue her teaching, she felt a deep obligation to care for the ailing Mrs. Stewart and her three children, and so returned to the United States with them.

After Mrs. Stewart's death in 1830, Stockton remained with the family for six more years, becoming, as Rev.

Ashbel Green later wrote, the "assiduous and unwearied attendant, and pious instructor of the motherless children." Later, she left Cooperstown and traveled to Philadelphia to become a teacher in an infant school, then was appointed by the state of New Jersey as principal of a large school for black students, served for a few months as an advisor to a Canadian missionary, and returned to Princeton, where she died Oct. 24, 1865. She was buried, as was her wish, with the Stewart family in Cooperstown.

The following tribute was engraved on her headstone:

Betsey Stockton
A native of Princetown, N.J.
Where she died
Oct. 24, 1865
Aged 67 years
Of African blood and born
she became fitted by
education and divine grace
for a life of great usefulness
for many years was a valued
missionary at the Sandwich Islands
in the family of Rev. C.S. Stewart
and afterwards 'til her death,
a popular and able principal
of Public Schools in Philadelphia
and Princeton
honored and beloved
by a large circle of Christian Friends.

Betsey Stockton was an uncommon woman for any age. She started from a position subordinate many times over- slave, domestic, and black unmarried woman- but with intelligence, faith and perseverance, she soared above society's restrictions to play influential roles in the lives of diverse groups of people; the beloved children of her family, the Hawaiians, and the children of her own race still fighting to melt the chains of bondage with the fire of education. She was exceptional in all her skills-as nurse, missionary, teacher, principal, and surrogate mother, a shining example and role model for any place and time.

Chapter 7

Nolle Smith/Iwalani Smith Mottl

Nolle Smith in Honolulu, 1937

Chapter 7 examines the life of Nolle Smith, civil servant, politician, statesman, and cowboy, and his family. One of his three daughters, the late Iwalani Smith Mottl, is also included in this chapter. Nolle Smith, cowboy, politician, and cultural diplomat, was born in 1888 on his parents' ranch in Horse Creek, Wyoming, but grew up in Cheyenne where he graduated as valedictorian of his high school class at Cheyenne High school in 1907. He was the son of a white father and an African American mother. Smith attended the University of Nebraska where he studied engineering and math while playing football, and basketball and competing in track. After graduation, Smith held engineering jobs briefly in River Rock, Wyoming and Denver, Colorado.

Nolle had met Purdy the famous Hawaiian cowboy and champion roper at a rodeo show in Nebraska, Purdy invited him to come to Hawai`i and see his beautiful island. After Nolle graduated with honors at the University of Nebraska in engineering, he applied for a job in Hawai`i and got it, working for the Matson shipping line. He quickly married the girl of his dreams Eva Jones from San Francisco, who had graduated from college and was a classic concert pianist. They moved to Hawai`i.

In 1915, however, he was offered another job in Hawai'i as an engineer with the Honolulu Department of Public Works. The following year he became the Superintendent of Docks for Matson Navigation Company, a major shipping firm in the Islands. In 1917, Smith married Eva Beatrice Jones, a childhood friend from Cheyenne who had moved to San Francisco.

In 1919 Smith established his own engineering and construction firm and obtained contracts for major projects throughout the territory. Smith was also active in Republican politics and in 1928 he was elected to the Territorial Legislature. He often addressed his constituents in their native Hawaiian language. After Smith left the Territorial Legislature in 1932, he was selected to be Hawai`i's Director of the Bureau of Research and Statistics and later held the job of Deputy Director of the Bureau of the Budget.

In 1942, Smith was appointed head of the Hawai`i Civil Service and in that position instituted numerous reforms including removing Hawai`i's poll tax as a requirement for voting. Four years later, Smith accepted an appointment as Commissioner of Insular Affairs for the Virgin Islands. In 1955, he accepted the first series of appointments with the United States Department of State that took him to Ecuador, Haiti and Brazil. He returned from the State Department in 1963. Nolle Smith died in Honolulu on February 9, 1982.

Tsulan Smith, 1949

Leinani Patricia Smith,
University of Hawai`i, 1943

Iwalani Smith demonstrates
an authentic hula,
International House,
University of Chicago, 1942

Nolle Smith, Jr., and bride,
Sookie Kim Smith, at Lihue,
island of Kauai, 1947

The Smith home in Honolulu, 1937. BELOW : Glee Club singers and hula dancers accompany the governor of the Lions International Club, 50th District, Hawaii, to the Lions convention in Oakland, California, June, 1937. Nolle R. Smith (second row from rear, second from right).

Nolle at his desk as Commissioner of Insular Affairs, Virgin Islands, 1954

Reception for Vice-President and Mrs. Richard M. Nixon, Virgin Islands, 1954. Foreground: Eva Smith, Nolle shaking hands with Charles Claunch, Secretary of the Virgin Islands. Background: Mrs. Nixon (head obscured), Vice-President Nixon, and Archie Alexander, Governor of the Virgin Islands.

Nolle as valedictorian of his graduating class, Cheyenne High School, 1907

Nolle, the freshman legislator (front row, second for left), attends opening day, February, 1929

Election card for Nolle R. Smith (Kamika), 1928

Nolle, University of Nebraska, 1908

The Assistant Director of the Hawaii
Territorial Bureau of the Budget
sets sail for a business trip to the mainland, 1939

Nolle as Assistant Director of the
Tax Foundation of Hawaii, 1947

Eva Jones Smith, Nolle's wife, 1949

Freshman football team, University of Nebraska, 1907.
Nolle Smith (back row, third from right) played tackle.

Beneath the portrait of Antonio José de Sucre, one of Ecuador's
national heroes, are Manuel Naranjo, ex-Minister of the Treasury,
Dr. Carlos Andrade Marín, Mayor of Quito, and Nolle Smith, Public
Administration Advisor. Taken in the Mayor's office, Quito, Ecuador, 1956.

Nolle, suited up for football
practice, University of Nebraska, 1908

The Nolle Smith residence in Quito, Ecuador, 1956

Melissa Boulware Smith,
Nolle's mother, Honolulu, 1920

Silas Peter Smith,
Nolle's father, Honolulu, 1920

The Smith family at their Kalihi home, 1927.
Clockwise: Eva (mother) seated;
Tsulan; Nolle, Jr.; Nolle, Sr., Iwalani, Leinani.

An old friendship is renewed in the nation's capital.
Senator Hiram Leong Fong (left) and
Nolle R. Smith, Sr., Washington, D.C., 1959.

Iwalani Mottl

Iwalani Looking Beautiful

Black History Month
Ayin Adams & Iwalani Mottl

Iwalani Mottl

Iwalani Birthday Party with Adesina

Another African American pioneer in Hawai`i was Nolle Smith's wife, Eva B. Jones Smith, who was also known as Eva Cunningham. She was the first woman to host a radio show in Hawai'i and her piano school was the "Place to go" before 1920.

Iwalani Smith Mottl Sneidman (b. Nov. 9,1917 - d. Jan.5, 2007 was the eldest child of Nolle Smith and Eva Jones. Iwalani was one of the first generation of African Americans born in Hawai`i in 1917, the same year that Queen Lili`uokalani made her transition. Iwalani's mother made sure her children were educated properly and as a young child Iwalani studied Japanese, piano, and she took hula lessons. Iwalani was an active part of her father's campaign for the legislature, helping pass out flyers to his constituents.

After high school in Honolulu, Iwalani attended the University of Chicago, where she was chosen to attend the world student conference in Tokyo, Japan, in the summer of 1939. Iwalani delivered the opening address because she could speak fluent Japanese. After graduating from the University, she became an elementary school counselor and advised many children to reach for their dreams and to better their education. She received the Counselor of the Year award for her efforts. During Iwalani's adult years, she became a Civil Rights Activist on O`ahu, supporting the black troops as they were discriminated against in hotels and other public places.

Adesina Ogunelese, a caregiver, remembers, "I met Iwalani in 2004, at age 87, after receiving a call to come to the island to give Iwalani care. Iwalani suffered a stroke which left her unable to speak, yet we found ways to communicate with each other. She moved around slowly in a walker. Iwalani was a social person and entertained in her beautiful spacious home frequently. She was well loved by the community. Iwalani enjoyed classical music, women in Jazz, World beat and New Aged music. Iwalani loved to be read to, and I read her father's book to her every night as she relived her family history. We often played dominoes together. She had a great game of dominoes, and used her skills to beat me frequently.

One of Iwalani's favorite pastimes was driving around the countryside. She also enjoyed cultural events at the Maui Arts and Cultural Center (MACC). Iwalani continued to dress formally when entertaining outside at events at the MACC when we went to see a jazz or classical music concert. Another favorite activity of Iwalani was participating in Black History Month events in February. I would take her to the library to see the children's excitement when I did a program on Black Inventors.

She enjoyed the poetry of award winning poet Ayin Adams and listened to her CDs daily. She often visited with Ayin in her home. In 2005, 2006, Iwalani rode in a wheel chair as she led Martin Luther King Jr. Parade. Iwalani was the oldest living African American woman on Maui."

Devastated by her passing in 2007, Adesina became inspired to study and research African Americans' contributions to the Hawaiian Islands, including Iwalani's father's book: *Nolle Smith: Cowboy, Engineer, Statesman* by Author Bobette Guglietta.

In the early 1890's, a number of other distinguished African Americans came to Honolulu and one was a well known daguerreotype photographer, James P Ball, Sr., who arrived with his son James Jr., who was an attorney in 1902 in Hawai`i. After leaving Hawai`i in the early 1900's, the Ball family moved back to Hawai`i for James P. Ball Sr.'s health reasons. He died in the Islands May 4, 1904 at the age of 79. James P. Ball, Jr. and his family again moved back to Seattle where they continued the photography business.

Alice Ball, James P. Ball, Jr.'s daughter, returned to the islands for graduate study in chemistry. She was another noteworthy pioneer as she was the first woman to graduate with a master's degree from the College of Hawai`i. She became a chemistry instructor. During her laboratory research, she discovered a breakthrough for

Hansen's Disease, commonly known as Leprosy, a disease which had devastated the Hawaiian community and broken up many families when the afflicted person was sent away to Kalaupapa on the island of Moloka`i.

Ball's discovery and this pioneering treatment was called the "Ball Method" found in Chaulmoogra seeds. She extracted the ether esters from the fatty acids found in Chaulmoogra tree oil. This chemical mixture was injected into leprosy patients to reduce the symptoms they suffered. This discovery brought relief to many patients who were suffering from the disease. Her research findings were considered to be significant and have a large impact on the cure for Hansen's Disease.

The knowledge of Alice Ball's research remained unknown for more than 80 years before it was coincidentally discovered during a literature search. She unfortunately did not receive recognition, or the acknowledgements and honor she was later to receive, because she died in 1916 at the young age of 24. The cause of her death was unknown.

This gifted and brilliant young African American woman researcher who pioneered the first effective treatment for Hansen's Disease, but received little credit for it, was honored by the University of Hawai'i, almost ninety years after her death.

On April 14, 2007, Alice Ball was awarded the Regents' Medal of Distinction for her achievements in a ceremony at the University of Hawai`i at Manoa emceed by Dean Emeritus Miles M. Jackson. The medal was formally presented by Allan R. Landon, Chair of the University's Board of Regents. The ceremony also featured University of Hawai`i professor Dr. Kathryn Waddell Takara. The Regents' Medal of Distinction is presented to individuals of exceptional accomplishment and distinction who have made significant contributions to the university, state, region or nation or within their field of endeavor.

Alice A. Ball, left, with two classmates, at her University of Hawaii
M.S. degree graduation in 1915. (University of Hawaii Archives)

Ninety-one-year-old
Nolle Smith in 1979
(Honolulu Advertiser, 1991)

Charles A. Cottrill, a lawyer, was appointed Hawaii's Collector of United States Internal Revenue in 1910 by President Taft.

Section II
Pioneering S/Heroes of the 20th & 21st Century

Chapter 8

Helene Hilyer Hale

The focus of Chapter 8 is Helene H. Hale. I traveled to the Big Island of Hawai`i to interview the high spirited 91 year old Helene H. Hale. Hale represents the political spirit of African Americans, and she was elected the first African American woman Mayor, then called Superintendent, of the Big Island of Hawai`i, a position that included all of the responsibilities of "Mayor."

Hale's spirit rises like the spirit all those African Americans who seek office in the political arena, in order to bring about positive changes to society. In this chapter, Hale's daughter, Indira Hale Tucker, writes and speaks of her mother's political moments in Hawai`i, both known and unknown to African American Hawai`i residents. Indira shares Hale's love for politics and the land. Indira openly shares her love and admiration for her mother in 'Growing Up with Wonder Woman'. Few people now remember that Helene Hale graced the cover of black owned *Ebony Magazine* in 1964.

HELENE HILYER HALE was born in Minneapolis in March 1918, to Ellen and Gale Hilyer, a lawyer like his father, Andrew Hilyer, who had been born into slavery but was in the University of Minnesota's very first graduating class in 1882. Born in a time when few women or African Americans went to college, Helene was the third generation of Hilyers to graduate from the University of Minnesota.

Born before women could vote, she became a political pioneer in Hawai`i: first woman elected to the Hawai`i County Board of Supervisors (1954) and first woman "mayor" in the state of Hawai`i (1962). Born during World War I, she promoted world peace, chaired the International Relations Committee in the Hawaii House of Representatives, and retired from politics in 2006 at age 88. By example and advocacy she encouraged women to run for office and serve on Commissions, and helped to create today's open door opportunities for women. Like the "Energizer Bunny," she keeps going and going and going. I call her mom.

During the Depressions, Helene Hilyer earned a Bachelor of Arts in Education (1938) in three years while working full time, followed by a M.A. in English. Because Minnesota school systems refused to hire African American teachers (or Jews, and her best college friend was Jewish), she found employment at Tenn. A. & I. State College, a Black College in Nashville, Tennessee. There she met and married William Hale, Jr., son of the college president.

After World War II, they moved to the island of Hawai`i with their young daughter Indira and taught in a local high school. Helene also later started a coffee farm, ran a bookstore, and sold children's books statewide until her husband entered her in a political race (without telling her) in 1954. Ten years later, she opened her own real estate office, promoted sustainable economic development, founded several local organizations from the Girl Scouts and 4-H clubs for her daughter to Business and Professional Women, The League of Women Voters, a foundation to promote the local astronomy industry (now the world largest astronomy complex), Sister City organizations, cultural organizations, political organizations, a local development corporation, and more.

Growing Up With Wonder Woman

There is really only one title for these remarks: "Growing Up With Wonder Woman." Long before I'd heard of the heroine of that name, Mom was Wonder Woman to me because she could do so many things so well and all at the same time. One of the things that used to amaze me was how she could cook a meal, serve it hot, sit down to eat with guests, yet leave a clean kitchen behind. She taught us to cook, but we never mastered that particular trick.

Before she was elected to the Board of Supervisors in the fall of 1954, she had run for Delegate to Congress, or actually my father had nominated her for Delegate to Congress. So my first election with my mother (my father had preceded her in politics and lost), was in July, 1954, exactly 40 years ago. It was an intriguing and fascinating experience for a 10 year old. I was "Press Secretary". I answered the telephone.

But even before she went into politics, Mom wasn't like anyone else's Mom I knew. She was fun to be around, always thinking up something interesting like hiking up to the Mauna Kea snowline, or down to the ocean on the lava flow next to our Kona house where I grew up.

She had a great sense of humor about herself and the rest of the crazy world around her. Nothing got her down for very long. In our house, hypocrisy was perhaps the worst sin one could be accused of, but being DULL was right behind it. She liked to quote the poem from the first page of the Book House set she sold, "The World is so Full of a Number of Things, I'm sure We should all be as Happy as Kings."

"Life is an Adventure", so her personal credo went, or maybe I should say, a play, since she once wanted to be a Broadway producer. We wrote the script. We played the leads. It was therefore our responsibility to make things happen. She wasn't much on the "victim mentality" even though I knew that when she had graduated from the University of Minnesota with a Master's Degree in English from the College of Education, she could not get a job anywhere in the state of Minnesota with any school system because they did not hire Negroes at that time (to use the old fashioned name for us).

Her outlook had a profound effect on me, influencing the Toy Loan Program I run which emphasizes personal responsibility and rewards individual effort.

Education has been a tradition in my home for several generations. Mom's father was a lawyer and her grandfather was in the first graduating class of the University of Minnesota. However, my parents' philosophy about education was not that education was simply a means to a credential for a better job, but that education was about learning, and learning was a lifelong process. Therefore it should be interesting.

Mom read Shakespeare, Chaucer, and poetry to me. At 10, I thought Shakespeare had a great way with words and Chaucer was pretty neat. Then came high school, Oh dear! English teachers tried very hard to convince me that Shakespeare was tedious and had to be admired and dissected but never enjoyed. Too late! Mom had already brainwashed me.

Three cornerstones of Mom's philosophy that I recall were "Where There's A Will, There's A Way," followed by "I Think I Can" from *The Little Engine That Could*" and finally, "If It's Worth Doing, It's Worth Doing WELL."

At about age nine, I wanted to take ballet lessons. The only class was 100 miles away, in Hilo. Of course Mom found a way. We left Kona at 7 am, reaching my class by 9. Mom never merely drove the car, she kind of did some low flying. She spent the day selling children's books. After my lesson, I took the sampan bus into town to the

Hilo Library. I stayed there and read until it closed. She picked me up and we drove another 100 miles back to Kona. Years later, the Librarian wrote me a letter when she saw my picture in the paper, recalling all those hours in the children's room and saying that she'd like to take some credit for the award I received because of all the reading I had done on Saturday afternoons.

Mom could apply "I Think I Can" to almost every situation. She took a woodshop class. Of course I tagged along. I was about nine years old, I believe. She made a high bunk bed. I liked to be very high, because our Kona house had lots of big brown spiders. Then she made a rollout trundle bed. I made the ladder. Needless to say, "The Little Engine That Could" showed up EARLY in my daughter's bedtime stories and sits on the Parent Education Shelf in my Toy Loan Center. "If It's Worth Doing, It's Worth Doing Well" learning to do something, keep improving it and mastering it. This was the goal to aim for, giving it your best effort was both the minimum and maximum requirement. The serendipity is that having done one thing well, people would think of you for something else. This seemed a good standard to pass on to my daughter, who has learned that one consequence of her doing well in school is a nomination to Who's Who Among High School Students, following in her grandmother's footsteps so to speak.

Finally, Mom believed in independence. We learned to cook, sew, garden, and run the generator, because South Kona had no electricity then, giving us responsibility early and backing us up with support. We'd often campaign with Mom, going to the Board of Supervisors' meetings, giving us insight into HOW things get done. Children of other politicians, I found, resented politics because their fathers were always away. Probably because of her inclusiveness, I have maintained a continuing involvement in political activity. Because inclusiveness is both the foundation and mission of her political philosophy, to bring greater participation into the process of democratic governance, this is a good place to end. My heartfelt thanks to Councilwoman Keiko Bonk-Abramson and all the committee members for convening this gathering and inviting me to share a slice of family history with you. It is such a pleasure to be able to say to her while she's alive, "Thanks for all the great memories and a super childhood." May I introduce my mother, Helene Hilyer Hale.

(Letter from India read by John Daggett at Helene H. Hale's 90th Birthday Celebration in Hilo, Hawai`i)

March 22, 2008,

To all the Guests: Thank you for coming to share this special occasion with my mom. You are some of her oldest and some of her newest friends and it is all the more meaningful and wonderful that you are here.

Her daughter, Indira Hale Tucker writes:

Dear Mom,

I've known you all of my life of course. Sorry for causing such an upset that you and Dad had to drive all the way from Arizona to the Mayo Clinic in Minneapolis to convince you that you weren't dying, it was just me on the way! When I was a child, you sure weren't like any other mom I knew…from getting into politics or hosting the women from India who showed me how to wrap a sari or starting the Girl Scouts and the 4-H club at my school to hiking down the lava flow next to our house to the ocean or making a complete trundle bed in woodshop or teaching me how to cook and sew my own clothes or reading Shakespeare and Chaucer to me. Thank you for a priceless gift of loving to learn new things. Sorry that your devotion to exercise did NOT take.

I called you Wonder Woman then, but I'll have to revise this because I still don't' know any other mom your age that is going full steam ahead…so I'm changing it to Energizer Bunny…you just keep going and going and going.

I really, really wanted to be there today but apparently it wasn't meant to be, so what I want to say most on your glorious milestone 90th Birthday is how much I LOVE YOU and am grateful that the universe picked out you as my mother. I've always admired your achievements, have been energized by your presence, felt supported by your continuing love, cheerleading when I've done well or encouraging and willing to drop everything and come help when the challenges seemed overwhelming.

The lessons of your extraordinary Life are enduring…commitment to family, passion for lifelong learning, involvement in community, and fearless advocacy for one's values. While I haven't been able to slow you down long enough to write your autobiography, I hope that the Helene Hale and Tucker and Hale Book Collections will introduce your example and that of others like you to a world-wide audience of women and men, young and old, who will be inspired to take up the cause of improving their communities with imagination a spirit of optimism, resilience, and above all, humor.

Life with Mom…always an adventure…and never dull!

With a Grateful Heart and all my Love,

Indira

Merrie Monarch Hula Festival

Hale also played a major role in creating the Merrie Monarch Hula Festival in 1964. In an interview she said," One of my best department heads was the late George Na`ope. George Na`ope and my administrative assistant, Gene Wilheim, and I, were trying to bat around ideas to improve our economy because we were a very depressed county. So, I sent George and Gene over to Maui to look at the Whaling Festival that they had over there in Lahaina. And when they came back, they came with this idea of having the Merrie Monarch Festival, and George and Gene put it on the very first year. We're very proud of George because he has been with it ever since and has carried on the hula idea all over the world."

In 1964, Hale lost her bid for re-election. Today she concedes it was because "a lot of people were very jealous, I think, and it wasn't the right place at the right time." After politics, she hosted a television show for six months, and then Hale started publishing a tour guide. "That took me all over the island, because I wanted to tell people about the island of Hawai`i. That kept me in touch with people," Hale recalled. "I'll learn to be a housewife again," she said after losing the election. But like Richard Nixon, after losing his bid to become California Governor in 1962, said, "You won't have Nixon to kick around anymore." But Hale was not through with politics!

Back in Office

By the mid 1970s, Hale had divorced, re-married and caught the political bug again. She was elected a delegate to the 1978 Constitutional Convention. Two years later, she won a seat on the Hawai`i County Council and served 14 years (no term limits existed back then). The Council seats were at-large until 1992 when a district system was established. Hale had been living in South Hilo, but figured she didn't have a chance to win there, so she built a house in nearby Puna.

A life long swimmer, Hale spearheaded the effort to build the Pahoa pool, the first public pool in the district. Then another opportunity opened up. Bob Herkes, then Puna's state representative, decided not to seek re-election in 2000. "I tried to get a younger person to run, but that particular person didn't want to run," Hale says. "In the middle of the night, I decided, 'I'll do it myself!'" She won and served three terms in the Legislature before retiring at age 88 in 2006.

A last bit of her local legacy is gradually coming to fruition. She said recently, "When I got to the state Legislature, I found the Pahoa school didn't have a decent gym. The Plantation gym was falling apart. So, I decided we needed a new gym. By getting the community excited about that, we were able to get them money. They should be letting out for bid shortly. I hope I live long enough for the groundbreaking."

At 91, she still exercises an hour every morning, loves to swim, and organized the local United Nations Chapter and a model UN for local students. Recently, the state legislature voted to ask the Department of Education to name a new high school gym (one of her legislative projects) in her honor. She is an inspiration to all.

On Thursday, August 13, 2009, the Hawai`i Tribune Herald staff writer Bret Yager ran the following story on Helene H. Hale: Pahoa High Finally Getting Gym. At long last.

After decades of promises and delays, Pahoa High and Intermediate has broken ground on a new gym, the first the school has ever had. "The class of 1972 was promised by the then-governor that they would have a new gym," Principal Dean Cevallos said Wednesday at a gathering of dignitaries, community members, school staff and students.

"It's finally here, and you'll be able to hit the ball high and it won't go into the rafters." The reference was a poke at the cramped county gym the school has used since 1942.

Speakers, including Mayor Billy Kenoi, state Sen. Russell Kokubun, Rep. Faye Hanohano and Puna Councilwoman Emily Naeole, handed much of the credit to Helene Hale, 91, who was in politics for the Big Island for one half a century. The gym will be named the Helene H. Hale State Gymnasium in honor of the former state representative, who represented Puna in the Legislature from 2000 to 2006, and fought tirelessly to get the gym built years earlier when she was on the Hawai`i County Council.

"She isn't just one servant leader, she's one servant warrior," said Kenoi, who promised to hold Hale on his shoulder so she could take the first shot when the gym is completed. "She's been fighting the good fight longer than many of us have been alive."

The $8.2 million gym will have hardwood floors, bleachers, a concession area and offices for the athletic director and athletic trainers. The 16,000 square-foot building will partially cover an area now being used for outdoor basketball courts.

With a 1,000 person capacity, it will be big enough to hold graduation ceremonies that now have to be held at the Afook-Chinen Civic Auditorium in Hilo. "It'll be a steel building with masonry walls and most likely will be used as a hurricane shelter," said Jack Ho, President of contractor Primatech Construction Company of Oahu, which will build the gym. The project should be finished within a year depending on weather. We understand the people are looking for jobs and we'll make local hiring a high priority," Ho said. Equipped with gold colored shovels, the dignitaries attacked the turf like they planned to complete construction themselves. The common theme was Pahoa finally getting its just desserts.

"It was supposed to happen in May two years ago," Hale said. "I told them I'm 89 and hope to at least see the groundbreaking." Cevallos said there have been at least three occasions he's aware of where the project almost got off the ground. Design money came through, but construction funds never materialized. "Helene and Kokubun pushed it through. We're the only school that doesn't have it's own gym," "Cevallos said. "Funds are there. I just don't want to see them disappear. The status of a $1.8 million request for a second phase that would add lockers and a wrestling room isn't clear."

The Legislature finally appropriated the gymnasium construction funds in 2007, but the project then ran into permitting delays with the county. Primatech plans to be on site with a work trailer in two to four weeks, put up temporary fencing and demolish portions of the concrete basketball courts. "My wife and I live in Mountain View, and I know this project is very important to the community," said Primatech project supervisor, Eric Horton.

National Front

In January, Hale received the National Association for the Advancement of Colored People Lifetime Achievement Award. In the bookcase of Hale's Hilo home, there is a framed photograph of her with another African American legislator from Hawai`i, Barack Obama. This past year, this tried and true Democrat admits she was in a quandary regarding the presidential race. "I'd like to have a woman (as president), but I also have to be for an African

American," she said. "I think anybody we can elect is better than the Republicans that they had and the one they have now."

Hale revealed why she remains tirelessly committed to the community. "I believe people shouldn't retire. You may have to retire from what you're doing right then, but you can always find new things to do. At one point in time, I took Aikido and we had an old sensei, and he said something I have never forgotten: 'As you get older and older, you get stiffer and stiffer until finally they'll put you six feet under as a stiff under the ground. So keep active!"

Over the years, Hale has been in and out of public service, has outlived two husbands and a son, and has battled breast cancer. Twenty years ago, the late Congresswoman, Patsy Mink wrote a birthday card in which she called her, "a valuable mentor."

Today, Hale's main public involvement is running the local chapter of the United Nations Association. "I want to see peace before I die," she says.

Indira Hale Tucker Family

Helene Hale On Front Cover of
Ebony Magazine 1964

Helene Hale Hilyer Family Photo

Helene Hale with Author Ayin Adams

Relaxing with Author Ayin Adams

June 2005 Hilo Public Library Helen Hale Collection

Helene Hale Collection in Hilo Hawaii

Helen Hale & family inauguration day 2001

Helen Hale & Barack Obama

Helen H.Hale & Indira Hale Tucker

Emily Naeole, Helene Hale, & Faye Hanohano

Groundbreaking Begins on "Helene Hale" Gymnasium in Pahoa

August 12, 2009 was the long anticipated groundbreaking of the "Helen Hale" Gymnasium that will be located on the Pahoa High and Intermediate Campus. Many dignitaries in attendance talked about how long this process has taken and all were very thankful that the process has finally started.

Helene Hale, who is a legend around this area, really pushed for this gymnasium many years ago and even today she was very grateful and joked that she was at least happy she was able to see the groundbreaking before she goes on to the next part of her life.

Community members from all parts of Puna came out to support this great project as most locals from around here… are actually graduates or attended Pahoa School at one time or another in their lives.

…The students of Pahoa are one of the last schools to get a gym built…

Chapter 9

Frank Marshall Davis

Dr. Takara shares with readers about black journalist and poet Frank Marshall Davis. Years later, President Barack Obama would become Davis' mentor. Takara takes us through political upheavals through Davis' eyes and uncovers while exposing the hardships and success, truths, and hidden lies between the pages of Davis poetry as well as his life as a journalist.

Frank Marshall Davis in Hawai`i: Outsider Journalist looking In
The Ethnic Studies Story: Politics and Social Movements in Hawai`i

Frank Marshall Davis (1905-1987), was a journalist, labor activist, poet, expatriate, and resident of Hawai`i for almost forty years. As an outsider looking in, he functioned as a significant voice in documenting the progress of the social movement in Hawai`i from a plantation to a tourist based economy. (1) In his weekly column, "Frankly Speaking," in the union newspaper *The Honolulu Record*, he acted as a commentator on the impact of the union movement on the plantation economy in the post war Honolulu scene. As a major national journalist and former editor of the Associated Negro Press, Davis was able to analyze the changing configurations of ethnic groups, class structures and strategies of control. His keen observation of the imperialist forces and his subsequent fall in status due to his outspoken editorials seem a paradox in a "so-called" paradise. His was a voice that inspired and threatened. His uniqueness as a black journalist and his middle class status showed that Hawai`i was indeed one of the few places in the 1940s and 50s where blacks held roles other than agricultural or service workers in a multi-ethnic setting. (2)

Blacks in Hawai`i had certain fluidity between several ethnic groups which afforded Davis a unique platform from which to observe and discuss the consequences of the new economy. He wrote of the parallels of laws and influences between the southern plantation system and plantations in Hawai`i, as well as parallels between Blacks and Hawaiians. His insight into colonial techniques and strategies for dividing the minorities/oppressed groups, his ability to see beyond the binary racism so common in the continental U.S., and his documentation of discrimination and racism in Hawai`i, are a testament to Davis's role as a significant voice and witness in the historical process of Hawai`i's economic development, inter-group relationships, and changing social consciousness.

Before and After Arrival in Hawai'i

The obvious question is why a prominent African American writer and intellectual would choose to go to the territory of Hawai`i in 1948 and not to Europe, Russia, or Africa, like so many of his compatriots. (10). Most African Americans were leaving the islands after the war to return to their African American communities. Davis was arriving. Why? The local Hawai`i newspapers thought they knew.

In December 1948, several articles in the *Honolulu Star- Bulletin* and *Honolulu Advertiser* announced the Davis's imminent arrival, then their delay, and finally their belated arrival. Several were accompanied by photos of the two. The press presented Davis as a successful journalist and as a poet and 1937 Julius Rosenwald Fellow. There were contradictory reports on the purpose of their trip. "Executive Editor of ANP Is Due Tonight" says that Davis is in

Honolulu for a visit that will combine a vacation with business . . . [that he] is planning a story on racial groups in the Islands . . . [and that] Davis also plans to visit army and navy posts" (December 8, 1948). "Negro Press Executive Here" says that Davis "is here on an inspection and vacation tour of the islands . . . [and] will tour army and navy installations and other territorial institutions" (*December 14, 1948, 10*). "Davis Considers Hawai`i Advanced in Democracy" says the Davises are in Hawai`i "for a visit of not less than four months." Davis will write a series of articles on his observations of the island scene and also will work on a book of poetry which he hopes will capture the spirit of the islands in verse," although the photo caption accompanying the article says the Davises are "in Honolulu for an indefinite visit" (10). Davis's wife was presented as an artist, writer, and executive editor of a national press agency, who planned "to do watercolors of the islands during her stay" (*Honolulu Star-Bulletin,* December 10, 1948) l2 "The obvious question is why a prominent African American writer and intellectual would choose to go to the territory of Hawai`i in 1948 and not to Europe, Russia, or Africa, like so many of his compatriots." (10). Most African Americans were leaving the islands after the war to return to their African American communities. Davis was arriving. Why? The local Hawai`i newspapers thought they knew. In December 1948, several articles in the *Honolulu Star- Bulletin* and *Honolulu Advertiser* announced the Davis's imminent arrival, then their delay, and finally their belated arrival. Several were accompanied by photos of the two. The press presented Davis as a successful journalist and as a poet and 1937 Julius Rosenwald Fellow. There were contradictory reports on the purpose of their trip. "Executive Editor of ANP Is Due Tonight" says that Davis is in Honolulu for a visit that will combine a vacation with business . . . [that he] is planning a story on racial groups in the Islands . . . [and that] Davis also plans to visit army and navy posts" (December 8, 1948). "Negro Press Executive Here" says that Davis "is here on an inspection and vacation tour of the islands . . . [and] will tour army and navy installations and other territorial institutions" (December 14, 1948, 10). "Davis Considers Hawai`i Advanced in Democracy" says the Davises are in Hawai`i "for a visit of not less than four months. Davis will write a series of articles on his observations of the island scene and also will work on a book of poetry which he hopes will capture the spirit of the islands in verse," although the photo caption accompanying the article says the Davises are "in Honolulu for an indefinite visit" (10). Davis's wife was presented as an artist, writer, and executive editor of a national press agency, who planned "to do watercolors of the islands during her stay" (*Honolulu Star-Bulletin,* December 10, 1948).

Other citizens of Honolulu, however, knew that Davis was more than a civic figure. As Henry Epstein, a local labor leader familiar with Davis's mainland reputation has said in an interview just before Davis's death,

> "What I remember about Frank was that he was a very prominent and well-known black poet who was very highly respected in Chicago. You'd see his picture once in a while on the society page of the Chicago newspapers and when they had fund raisers for progressive organizations in Chicago, if Frank Marshall Davis was coming you had a real attraction, a prominent person that would help bring people into the event. . . . You saw him in what's now called civil rights affairs. . . . I don't think Frank was recognized as the prominent person that he was back in Chicago." (Rice & Roses 1986a, 2:1 & 5)

Epstein was right. In Hawai`i, few people accorded Davis the status and respect that was his due, partly because they were unfamiliar with his past, and partly because it was a time when people were afraid to take risks due to the shadow of McCarthyism.

Davis's own reasons for coming to Hawai`i were less overtly political. In an interview shortly before his death for the television series *Rice and Roses*, he recounted how the internationally famed singer Paul Robeson, whom he knew from Chicago and the progressive movement there, influenced him to come to Hawai`i: " [Robeson] had been over here the previous year on a concert set up for the ILWU. And he was telling me how much he liked it and he said he was going to come back every year. He never did show up again. But anyway, he was instrumental in helping me to form my desire to come over." The welcome proved to be impressive. When the Davises first arrived, the extensive media coverage made them feel accepted. They were stopped on the street and warmly greeted by many local residents. He and his wife were offered rides when waiting for a bus, and were invited to dine at the Willows, which refused to serve most African Americans at that time. Davis in short sensed that Hawai`i would be a relaxed and friendly place to live, and "Within a week I had decided to settle here permanently, although I knew it would mean giving up what prestige I had acquired back in Chicago where I was now appearing each year in *Who's Who in the Midwest* and had been told by the editors that in 1949 my biography would be included in *Who's Who in America*." Clearly, Davis was willing to sacrifice a great deal to escape the tensions and demands of his experiences on the Mainland, for he concluded that "the peace and dignity of living in Paradise would compensate for finding a way other than as a newspaperman to make a living."

In certain ways, Hawai`i was a welcome change. Davis for instance marveled that he had many white friends in the islands:

> "I was somebody who came from the same general environment and over-all background. At first it was shocking to hear Caucasians tell me what "we" must do when, on the Mainland, they would likely say "you people." Many whites of considerable residence here are as bitter about racism as any of us and are glad to live in a place where overt prejudice is not customary. I have known *haoles* to go back home for a long visit but return ahead of schedule because they couldn't stand the attitudes of their old friends." (1992, 317)

But Davis almost immediately came to realize that some of these "strong friendships with many haoles" developed because he was not Oriental, and in fact, his anomalous position as an African American in Hawai`i would become the source not only of his own sense of Hawai`i as both a multi-ethnic and colonialist culture, but also of his outspoken sympathies and opinions in print, which would markedly affect his own life in the islands. And yet, because he felt that, with his arrival in the islands, he had at last found dignity and respect as a man, as a human being, Davis proved slow to complain. He had resolved that even politics was never to take this dignity away from him again.

The ILWU and the Honolulu Record

His expectation that he could not support himself through his writing soon proved accurate. Although when he arrived in Hawai`i his welcome led him to assume that finding a job would not be difficult, especially with all of his experience and expertise in journalism, when he tried to get a salaried job with a large local daily, word had apparently gotten around that Davis was pro-labor, and the paper, which was controlled by the Big Five (American Factors, Theo H. Davies, Alexander & Baldwin, Castle & Cooke [Dole], C. Brewer and Co.), ignored him. The word was in fact correct, for Davis's initial contacts with Hawai`i all had extremely strong ILWU ties. Paul Robson's own Hawai`i acquaintances, which he passed on to Davis, insured that "when I came over, one of the first things that I got involved with--well, I met all the ILWU brass, Jack Hall and all of them, and I went--they had both of us over to various functions for them--Harriet Bouslog was also a good friend" (Davis 1986a, 5:29-30). (3) Davis soon realized that he had arrived at a very important moment in Hawai`i labor history. The huge International Longshoreman's Workers Union (ILWU) strike was imminent, pitting labor against the Big Five. For Davis, this was the kind of political ferment and struggle between the powerful and powerless that he thrived upon:

> "When we arrived in 1948, the Big Five had an iron grip on island economy. Organized labor led by the ILWU with Jack Hall at the helm was still struggling to break its hold. Groups of oriental businessmen were forming cooperatives and attacking from another angle." (Davis 1992, 313-314)

On the eve of the famous ILWU strike of 1949, the big issue was wage parity. Labor (non-white) was demanding from management (white) equal pay with workers on the West coast. The white executives and employers were starting to fight back against the union, and even their wives organized the "broom brigade," an anti-labor group to oppose the strike. (4) They named themselves *imua*, a Hawaiian word which means to move forward, and they tried to convince the wives of the striking workers to side with management and join a presumed better life. They also launched a publicity campaign supported by the commercial newspapers accusing the ILWU of threatening to starve the people of Hawai`i with the impending strike because much of the food came from the United States.

Davis and his wife both publicly aligned themselves with the ILWU. (In response to the "broom brigade," Helen picketed with other labor wives.) This did little to endear them to the power elite in the islands, who of course controlled public images. As Ah Quon McElrath recalls,

> "Generally, the community didn't look upon trade unions with a great deal of love and affection. Besides which the Izuka pamphlet about Communism in Hawai`i had just been issued so there was fuel added to the fire which had started during the 1946 strike when they said that outsiders were coming in and taking over . . . Hawai`i and destroying the sugar industry as well as the pineapple industry." (1986, 24:1)

Since as Davis recalls, "Not too long before my arrival, all Democrats were tarred with this same brush by the ruling Republican clique (1992, 323-24). His problems multiplied when it became clear that there were concerted efforts to brand him an outside instigator, and even a Communist. "The local establishment, which evidently had been given a file on me by the FBI, flipped," Davis recalls, they said "I was a Communist and a subversive and a threat to Hawai`i."

The ILWU sought to unify the workers and encouraged them to transcend their diverse ethnicities and cultures:

> "When the ILWU started organizing . . . they were advised that they must have an inter-racial leadership or the ILWU would not charter them or would not help them organize. . . . This spirit of all the people working together is what built up the ILWU and it's what gave them a lot of strength." (2:9)

And one of the strongest and most sustaining forces for this strength and solidarity would prove to be a publication which Davis's previous experience made him perfectly suited to help.

In speaking of the origins of this paper, Epstein notes:

> "The *Honolulu Record* was started by Koji Ariyoshi and Ed Robo with the help of the ILWU and the idea was to have an independent newspaper which was friendly to the labor movement and could present the other side of the news. . . . They had a lot of articles that you wouldn't read anyplace else." (1986a, 2:1 & 5)

Davis himself recalls that even before he left for Hawai`i, "[Robeson] and Bridges who was head of the ILWU and the CIO in the Pacific Region, (5) suggested that I should get in touch with the *Honolulu Record* and see if I could do something for them."

When Davis became a columnist for the *Honolulu Record*, the newspaper was just beginning to document the imminent strike of the ILWU and the subsequent breaking up of the monopolistic power of the Big Five over the various immigrant labor groups, including the Japanese--who were the most powerful and radical, Chinese, Filipinos, and Portuguese. As Davis later commented in an interview, "During this time when there was this controversy between the ILWU and the big five firms, I was obviously on the side of labor . . . and the strike was something that was opposed by virtually all of the haoles of importance around here and many of the oriental business men . . . who had a vested interest in keeping things going with the Big Five" (1986a, 9:52).

Davis observed how the ILWU publicized itself through a daily radio program and labor newspapers such as the *Honolulu Record*. It offered a pro-labor viewpoint to answer the conservative *Advertiser*, the *Star-Bulletin*, and a radio show by celebrity DJ AKU; and Davis, with his vanguard ideas and deep understanding of class struggle, and his ability to discern the local ethnic struggles and exploitation, was quick to become a writer for the *Record*. Or in his own words, "Not long after arriving in Hawai`i, I began writing a regular weekly column for the *Honolulu Record,* supported mainly by the ILWU membership, and was openly friendly with its leadership." This was hardly a career move, since "The *Record*, of course, was not financially able to add me to its payroll." But Davis felt an affinity with Koji Ariyoshi and Ed Rohrbough, "who were its editorial mainstays" (Davis 1992, 323), and since the *Record* was created to provide an alternative perspective to the news, Davis found it to be the medium through which he could critique the socio-political structure of the Territory of Hawai`i and keep in touch with the common people. When Ariyoshi offered him a column, which became known as "Frankly Speaking," therefore, Davis couldn't resist.

Davis as Columnist

What Davis could bring to the *Honolulu Record* was an acute sense of race relations and class struggle throughout America and the world. In his column, for instance, Davis openly discusses imperialism and colonialism. He compares Hawai`i with other colonies and attacks the press for its racist propaganda. He identified and connected the non-white people of different cultures and colors as victims of exploitation. One "Frank-ly Speaking" column dated Jan. 12, 1950 states:

> "To the people of Hawai`i, Africa is a far-away place, almost another world. And yet in many ways it is as close as your next door neighbor. The Dark Continent suffers from a severe case of the disease known as colonialism which Hawai`i has in a much milder form. The sole hope of the dying empires of Western Europe is intensified exploitation and continued slavery of African workers through U.S. money and munitions. There are strikes in Africa against the same kinds of conditions that cause strikes in Hawai`i."

> "Maybe you think of Africans as black savages, half-naked, dancing to the thump-thump of toms-toms in jungle clearings, if you think of them at all. You may have gotten your impressions through the propaganda of press, radio and films, intended to sell the world on the idea that Africans are inferior and backward. It comes from the same propaganda mill that sells Mainlanders the idea that Japanese and Chinese and Filipinos and other people of different cultures and colors are also inferior and backward." (Vol. II, No. 25, 8)

More typically, though, Davis drew on his own experiences on the Mainland. He often grounded his critiques by referring to contradictions between social practice and American constitutional ideals. In one column dated Jan. 19, 1950, for example, Davis writes that we "should bring the Bill of Rights back to life in our constitution":

> "It has been a casualty of the cold war, yet it is as important today as it was when it was first framed. For, to paraphrase Lincoln, we have come to the evil day when none but the supporters of our bi-partisan foreign policy are entitled to life, liberty and the pursuit of happiness. That is not the kind of democracy Washington and Jefferson built in the young days of our nation; it is a dictatorship of thought absolutely repugnant to our national traditions. Let Hawai`i lead the way back to Americanism."
> (1949-1952, Vol. II, No. 26, 8.)

His eye for class analysis, and his former experience with institutional racism, led him to discern quickly the exploitative role of big business and landowners in the lives of the ethnic non-white minorities. He had already written an editorial on the Massie case when he was living in Chicago, so he knew that Hawai`i residents experienced virulent episodes of racism. Once in Hawai'i, he soon recognized various ways racism permeated the society. He became familiar with the subtle forms of discrimination, and on occasion the more blatant ones as well; for example, the segregated housing facilities at Pearl Harbor, and particularly Civilian Housing Areas 2 and 3 (CHA 2, CHA 3) (See Takara 1990:202) He learned about the hostilities between Okinawans and Japanese, and various other inter and intra ethnic group prejudices and discrimination. (Davis 1992: 314)

He observed the discrimination in certain bars and restaurants, and the reluctance of the legislature to pass a Civil Rights law, because by passing such a law the myth of Hawai`i as a racial paradise would be shattered. And soon, within his columns, he was speaking about these matters. He attacked big business, the HUAC witch hunts, thought control, the loyalty oath, fascism, the Smith Act, white supremacy, Jim Crow, the War Machine, imperialism, racism and prejudice, reactionaries, discrimination on Supreme Court appointees, dictatorships, and ultra-conservative wealthy people. He exposed unemployment, land and housing problems, blacklisting, and the exploitation of minority groups. He espoused freedom, radicalism, solidarity, labor unions, due process, peace, affirmative action, civil rights, Negro History week, and true Democracy to fight imperialism, colonialism, and white supremacy. He urged coalition politics. He called for people to investigate the real threats to democracy, such as big business interests, repression, censorship, thought control, the war machine, anti-communist hysteria, unemployment, reactionaries and fascism, segregation and racism. He called for the ordinary person to fight for democracy, to revise the land and tax laws. He exhorted the people of Hawai`i to wake up from indifference, to challenge police brutality, to support democratic politics, to gain economic power from land reform.

In speaking of his writing and influence, McElrath notes in an interview:

> . . . (H)e wrote some very prescient articles about race relations in Hawai`i and given the fact that Frank, a black married to a white, had come from that kind of situation in Chicago, it's utterly amazing how he was able to size up the race relations here in the . . . Territory of Hawai`i. As a matter of fact in the first article that he wrote, I have the date here, January 13, 1949, he talked about Anglo-Saxon culture being not better, but different from Hawaiian culture, Japanese culture, Chinese culture, and he talked a little bit about the typical reaction of the whites to different cultures . . . started a whole series of articles on race relations. As a matter of fact, one of his articles ended with this phrase.

"These beautiful islands can still chart their own future." I'm not sure that Frank would agree that the future which we have since chartered has been a good one or a bad one. (McElrath 1986, 24:3)

Nor was the course he charted a particularly comfortable one for himself, since it so clearly revealed the racial underpinning of so many supposedly "social" or "economic" problems.

Indeed, during this period most whites, commonly called *haole* in Hawai`i-- descendants of missionaries, merchants, and/or landowners--had a colonialist attitude, and looked down on the local Hawaiian people and immigrants who worked for them. Class and ethnicity were well-defined and obvious. (McElrath 1986, 24:3)

As Epstein recalled, "When I first came to Hawai`i, my understanding was the banks had dual salary schedules and that Haoles had one rate of pay and local people had another. I don't know whether it was justified by classification or how they covered it up but it was commonly accepted. (McElrath 1986, 2:2)

Traditionally, *haole* were discouraged from seeking employment in subservient roles and were permitted neither to work as laborers on the vast sugar and pineapple plantations, nor for the most part to join the trade unions. Management kept the different ethnic groups in segregated housing areas with discriminatory salary schedules, playing one group against the other. Davis himself was certainly cognizant that the whites were still in control in Hawai`i: the acting Governor at that time was Gov. Steinback, a native of Tennessee, and his unofficial attitude often coincided with that of the many southern whites imported to work for the military (1992:313).

Davis was very familiar with how civil rights issues often worked themselves out in racial terms. He relentlessly focused on the socio-economic and political problems which he observed and could expertly analyze due to his twenty years of newspaper experience, labor union work, familiarity with global politics, and the many years of experience browsing thirty-five newspapers a day. Moreover, Davis was used to hostility from the white community; he had always been an outsider, a *malihini*. He was not easily thwarted. He was not intimidated by the FBI--although his influence was diluted by its discriminatory practices and harassment--since he had previous experience with it in Chicago at the ANP, where he had developed a strategy for giving them misinformation (Davis 1986, 5:28). "I was vice-chairman of the Chicago Civil Liberties Committee," Davis recalled, "and so the Civil Rights Congress was in existence when I came over here. And we were, the local civil rights chapter, was affiliated with the Civil Rights Congress, which was another thing which did not sit well with the powers that were (1986, 6:34).

Not surprisingly, such activities were not appreciated by the status quo in Hawai'i. Though welcomed at first, when Davis turned his past experience on present-day Hawai'i, those in power became upset. This was especially the case when he advocated the creation of a union or committee of the various ethnic groups, often by illustrating how in the U.S., African Americans had worked together with other groups in coalition politics to get things done. The result, predictably, was accusations of anti-haole bias and hatred:

In my column I tried to spell out the similarities between Afro-Americans and local people and local leaders thought my fight against white supremacy meant I was anti- white. I opposed any and all white imperialism and backed the nations seeking independence following World War II. I so incensed members of the White Power Structure that I became the constant radio target of an anti-labor organization known as IMUA, formed to combat the long waterfront strike in 1949, and whose membership was overwhelmingly haole. Even the two dailies were not above taking occasional potshots at me. (1992: 323-324)

In the late 1940s and early 1950s, many who were opposed to the status quo were also considered Communist, but this did not deter Davis from continuing his path as a social realist, a militant voice in a gentle land. In a remarkably brave move, he even attacked the HUAC for failing to investigate flagrant abuses of democracy such as restricted housing, and for wasting their time by protecting the interests of big business. In his "Frank-ly Speaking" column, dated Dec. 28, 1949, he notes:

> The Hawai`i un-American Activities Commission has an excellent chance to break with tradition and win respect for such investigations, by probing the activities and programs of powerful groups that use color, religion or national origin as a basis for denying equality to all.

The matter of restricted housing should be thoroughly aired and those who perpetrate this evil practice should be forcefully exposed. Naturally, it would hit some of the Territory's most influential persons, many who dominate our economy. Is the commission willing to step on big toes or will it confine its investigations to the weak and powerless?

Restrictive housing covenants hit the majority of the Territory's population, since most are non-haole. In the year that I've been here, I have been blocked by this evil and totally un-American practice. Twice it came up when I sought rental units; last week it was raised again as I contemplated purchase of a home in an area off Kaneohe Bay Drive. It was Castle leasehold property and restricted, I was told. And so the deal was off. (*Honolulu Record*. 1949-1952, Vol. II, No. 22, 16)

And yet, it was precisely because such exposes and attacks seemed to be targeting the white powers that be that Davis was able to serve as a spokesman for many who were neither white nor African American. Davis wrote about this phenomenon--appreciatively, but with clear insight as well:

> Despite propaganda spread by southern whites imported to work for Uncle Sam during World War II and the unofficial attitude of the territorial administration then headed by Governor Steinback, a native of Tennessee, local people generally were ready to accept Afro Americans at face value. Of course many had strongly warped ideas, drawn from traditional stereotypes perpetuated by press, movies and radio, but in the final analysis they based attitudes on personal relationships. I soon learned many Japanese went through a sizing up period when blacks moved into a predominantly Japanese neighborhood or they came in contact at work, but when they decided to accept you it was on a permanent basis, not as a fair weather friend. Dark Hawaiians tended to dislike Afro Americans as a group (many lived in mortal fear white tourists would mistake them for Negroes) but developed strong friendships with individuals; Hawaiians are traditionally warm and outgoing. (1992, 314)

From very early on he felt this support after he invested in property on the Windward side of O`ahu, first in Kahalu`u, then in Hau`ula where the family remained for seven years with the addition of several children. Davis seemed to feel welcome in Hau`ula, and only moved to the leeward Kalihi valley in 1956 for its convenience and proximity to hospitals, schools, and work in Honolulu.

For seven years Helen and I lived at Hau`ula, a predominantly Hawaiian village on the ocean some 31 miles from Honolulu. When I began driving daily to town and back, local boys who knew my schedule often waited beside the highway, sometimes for as long as three hours, to flag me down and ask questions about their personal lives, explaining, "you're not haole [white] so I know I can trust you." In Hau`ula I joined the Democratic precinct club, virtually ran the organization and was sent to the state convention by the predominantly Hawaiian membership who told me that since I was educated and articulate, I could speak for them. (Davis 1992, 316)

When Davis became well-known for his writing for the *Honolulu Record*, he found this support only increased:

> I found that many of the people around here . . . were quite . . . on my side. And I would
> sometimes be in my car, and I would stop at a light and, this was after I was writing
> this column for the *Honolulu Record*, . . . an Oriental businessman . . . would tell me
> that he recognized me from my picture which accompanied my column, and he'd say,
> "You know, you're writing exactly what I would say if I could. I just don't know how
> to say it." So therefore I got a lot of friendships which grew that way. (1986a, 9:52)

So too did support from less likely sources, all because the implications of Davis's writing did point out the haole dominance in Hawai'i. His columns later had the effect of getting him customers for his paper and office goods business, since Oriental businessmen appreciated that he had defied "the big haoles."

With this kind of support, and with the examples of experience, Davis came to advocate reform measures which either took years to achieve, or are still challenges for the state. Land reform laws were finally enacted in the 1960s to resolve some of the problems which Davis addressed and spoke out about in the 1940s and 1950s. And his comments on the nature of Hawai'i's agricultural economy, and the future it must move toward, sound very familiar today, at a time when such issues as lease to fee conversion and sovereignty for Hawaiians are so centrally a part of public discourse. One column dated Jan. 19, 1950, for instance, states that

> Provision should be made for breaking up the big estates which control so much of
> this territory and force Hawai`i to depend upon a sugar and pineapple economy. Small
> independent farmers need to have access to land at a reasonable fee so that they can
> engage in diversified farming and thus make the people less at the mercy of the
> shipping industry and importing monopolies for food. For we have reached a period
> in our history when not only political and social rights need to be spelled out, but
> economic rights as well. (1949-1952 Vol. II, No. 26, 8).

Other Modes of Comment: Poetry

One of the most important sources of information about Davis's positions during this time, however, comes from work written long after and therefore more concentrated and coherent. I am referring to his poetry, which he wrote up to his death. Of several poems about Hawai`i, two are exceptional, "Tale of Two Dogs," and "This is Paradise," because Davis addresses the class and ethnic problems in Hawai`i: the exploitation of the indigenous Hawaiians and immigrant workers by the haole oligarchy.

"Tale of Two Dogs" attacks the United States imperialism in a historical poem about the sugar and pineapple industries:

Then the strangers came;

They loosed their chained terriers

Of pineapple and sugar cane;

Sent them boldly into the yard

To sniff with eager green noses

At the sleeping old.

Long since

Pine and Cane

Have taken over the front lawn.

Snapping impatiently at obstructing ankles;

They run between

The tall still legs of the motionless mountains

As if they originated here

And the silent ancients

Were usurpers.

Here in this cultivated place

Growing the soft brown rose of Polynesia

The dogs have scratched

Digging for the buried pot of cash returns

Killing the broken bush

Under the flying dirt

of greed and grief.

. . . There is none so patient

As a tired mountain drowsing in the sun;

There is no wrath so great

As that of a mountain outraged

Destroying the nipping dogs

Loosed on the front lawn

By the Strangers. (1987, 4-5)

The accusatory voice, the exposure of the raw power of the usurpers, and the suggestion of revenge make this poem powerful, especially in contrast with the ancient silence of the motionless mountains.

"This is Paradise" is an epic five-section poem. Davis offers an ironic travelogue in which a superficial tourist from Iowa might find a quaint, exotic paradise peopled with friendly, peaceful, prismatic natives contented to serve. In the second section of the poem, he reveals the "soiled slip" of the real Hawai`i behind the props and stage setting: "Captain Cook . . . sweeping over the old way / inundating the ancient gods / flooding the sacred soil of custom and tradition" (1986b, n.p.). He speaks of the missionaries as "magicians, the conjure men of Christianity / placed the vanishing cloth of Mother Hubbards on the women / Then whoosh and presto/ Nudity into nakedness" (n.p.). He points to the irony that:

Now that it was uncivilized to kill by spear or club, guns became a symbol of progress:

and at the end of Part II he writes,

The missionaries came with Bibles

The heathen natives had the land

Now the natives are no longer heathen,

They have the Bible and Jesus

and in this equitable trade --

This oh so reasonable swap

The missionaries got the land. . . . (Davis 1986: n.p.)

In Part III, Davis begins his critique of the Big Five: "Under the manure of the missionaries / sprouted the Big Five / Time was / When the Big Five had God on their payroll. . . . But that was before the Union/" (n.p.). He proceeds to describe the struggle between the ILWU and the Big Five; the plain people finally become freed from fear but still remain victims of poverty.

In Part IV, Davis speaks lovingly of the ethnic mix of the inhabitants of the island but adds irony. A haole tourist from Birmingham states: "Went home after two days of his intended month: / 'You can take these Goddamned islands,' He told friends in Dixie/ And shove them up your ass / I don't like Hawai`i --/ Too many niggers there'" (n.p.). Davis points out the divisive irony of color as a dark Hawaiian speaks to a lemon-light Negro using the expression "boy" in describing his best friend who was an African American in the army. Later Davis uses Asians in the poem to ridicule the "funny kind names" of the *haole*. The more subtle problems of miscegenation are addressed when two *haole* parents referring to the Japanese bride of their son say "It's all right to sleep with 'em / But for Christ sake/ Why do you have to marry 'em?" The bride subsequently returns to the islands.

In another ironic passage, the Keakana family goes to the beach on the weekend to fish, "And the tourists from Topeka riding around the island in the prancing buses smile pinkly and murmur: 'How quaint, how carefree the Hawaiians are, not a worry in the world, nothing to do but loaf and fish just like their ancestors'" (n.p.). Davis finishes the vignette with the comment that John Keakana weighs his fish to sell and to eat in order to "stretch monthly pay within $40 of what the social scientists call necessary for minimum health standards." Davis reveals the low standard of living and poverty which a typical native-Hawaiian family might be confronted with in contrast to the tourist-oriented, technological society in which they find themselves in modern times, and in contrast to their original relationship to the land (`aina) in the islands.

In Part V of "This is Paradise," Davis satirizes the cliché that there is no race prejudice in Hawai`i, creating imaginary scenes where skin color and ethnic identity are equated with attitudes of superiority and inferiority:

One week in the country

And the navy wife phones her landlord:

"Across the street

Lives a bunch of dirty Hawaiians;

Next door on our right

A family of lousy Japs;

On the other side

A house full of slant-eyed Chinks;

And in front of us

On our very same lot

A white bitch married to a nigger --

I want our rent money back." (Davis: 1986 n.p.)

Davis ruthlessly exposes the color line in Hawai`i and the racism in Paradise brought by the white Americans, and for that he did not find, or in the case of this poem did not even seek, an audience.

Davis's Hawai`i Legacy

Was there any way that Davis, as an African American man in Hawai`i, could remain unconventional, radical, and defiant in the face of strong political and economic machines, and be financially successful? Was there any way to maintain his political views and aggressive nature and prosper with no allegiance to a power base in the community? The answer is an unequivocal no. Unfortunately, no significant African American community existed in Hawai`i to provide Davis with emotional and moral support, and an expanded audience and market for his writing. Also, because he was still concerned with the issues of freedom, racism, and equality, he lacked widespread multi cultural support. Many islanders felt economic issues were more important, or, they simply dared not challenge the system again after the strike, and risk their jobs, security, and well-being, since most had come to Hawai`i as immigrants and had only recently moved into a tenuous middle-class status.

One can only imagine Davis's frustrations at his inability to become a successful writer in Hawai`i after his promising beginnings in Atlanta and Chicago. He rarely complained, but he must have felt incomplete if not bitter when he found dignity but not freedom to develop his potential and lead the distinguished life to which he was accustomed. Considering the controversial subject matter of Davis' writing, it is little wonder that some whites looked askance at his presence in the islands. He worked quietly, he wrote even when he no longer published his writings, and he talked with those who came to visit him, always seeking to present the truth of his vision, confident that social justice and human dignity would finally prevail. Indeed, despite his radical rhetoric, Davis was optimistic that good relations between ethnic groups could and would lead to a better world.

Davis was a pioneer to Hawai`i in the sense that he was a tireless witness recording the race and class history of his time, thinking of himself not as a local person, but rather as an expatriate who found a community which accepted him, and a personal level of human dignity and peace which he treasured. If Davis did not succeed financially, why did he not succeed literarily and gain status and renown? Did Davis eventually tire of carrying the race struggle and protest message on his shoulders, or did he simply carry his battle to another level? Although certainly not "successful" in the traditional, capitalistic sense of the word, could the life of Davis be said to end in defeat? What constitutes defeat?

It can be argued that Davis escaped defeat like a trickster, playing dead only to arise later and win the race, although the politics of defeat were all around him. If society seemed to defeat him by denying him financial rewards, publication, and status, he continued to write prolifically. He stood by his principle that the only way to achieve social equality was to acknowledge and discuss publicly the racial and ethnic dynamics in all their complexity situated in an unjust society. He provided a bold, defiant model for writers to hold on to their convictions and articulate them.

His testimony remains. The social criticism and perceptive analyzes are just as relevant today when the conditions of exploitation continue to thrive, and deprive many people of color, minorities, and those who are poor.

Notes

1. For more information on the labor movement and transition of Hawai`i to a tourist based economy see Beechert, Working in Hawaii: A Labor History.pp 225, 285.

2. See Beechert.

3. For more information of Hall and Bouslag see Beechert, p 227.

4. For further information on colonial wages see Beechert, p 311.

5. For More information on Harry Bridges see Beechert, p 228.

6. For more on the end of colonialism in Hawaii see Beechert, p 310.

THIS IS PARADISE
by Frank Marshall Davis

I.

Here is the peaceful postcard paradise

A considerate sun slaves overtime

The moon dances to a soft guitar

The champagne rain bubbles and warms

And June lasts a full twelve months;

Sun-washed, moon-dried,

Diamond set in the lava ring

Of brown green mountain and rainbow valley

In the blue jewel case

Of the Pacific.

The seven main islands of Hawai`i

Born two thousand miles from California

Are inhabited by people, pineapple

Sugar cane and Pearl Harbor

Grown dependently together--

This much is in the travel folders.

The rich cruise here in winter

Planes bring the middle class in summer

(The poor see the sights any time

At their neighborhood movie or on T-V:

Who says there's no equality in America?)

With air above and water below

Subject to municipal regulations

And official boundaries

Afloat on the ocean,

You enter the City & County of Honolulu

A thousand miles

Before you reach

The City & County of Honolulu

(Discount any comments

From birds and fishes--
They have neither voting rights
Nor civic consciousness)
Bring along a blank paper mind
Until the Island of Oahu
Inflates from dime to dollar
And then a sack of bulging bullion
Split by the worried brow of Diamond Head;
See the languid palms
Dressing the shining coral shores;
Bright houses and slick buildings
Like quarters and dimes
In a pocket of greenbacks;
Come luxury liner
And see the little welcoming boats
Like chicks around a mother hen;
Brown boys in bright trunks
Diving to spray tourists
With splashes of Local Color;
Hula dancers waving their hips
To conduct the Royal Hawaiian Band;
Come by air
And see the Flyspeck Mountains
Spring into gaunt giants
As the land reaches up
Like a friendly hand;
Come either way
And wear a lavaliere of flowers
On that greeting drive through strange streets
Glowing with the brights prismatic people;
Now enter into the baited door
Of your tourist trap in Waikiki,
Pour your eager flesh and bone
Into a bathing suit,

Dash to the nearby beach

And sit;

Sit while barefoot boys bob by

Twanging ukes;

Sit while waves regularly report

Their quotas of spray and surf board riders;

Sit for dinner under soft stars

Sit until the night grows confidential

And solicits for his scented woman, Sleep

Now take a postcard to your room

Write "Having wonderful time---"

And go to bed, murmuring

"It's really true!

This really is Hawai`i!"

Tomorrow, long after the sun

Has wandered into your room

Sat awhile, and left his calling card

You will leisurely arise

Breakfast on papaya,

Guava jelly and Kona coffee

Then buy a gaudy Aloha shirt;

Now start your conducted tour

Of the island,

See for yourself the fabled sights

Leap to life from the guide book;

Go to a luau and eat like the natives--

The quaint, friendly, childish natives;

Pinch the buxom bottoms of the islands girls

While your wife makes eyes

At the sleek brown boys;

Loaf and live

By all means live;

Go to the Outer Islands

Visit the bubbling volcanoes on Hawai`i

Huge Haleakala crater on Maui

Wonderful canyon on Kauai

Or stay in Waikiki;

This is Paradise

Any way you take it--

And so two weeks, a month slip by.

Now it is time to leave

Return as president of that Iowa bank

(Good old Iowa, the REAL U.S.A)

Back as buyer for that Boston store

(Good old Boston, pride of New England);

You've had as good a time

As money could buy

At prevailing prices;

(That explanation

By the Hawai`i Visitors Bureau

Was logical:

Everything's shipped in, you know")

You'd like to come again

Not next year but sometime

But no matter

You've plenty to tell the folks back home,

You've seen the peaceful postcard paradise,

You've seen the bright prismatic people

And now you know Hawai`i!

Chapter 10

Kathryn Waddell Takara, Ph.D.

Kathryn Waddell Takara, Ph.D., born and raised in Tuskegee, Alabama, taught at the University of Hawai`i at Manoa for more than 31 years in the Ethnic Studies Department and in interdisciplinary studies. She developed courses in African American politics, history, and culture.

In 1971 she was the only African American lecturer and later Professor teaching Black Studies in the University of Hawaii academic setting for many years. She earned a BA. in French from Tufts University (Jackson College), 1965, a M.A. in French from the University of California, Berkeley, 1969 and a Ph.D. in Political Science from the University of Hawai`i at Manoa, 1993, and has been a Fulbright Scholar twice.

Dr. Takara wrote the following article for Honolulu magazine in 1971 based on some of her observations and revised it recently.

"It Happens All the Time" or Does It?

It happens all the time, even in Hawai`i, especially if one is an African American. Stereotypes and selective memory are common, even in Hawai`i, where I have lived now for more than 40 years. Today 2009, Bell Hooks speaks of 'talking back.' Bessie Head speaks of the man who came to the realization that "I am just anybody." Somehow I combine these two points of view and reflect on my experience as an African American immigrant to Hawai`i.

After graduating with an M.A. in French from U.C Berkeley, leaving behind the turbulent black power revolution, the Black Panther movement, the anti-war movement, and radical organizations like Students for a Democratic Society (SDS), the Weathermen, the hippies, and the peaceniks, I arrived in Honolulu with my Caucasian husband, our baby daughter, lots of energy, yet few preconceived notions about the islands, except that I had listened to melodious strains of Hawaiian music when I was young, since my dad enjoyed it. I had heard that it was a place of racial harmony, good for people with interracial marriages, nurturing for children, and a kind of paradise with fragrant air, balmy weather, beautiful beaches, and full of romance.

Being an Alabama girl, of course all this was alluring. I had been raised in a time and place where fear hung like a razor's edge, where Jim Crow and prescribed behavior was the status quo, where it was against the law for me to marry my former husband, where my closest cousin, a civil rights worker, was shot and killed for trying to use a whites' only bathroom, and the accused killer was acquitted, in spite of convincing evidence against him. I became bitter, enraged, carried my recollected racial experience to the East Coast where I received my private education, to Europe where I lived and studied French, and finally to West Africa. Still, I was somewhat utopian in my philosophy, artistically inclined. I had long worn flowers in my hair and loved to go barefoot, even though my mother hated the latter and thought it was a "country" way to act.

So when we deplaned in Honolulu one balmy evening marveling at the sweet air and exotic flowers, I hardly noticed the black porters at the airport. In fact, it didn't immediately strike me that I saw no other blacks around for several weeks, as we hustled and bustled and got settled in at the elite private school where my husband had been recently hired to teach. What I did notice was, whenever I was not with my husband in a public place, friendly local people would inevitably ask me if I or my husband (whom they assumed was black) was in the military.

After a few months, I began to substitute-teach at public and private schools on O`ahu and soon began to realize, by the curiosity of the students, that there were few if any African American teachers or students in the community. The more I read the local newspapers and watched television in those days, the more I was offended and embarrassed by the sensationalized stories about blacks: riots, unemployment, welfare, and crime. And there were few counter stories or role models to make people think we were not all in some way stigmatized. I began to feel anger and pain that even outside of the continental shores of America, people were still learning how to be prejudiced.

My second year, I was offered a job teaching French at a small private college, where I worked for two years, and then I was hired in the university system in the new Ethnic Studies program to teach a course on African Americans. The following year I enrolled in the Ph.D. program in political science, prompted by my recent divorce, and my desire to teach and inform the public on our neglected black history and contributions to society. As a single mother who now had to support my daughter, I realized that I would need a Ph.D. to advance in my profession and to gain the respect of my colleagues. I also remembered the words of my father, who had constantly reminded me since I was in elementary school that I had to always do more and be better than anyone else in order to be considered equal.

I chose to study political science for a number of reasons: (1) the university did not offer a doctorate in French; (2) my cousin had been slain in the civil rights movement; (3) I knew that to gain tenure in Ethnic Studies, I would need a doctorate; and (4) political science seemed relevant to Ethnic Studies and the political science department had an excellent national reputation at that time. When I began my coursework, there were no African American professors in the College of Social Sciences, and only one tenure-track, full-time African American professor out of more than two thousand faculty members. There were no more than five or six black graduate students at that time.

Moreover, as a mother I realized that the local community did not offer information about African Americans in the public schools, mainly because the majority of teachers were not informed, had little if any contact with blacks, and had not been exposed to any academic courses taught by or about blacks. Indeed, there seemed to be little knowledge or understanding of the historical African American experience beyond the public and often demoralizing fictions. I was surprised that the Hawaiian Islands and local community did little to encourage support, or sustain a noticeable African American presence or community, which could in turn develop and promote cultural awareness, business interests, political power bases, and intellectual forums. As I actively searched for African Americans, I found a few black churches, social organizations, and entertainers in town, and of course athletes at the university. (Out of 20,000 plus students at the university, about 100-200 African Americans were full-time students, and about 80 percent of those were athletes. Unfortunately, the statistics at the university have not changed very much).

Of the approximately 29,000 African Americans living in Hawai'i when we arrived, the military was by far the largest representative group, numbering perhaps around 20,000. The several thousand permanent residents were living and working throughout the islands, and many had assimilated into the local community and culture through intermarriage. This was fine, but when other ethnic groups had a visible economic and cultural presence, it made me want to promote the same in order to enhance the self-esteem and dignity of our children and our group. I also knew that we had many positive qualities and talents to share with the world. Therefore, whenever there was an opportunity, I had my daughter do a report on an outstanding African American or African to instruct her class and teacher.

I slowly began to meet other African Americans, and after a small racial riot at the marine base, I began to work as a mediator between black G.I.'s (who were often incarcerated in the brig) and the predominantly white officers. Perhaps what struck me the most was how alienated these young black men felt here. Of course, much can be said about socio-economic factors predetermining their attitudes, but many said it was the most prejudiced place they had ever been. I certainly never felt this way, although in retrospect perhaps part of their complaint was the lack of a feeling of the support and understanding that comes from a visible, supportive, and representative community. As a result of racial problems in the military during this period, several people of diverse ethnic groups created a black cultural center featuring food, music, books, and discussion groups in downtown Honolulu, which catered to the military. However, many longtime black residents no longer felt the need for an active African American community center since they had assimilated into the island lifestyle.

Meanwhile, my daughter seemed to be accepted into the local community since she looked "local," and unless/until I showed up with my afro and obvious continental connection, most assumed she was another ethnic mix like a majority of the children in these islands. But even here in "paradise," *hapa* (half) black children can be maligned as a result of the stereotypes, institutional and interpersonal racism, historically generated fears, and racialist ideologies which have come to the islands with the missionaries, the plantation owners, the military, tourists, and of course the media.

Yet on an individual level, my daughter and I soon felt quite at home here, comfortable without the constant tension between black and white, secure in a community where the majority were many minorities, where an individual could be rewarded by his/her contributions and not only because of skin color or ethnic affiliation. Of course I would be lying if I did not say that people of darker hue, the Hawaiians, Filipinos, Samoans, Fijians, Tongans, and more recent immigrants, including African Americans, have fewer connections, advantages, and privileges than do the whites, Japanese, Chinese, and Portuguese, to mention a few with obviously lighter skin color, have better jobs, and more power. Nonetheless, there is considerably more diversity, mingling, and opportunity for anyone who is well trained, prepared, and willing to compete as an outsider, that is, someone who was not born and raised in the islands.

For several years I worked hard and went to school, and eventually remarried, this time to a "local" man. We had a daughter and struggled to buy a home in the country (where we could afford one), raise the children, and later send them to private high schools and colleges.

In 1976, I began to work on an oral history project on African American women in Hawai'i, and to my surprise I discovered that a few black men and women had been in the islands since the late 1700s and early 1800s. However, due to the great amount of intermarriage and the various and erratic historical methods of categorizing black people in the islands, in the Census, research was very difficult and tedious, not helped by locals who seemingly found it disturbing to learn not only of our small yet long and consistent presence, but also the institutional discrimination which discouraged our coming and staying. Unlike the process on the mainland, where persons of African descent were automatically classified as "negro," "Colored, " "Black" or "Afro-American," the census takers often labeled blacks as Portuguese, Puerto Ricans, part Hawaiian, part something else, or "other."

Even in 1995, perhaps because of our small numbers (3 percent of population), we are still often categorized with Samoans, Tongans, and other small minority groups as "other." I also discovered that there were other African American immigrants, some as early as 1913, who were well educated and of light complexion, who wanted to forget their haunted heritage and who preferred to pass for white, thereby escaping the restrictions, handicaps, and stereotypes of being born "black" in America. Amongst these were a few outstanding women who contributed actively to the Hawaiian community in politics, art, entertainment, and business. For example, some blacks who called themselves part-Negro in the 1910 census found it easier to become part-Hawaiian in 1920.

It was some years later, after I had had my second child, that I renewed my research and read about Alice Ball, a "Negro" chemist at the University of Hawai`i, who in 1915 started research on a leprosy serum that was later used at hospitals and at the leprosy colony at Kalaupapa, on the island of Moloka`i.

I wondered why there were so few black residents in Hawai`i for so many years, and I discovered some amazing facts. It seems that although individual blacks were readily accepted and assimilated into the community, mass immigration was discouraged as early as 1882 when the Honorable Luther Alolo introduced in the legislative assembly a resolution that efforts to repopulate the islands with Negroes be discouraged (the Hawaiians had been largely decimated by diseases). In 1913, there were strenuous efforts to keep the U.S. Army's 25th Negro Infantry Regiment from being stationed in Hawai`i. Yet they did come, made quite a favorable impression, and again, some stayed on to marry, have families, and create more daughters and sons, most of whose descendants were subsequently also classified as "part" or "other". These people gradually faded into the local community, most never learning African American history or culture, many not even knowing that they had a rich black heritage.

During World War II, several thousand black men and women came to Hawai`i as soldiers and civilian defense workers. In this period, there was reportedly much friction between the races, perhaps due to the seeds of prejudice planted previously by those missionaries and planters who came or returned from the mainland, as well as by the military population itself. To balance flaring tempers and incidents, the military largely maintained segregated housing during the 1940s, called "Little Americas" for its personnel.

At Hickham Air Force Base, black women were housed separately until a petition was filed. During this time, their barracks were neglected, habits of visitors and guards became lax, and finally two black women were attacked by unauthorized visitors. An investigation followed, and eventually segregated housing was abolished.

The Navy was also flagrant in its discriminatory treatment toward those of African descent, even in the islands. In an interview, Clarissa Wildy said she joined her military husband in the islands, only after a long and inexplicable delay in California, even though white women and their families were constantly being sent on to Hawai`i to join their husbands. Finally, after as much as months of waiting in some cases, the black women registered a complaint with an admiral, who assumed no responsibility for the delay. However, a few days later, a freighter with thirty black women aboard set sail for Honolulu. Had they in fact been waiting to have enough black women from around the country so that they could ride together in segregated accommodations across the Pacific? The structural patterns of racism and oppression seemed to spread over land and sea, but I was philosophical, the more I learned, and again noted, "It happens all the time."

Like many others who have chosen to settle in the islands, Wildly commented that after the initial adjustment in CHA2 and CHA3, segregated housing (two streets on base where only blacks were permitted to live), and after the war when many returned to the mainland, she had no particular problems, and grew to love her home in a multiethnic, multicultural environment.

Through the years, a few blacks have been active in public life and politics. Helene Hale arrived with her husband, both educators, in 1947 to escape the racial discrimination on the mainland and to raise her family in a place with less discrimination. (See Chapter 8 on Helene H. Hale)

Meanwhile, I struggled with my part-time job at the University of Hawai`i and became active in civil and human rights issues, gender issues, and race relations. For a while I worked with and taught blacks in the military, became involved with the literary arts council, coordinated events featuring African American scholars and artists, and began to use public speaking and poetry as a forum for black history and culture. The longer I lived in the islands, the more I realized how isolated the local inhabitants were from a spectrum of African Americans not affiliated with the military.

Civic and Social organizations were established from the 1940s on. In addition to the NAACP, there were other social groups, the Wai Wai Nui, the Eastern Stars, several sororities and fraternities, an African American Association, and most recently an African American Chamber of Commerce. Moreover, there are two black newspapers, several black businesses, a Black Pages publication, several large annual social events including the Martin Luther King Jr., dinner dance at the Hyatt, which has featured such outstanding speakers as Martin Luther King III and the Reverend Louis T. Farrakhan. There are also more black tourists. However, rarely are blacks included in the tourist industry, which caters to Caucasians from the mainland and Europe and Japanese from Japan, both groups that often hold negative stereotypes about African Americans.

Many African American women would agree that there is a sense of alienation here in the islands, especially for the new arrival. There is no geographic community, although African Americans often settle in centers near the numerous military installations around the islands. Some have observed that the cultural sensitivity, traditions, music, and events so significantly lacking beget the crisis of violence, poverty, low self esteem, and the deterioration of our communities. However, there is also optimism, especially among those with creative ideas or those who are well prepared in their fields, as doors sometimes open more readily than one would find on the mainland. In other scenarios however, the many local minorities, Filipinos, Hawaiians, Pacific Islanders, Chinese, Japanese, and even Caucasians, are the ones who are able to benefit from economic opportunities for "under-represented" groups, sometimes at the expense of African Americans, who are a less visible, more highly suspect minority.

So, if this be paradise, a place of racial and ethnic harmony, a haven for interracial couples, it is also a place where prejudice is overlooked, discrimination is subtle, and corporate ceilings are clear as glass. Overt discrimination is rare, dehumanization is not uncommon; yet the illusive "it" of marginalization persists, it happens all the time, but less here than in many other places.

Trailblazers, by Dr. Takara was recently published in *Hana Hou Magazine*.

TRAILBLAZERS

It is 1915, in a rugged, parched terrain, a work crew labors, clearing a trail. They toil partway up the flank of a massive volcano, breaking lava rock with picks. They angle their mules for protection against the cutting winds and the burning sun. Draw closer and you will see they are all black (except for their white supervisor, who casually leans against a wagon, directing them). The men sing a work song as they hack at the bare lava. Closer still, and you can see that the men wear uniforms. They're soldiers, Buffalo Soldiers.

From 1913 to 1918, the U.S. Army's 25th Negro Infantry Regiment was headquartered in Hawai`i. At that time, just two decades after the overthrow of Queen Lili`uokalani, few in Hawai`i had heard of the Buffalo Soldiers or knew their distinguished history. Even today not much is known about the Buffalo Soldiers contributions in Hawai`i, and little documentation survives in the state, if it ever existed. We do know that beginning in 1913, they built an 18 mile trail to the summit of Mauna Loa. They also built a cabin so that scientists could spend extended periods of time studying the volcano. The trail and cabin, which are still in use today, are perhaps the only visible signs of the Buffalo Soldiers' presence in Hawai`i.

Even as far back as the War of Independence, black soldiers had served in the military while struggling to overcome prejudice, discrimination and invisibility. Not only did they fight with distinction, they helped open the American West after the Civil War. Yet their contributions often appear as little more than marginalia in the annals of military history.

"Buffalo Soldier," a phrase made world famous by Bob Marley's song, is a term for any black soldier who served in the segregated troops from just after the Civil War until the integration of the armed forces during the Korean War. They served primarily in the 9th and 10th Cavalry and the 24th and 25th Infantry divisions, fighting in numerous wars including the Civil War, the Indian Wars and in the Spanish-American conflicts in both the Caribbean and the Pacific.

Some were sent west (sometimes transported in cattle and freight cars because blacks were banned from traveling in passenger cars) to carry out work considered too menial or laborious for whites. With secondhand, obsolete equipment and horses rejected by the white cavalry also stationed on the frontier, they built roads and outposts, escorted wagon trains, monitored watering holes, safeguarded railroad crews and constructed telegraph lines. They secured the Mexican and Canadian borders, defending white settlers from marauders and bandits. They patrolled, protected and sometimes subdued ninety-nine Native American tribes scattered over the thousands of miles between Montana, the Dakotas and Mexico.

It was after skirmishing with the black troops that one of those tribes, the Cheyenne, dubbed them "Buffalo Soldiers." Many black soldiers had "wooly" hair and dark skin like the buffalo, but the name also connoted courage, spirit and fighting prowess. The name, which caught on with other Plains tribes, was considered an honor. Buffalo were sacred to the Native Americans. Though they often fought with the tribes, the Buffalo Soldiers also enjoyed a respectful relationship with them, learning how to survive the harsh winters; how to use buffalo for food, clothing and shelter; how to scout. Some Native Americans became guides for the black soldiers and taught them their guerrilla combat style and their stealth and skill on horseback.

With their distinguished performance in harsh conditions, the Buffalo Soldiers challenged racial stereotypes; for example, they debunked the myth that blacks could not survive in extreme cold climates.

Again and again, black soldiers performed admirably under difficult circumstances, exceeding expectations. It is not surprising, then, that they were tapped to build an 18-mile trail up a barren volcano.

When the Buffalo Soldiers arrived in Hawai'i in 1913, no one had yet written a history of blacks in the Islands. The Buffalo Soldiers in Hawai'i probably weren't aware that Honolulu once had a small but vibrant community of black businessmen, many of them musicians who played in King Kamehameha's band before the Civil War. Most of those men married Hawaiian women, had children and blended into the community after a couple of generations.

It's unfortunate but perhaps not surprising, then, that when the black soldiers of the 25th Infantry arrived in the Territory of Hawai'i, they encountered hostility and fought with distinction in the Philippines and with Teddy Roosevelt's Rough Riders in Cuba. Even other minority groups had more privileges than blacks; the census classified Portuguese and Puerto Ricans as white for election purposes and special status. By 1918 the Selective Service classified Native Hawaiians as white for the WWI draft. But the black soldiers were tough men who were used to segregation, poor living conditions, dangerous assignments and hostile environments.

About 800 black soldiers settled in at Schofield Barracks (named for Lt. Gen. John McAllister Schofield, whose younger brother, Maj. George Wheeler Schofield, had commanded the all-black 10th Cavalry in the Indian Wars and had led them against the Mexicans in a border skirmish in 1875). Lt. Gen. Schofield was a friend of Hawai'i businessman Lorrin A. Thurston, who in turn was a friend of the famous volcanologist Thomas Augustus Jagger, founder of the Hawaiian Volcano Observatory. Jaggar had tried to lead several expeditions to the top of Mauna Loa in 1914 but was unsuccessful due to the elevation (13,678 feet) and the harsh conditions: rough lava, violent winds, noxious fumes, shifting weather, extreme temperatures and a lack of shelter, water and food.

The ancient 34-mile Ainapo Trail was in poor condition, unsuitable for transporting cumbersome scientific equipment. So, Thurston asked the military to build a better trail and campsites in the desert of Mauna Loa. Who better than the Buffalo Soldiers, who had already built trails through the difficult terrain of the high Sierra, in Yosemite and Sequoia national parks?

In October 1915, about sixty black soldiers in Company E shipped out for Hilo. They set up camp near Volcano House among the mist-hung *ohi'a* forests. In a little more than two months, Company E completed the Mauna Loa trail and built the ten-man Red Hill Cabin and twelve-horse stable. Of their work on the mountain and the hardships they endured, no record- either photographic or written-has yet been discovered. Only a cabin, a stable and a trail winding silently up to a summit survive.

But one account of the soldiers' experience in Hawai'i does exist. In 1917, two years after the project's completion, George Schuyler, a famous black writer of the Harlem and Chicago Renaissance who served in the 25th Infantry at Schofield, returned to the Big Island. He recorded the soldiers' fascination at the strange volcanic landscapes they encountered.

"H Company spent a pleasant week on the island of Hawai'i, camped in a barrack on the rim of the Kilauea volcano. We traveled by inter-island steamer to Hilo, then by wide-gauge railroad to the railhead at the foot of

Mauna Loa mountain, the twin of Mauna Kea, and from thence we hiked up to the 4,000 foot plateau where the fiery crater of Halemaumau was inside the Kilauea volcano. We passed through the fantastic fern forest, saw the garden where Russians raised strawberries as large as crab apples in steamheated soil, visited the Petrified Forest and went over the whole volcano area. We journeyed through the Devil's Throat connecting two small volcanoes, scrambled the 900 feet to the bottom of the crater, Kilauea-Iki, which was as flat as a tennis court, sweated in Pele's bathhouse, a deep cave in which volcano steam rose every fifteen or twenty minutes."

By the time Company E returned to Honolulu from Mauna Loa, the local community's attitudes about the Buffalo Soldiers had begun to change. Crowds started showing up to support the black soldiers: In the military band their musical talents were admired, their precision marching attracted spectators and their baseball team was reputed to be one of the best in the nation. Before departing the Islands in 1918 for reassignment in Arizona, some of the soldiers of the 25th served in the honor guard at Queen Lili`uokalani's funeral.

It would be decades before black soldiers in Hawai`i regained the acceptance of the Island community. In the years after 1918, when Jim Crow laws ensured segregation, many Buffalo Soldiers coming through Hawai`i on their way to the Philippines experienced blatant discrimination. At the outbreak of WWII, there was a mass movement to keep a black labor battalion of 600 men out of Hawai`i. During the war, several thousand black military and civilians came to the Islands to help with the war effort, but most facilities off base were closed to blacks, even in Waikiki. After the world war, a few black soldiers stayed on in Hawai`i and helped to slowly dispel negative stereotypes as they assimilated into the local communities, mostly on the Leeward coast of O'ahu. Their work to overcome more than a century of racism in Hawai`i continues to this day.

In 1972 a former Buffalo Soldier named William Waddell retired in Honolulu with his wife. He had distinguished himself as the first black veterinarian to graduate and pass the Pennsylvania state board exam in 1935. He had co-founded the School of Veterinary Medicine at Tuskegee Institute in Alabama, where he worked with George Washington Carver on peanut research and oil therapy. He joined the Reserves and served in the 9th Calvary. After the death of his wife, he moved to Ka`a`awa, on the Windward side of O`ahu, where he happily spent the remaining eighteen years of his life with his family. Dr. William H. Waddell, one of the last living Buffalo Soldiers, was the father of Dr. Kathryn Waddell Takara.

While living in Hawai`i, he maintained his connection with the 25th Infantry (now integrated) and was often invited to speak at ceremonies at Schofield Barracks. Until three months before his death in January 2007, at the age of 98, he continued to address military audiences with words of courage, patriotism and hope. He told riveting stories of his days on the Mexican border, and of his adventures in North Africa and Italy, where he was the veterinarian responsible for the care of 10,000 horses and mules. He accepted the military's invitations to speak even when he could no longer walk. After his speeches, he would treat his escorts to lunch at the Crouching Lion Inn, where he was a welcome icon.

Buffalo Soldier daughter, Dr. Kathryn Waddell Takara writes, "My father was a humanist who challenged injustice and believed that through service to his country, he could gain acceptance for himself and others. He opened doors for minorities in federal hiring, promotions, housing, education and science .He was both an inheritor and a torchbearer of the legacy of the Buffalo Soldiers. He and all the others excelled in the face of overwhelming odds to blaze a trail to the summit…for anyone who might come after.

Dr. Kathryn Waddell Takara

Kathryn Waddell Takara, William Waddell,
and Karla Brundage

WHO IS THE BLACK WOMAN IN HAWAI`I?

What pulls a person/to a family/to a group? /What does one seek/in a race? /if there is no family/no group/of one's own/how does one satisfy/the taste? /Mechanical to seek/Inevitable to greet/those others from/another tribe and place/Survival is the aim/ Communication tames/and trust, not fear/Fills the space.

Kathryn Waddell Takara

Historically a study of Black women in Hawai`i is complicated. It is sometimes difficult in fact to know who the Black woman is in the Islands. There are several reasons for this.

First, the process of categorizing Black people on the mainland is different from the traditional process of census-taking in the Islands. On the mainland, due to the previous inferior status designated to Negroes who were forcibly brought to the United States as slave labor, all people of any Negro ancestry were classified as Negro.

By contrast, the former census-taking policy in the Hawaiian Islands was radically different. For example, a person with any Hawaiian blood could be considered part- Hawaiian. A person who was part-Japanese or part-anything could claim and be claimed by the family of the parent who was other than Negro. Thus, in the census, many of Negro descent were listed as part-Hawaiian, "colored" sometimes (which for a while included all non-whites such as Japanese, Hawaiian, Chinese, Indian, etc…) or "part" plus the preferred ancestry.

Many others who would have been classified as Negro on the mainland were often listed with the Portuguese and Puerto Ricans, according to their country of origin. Some of the Puerto Ricans who came to Hawai'i in about 1902 were of Negro descent, although in the census they were listed as Caucasian until 1940!

Then there were also the descendants of Black Portuguese men from the Cape Verde Islands who arrived in Hawaii on whaling ships between 1820 and 1880, many of whom jumped ship and remained in the Islands with Hawaiian wives and families. Again, unlike the census policy on the mainland which classifies anyone of known Negro descent as Negro, these men were classified as Portuguese according to their country of origin before 1900.

There were also those Negroes who came to the Islands, some as early as 1913, who were well-educated and of fair complexion, who wanted to forget their haunted heritage and who preferred to pass for white, thereby escaping the restrictions and handicaps of being born "Black". Amongst these were a few outstanding women who contributed actively to the Hawaiian community in politics, art, entertainment, and Business. It should be no surprise, therefore, that some Black in the past chose another race with which to identify that was more acceptable to the community in order to avoid the latent antagonistic feeling indirectly introduced into the Islands against Negroes as a group. For example, some Blacks who called themselves part-Negro in the 1910 census found it easier to become to become part-Hawaiian in 1920. There is a fear even today among a few of the possible or imagined repercussions of being discovered to be of Negro origin. With theses considerations, one can now examine the first available history of a Black woman in Hawaii and brief biographies of other black women in the Islands.

Betsey Stockton (See chapter 6).

Annie V. Crockett, also known as Mother Crockett, went to Maui with her husband who became District Magistrate of Wailuku. She herself was distinguished as an outstanding teacher, and her daughter, Grace, in 1918, received a master's degree in education at the University of Michigan, an unusual accomplishment for a Black woman in that historical period. Both mother and daughter were responsible for the education of many fine women who later became principals and leaders of Maui.

Mrs. Crockett also had a fondness for and a certain touch with plants, especially flowers, and she was in fact the creator of many of the hybrid hibiscus flowers that now enhance the beauty of the Islands.

Why were there in fact so few Blacks here in Hawaii for so many years? It seems that although individual Blacks are readily accepted and assimilated into the community, mass immigration was discouraged as early as 1882…while many Black women have come to the Islands with their husbands who have been affiliated with the military of federal government, others have come for other reasons.

Helene Hale (see chapter 8).

Marva Chaney Garrett, an arrival in Hawaii in 1955, perhaps was most responsible for reorganizing and creating an effective organization of the local chapter of the National Association for the Advancement of Colored People (NAACP). She was president from 1960 to 1966. She was responsible for pioneer work in investigating and opening the housing available to Blacks. She co-organized the Wai Wai Nui, a Black women's social club, and has been involved in much community work.

Ms. Garrett often observed hostile attitudes and name-calling among many youths in the school system and felt responsible to work toward elimination of such fears and prejudices. She provided an intensive educational campaign through the NAACP to the local community on the history of Black people, with the result of more understanding and fewer stereotypes and fears by Hawaiian residents toward Black people.

She also turned her attention to the local community in Waianae, her place of residence, where she found many dark-skinned Islanders shunning association with Blacks because of a fear of being considered Black with all of the negative connotations implied.

Ms. Garrett was one of eight chosen for leadership training to head the Waianae Model Cities Program. After receiving a bachelor's degree from the University of Hawai`i in 1973, Ms. Garrett went to Harvard University where she received a master's degree in 1974 and an advanced degree in the School of Education in 1975 in Administration, Planning and Social Policy.

She planned to continue to work in Waianae where she was a long-time resident and where she felt needed due to her strong emotional commitment to the struggles of the local community.

Carol Mengesha, proprietor of Carol's International Beauty Salon in downtown Honolulu, arrived in 1956. Initially she had a husband and child. After a divorce she became a single woman with a child. Ms. Mengesha joined the NAACP and found it to be a good referral group and helpful in times of difficulty.

To support her child and herself, she found herself forced to work at several odd jobs. She was unable to find employment as a cosmetologist, the area in which she was trained. There were other obstacles, like a feeling of alienation and the difficulty of finding a place to rent. A Black woman alone with a child was considered a risk.

Finally, the decision was made to go to barber school. The custom here at the time was for Black women to have beauty shops in their homes. It was her aim and her dream to establish her own salon.

After several years of odd jobs and part-time cosmetology, an important opportunity finally arrived in 1961 through a Chinese woman who owned a beauty shop in Kalihi. Mengesha rented a booth on a percentage basis, but she was allowed in the shop only when the owner was present. Three years later, through persistent efforts, she found a space for a salon in downtown Honolulu where she was located for many years.

It was still necessary to maintain two jobs until her clientele grew. Her clientele became a mélange of different ethnic women, which provided variety and creativity. Carol liked it *this way!*

Doris I. Ray, whose mother was a minister, lived in the rural area of Oʻahu since 1962 with her two children. It was her opinion that one's personality and attitude have much to do with one's reception here in Hawaiʻi.

Upon moving to Hauʻula, where she went to be close to those of Hawaiian descent, she was enthusiastically welcomed. In fact, two families "adopted" her and the children and went so far as to see that she reached work and was picked up from work everyday in Honolulu. There was also a hot dinner waiting for her upon her return from town.

Initially, Ms. Ray found it difficult to find a job in the area in which she had been previously employed (a secretary for the College Department at Random House/Alfred Knopf, Publishers in New York City). In order to support her children, she found it necessary to accept various other types of occupations: a packer at Dole Cannery, a wrapper at Sears, a checker at Pacific Laundry, and a professional dancer on all the major islands.

Subsequently, she became a secretary, an actress, a playwright and a director. She was able to return to school and earned master's degree in Fine Arts at the University of Hawaʻʻi.

Iwalani Mottl, one distinguished Black woman born and raised here, was a mother of three children and a retired educator. Aside from rearing a family, Ms. Mottl was active with the feminist movement and in the Democratic Party. She was honored by the Hawaiʻi State Legislature in 1976 on the occasion of her retirement and also received an award from the Hawaiian Personal Guidance Association for her work in that field.

Ms. Mottl was tireless, charming and full of grace, yet determined and firm when necessary. She was currently Chairperson on the Advisory Board of the Salvation Army Facilities for Children and Youth and a member of the State Council of Federal Projects through the State Department of Education. She was one of those special women who has been included in **Men and Women of Hawaiʻi** since 1960 and was considered worthy enough to be included in the **World's Who's Who of Women,** which indicates her level of achievement as a woman internationally.

She greatly valued her family and assumed the responsibility for their formal, cultural and social education. The late sixties and seventies have brought a new breed of Black women to the Islands. These women have brought with them certain new attitudes from the mainland that are relatively more sophisticated and politically aware than previously and reflect their education and experience in a country still grappling with the specter of racism. One can feel from their presence a certain pride, understanding, and togetherness which reflect a different level of consciousness, a new experience.

Cassandra Burnett arrived in 1967 with her husband, a Navy man, and her two children. Affectionately known to some as "Mau Mau Cass," she often told the story of trying to obtain a haircut in a "natural" style and being refused and referred to Hotel Street over and over again. No one, it seems, wanted to take the responsibility for cutting her kind of hair and possible ruining it. Finally, she ended up in Ewa Beach where she found a poodle groomer who was not afraid and sheared her soft and kinky hair into a "natural."

In 1968, she joined the NAACP to help in the fight against discrimination in housing and jobs. Feeling a need for another type of organization, in 1970 she became actively involved in the plight of Black military men and became a charter member of the Committee Opposing Racist Practices and Sentiments (CORPAS), which, with the help of the Council of Churches and other interested groups, established a Black Cultural Center in Waikiki to serve primarily the Black servicemen as well as Black people in the community.

When asked about being a Black woman in Hawaiʻi, Ms. Burnett answered that she is often asked to be a kind of spokesperson for Black people as a whole, which she is not prepared to be. The many referrals and allusions to "you people", "your people", and the ceaseless curiosity about the Black person's attitudes and ways of life, have to her seemed to be a manifestation of subtle racism and stereotyping in Hawai`i.

For Ms. Burnett, vigilance is a key. She sometimes feared that Hawai`i was developing its own type of discrimination based on the size of the bank account and the color of the skin. Somehow, even here these two factors seem to come together.

Audrey Fox Anderson is a lawyer. She arrived in Honolulu in 1968, after a distinctive practice as a criminal lawyer in New York City. Educated at Howard University and Fordham University School of Law, Ms. Anderson was extremely active in the Honolulu community. She had an extensive general practice in the state and the federal courts, and the Workmen's Compensation Board. She was a candidate for the State Senate in 1974.

Her practice involved setting up corporations, wills and real estate matters. She was also affiliated with a number of professional organizations. Her professional experience made her perceptive and strong whereas her experiences as a Black woman provided her understanding and insight. She asserted a control in her life through choice and perseverance, thereby overcoming certain liabilities of being a woman and being Black.

Winifred Simmons, a psychiatrist, arrived in the Hawaiian Islands from Washington, D.C. in 1970 with her husband. She found the transition to be extremely smooth, probably due to friends already established here in the islands. She came to the Islands to expand her life experience.

In her work, her clients were mostly women and, as women, they faced similar difficulties be it here or on the mainland. The difference here is that there were fewer Black clients. She observed a cultural sensitivity on the mainland with Black women that is lacking here, probably due to the lack of a Black community and a unique experience where attitudes, beliefs, and values with a Black perspective are often cultivated and exchanged. The experiences of Black women here do differ from the experiences of their sisters on the mainland.

Many Black women here would agree that there is alienation, especially for the new arrival. There is no Black community physically speaking, and Blacks have arrived as individuals. Many miss the opportunity of association, the culture, music, and traditions that are shared within a traditional Black community.

In Hawai`i, distance separates Black women as most tend to live in separate communities and neighborhoods and it is often by mere accident that one meets other Blacks, except for a few clubs which meet infrequently, among them the Wai Wai Nui, the Eastern Star, the NAACP, the Links, and a few others, or by an introduction through a friend.

Moreover, aside from the NAACP, there are no large institutions here to focus on the problems of Black people, which somehow do not just disappear by crossing the ocean, nor is there an emphasis to encourage the development of Blacks as a group, despite the current trend toward ethnic pride and history in Hawai`i. Thus, if a Black community per se is lacking, so is a political base. There is no pressure felt by institutions to make provisions for a Black constituency, be it ever so small. In fact, often Blacks are not even viewed as a minority here, but are rather silently ignored as an ethnic group.

Nevertheless, there remains a psychological bond between Blacks due to the historical experience of oppression and racism on the mainland. There are also decided advantages to living in Hawai`i, that must not be overlooked. There is the absence of peer pressure to be constantly politically active and one has the time to reflect upon and evaluate life and its myriad of possibilities. Moreover, if one is qualified, there are jobs available here, and there are currently Black women working in a great variety of positions.

There are still the expectations and the stereotypes that trail behind like a shadow, but one can step out as a person, a Black woman, and see hope for the future, the children, the world.

To gether

To gather

A harvest

  Of woman

   In we.

Chapter 11

Miles M. Jackson, Ph.D.

Dr. Jackson is a retired Professor and Dean Emeritus of the University of Hawai`i at Manoa. He served for twenty years in the School of Library and Information Technology and was Dean from 1982 1995. Dr. Jackson is a graduate of Virginia Union University and earned a masters degree from Drexel University's College of Information Studies and a Ph.D. in Communication from Syracuse University. He began his career as a librarian/ information specialist with the Free Library of Philadelphia. Following a few years in Philadelphia he held positions as Head Librarian at Hampton University, 1958-1962, Territorial Librarian in American Samoa, Chief Librarian at Atlanta University Center, and Associate Professor at State University of New York.

Dr. Jackson has written over 50 articles in various professional publications and as a freelance writer he is an occasional contributor to the Honolulu *Advertiser*. Among the seven books he has written or edited are *Pacific Islands Studies*, (1986), *Publishing in the Pacific* (1985), *Linkages Over Space and Time* (1986), *And They Came* (2001), and *They Followed the Trade Winds: African Americans in Hawaii* (2005). He writes a monthly column for Mahogany, covering people of color.

Dr. Jackson has served as a consultant to the People's Republic of China, Taiwan, Pakistan, India, Fiji, Papua New Guinea, Australia, New Zealand, and Indonesia. In 1968, 1969 he was a Senior Fulbright Professor at the University of Tehran, Iran and received a Ford Foundation award for travel in East and West Africa. His work in Asia and the Pacific was for the United States Information Agency and U.S. State Department Specialists Program.

Holding Fast the Dream was the featured centerpiece of February's Women's Studies Colloquium Series at the University of Hawai`i-Manoa. Producer and U.H. Dean Emeritus Miles Jackson and U.H. faculty members Dr. Kathryn Waddell Takara and Elisa Joy White discussed the history and issues of Hawai`i's African American community with a focus on the role and achievements of women.

Special preview excerpts of footage from the film were presented, featuring both Dr. Kathryn Waddell Takara and White, along with *Honolulu Advertiser* Managing Editor Marsha McFadden, community activist Faye Kennedy, retired teacher Gwen Johnson, and Honolulu resident Denise Boyce.

When we think of African-American history, it is usually within the geographic regions of America's contiguous states. With an African-American population hovering at only about 3 percent of the total, it is easy to overlook the important contributions of blacks in Hawai`i.

For those on the Mainland, this is probably more difficult to consider because Hawai`i is a latecomer, it became our 50th state in 1959, and has an "exotic" image in a remote location. Over the past few years, with the rise to prominence of Honolulu born Barack Obama, there is more interest in this state's African-Americans.

Fortunately, the University of Hawai`i Press has published two books to remedy this lack of generally available material on the state's black history: *They Followed the Trade Winds: African Americans in Hawai'i* edited by Miles M. Jackson. Dr. Jackson also wrote *And They Came: A Brief History and Annotated Bibliography of Blacks in Hawai'i.*

They Followed the Trade Winds is volume 43 in the Social Process in Hawai`i series. The articles range in topics from the historical "The African Diaspora in Nineteenth-Century Hawai'i by Dr. Kathryn Waddell Takara to the contemporary "Striving towards Community" by Dr. Miles M. Jackson. They are presented with solid, academic research but are quite accessible to most interested readers.

There are fascinating stories of some of the early African Americans who had the courage and foresight to leave their homes on the Mainland to help create new lives for themselves and others. Some stayed, others did not but they all left their mark.

Dr. Jackson co-produced *Holding Fast the Dream,* a one-hour documentary highlighting the two-hundred year history of African Americans in Hawai`i. The film explores the importance and the challenges of building community, the individual and collective search for security, and the dichotomy of race even in a multi-ethnic society. Untold stories of achievement and success illustrate the tenacity of human spirit and courage of the individual despite isolation and even ostracism. It celebrates the true meaning of community: the "process of building a shared story, built upon respect for all individuals.

The following people to be included as subjects of the documentary, "We've Come This Far by Faith"

Ernest Golden, who moved who moved to Hawai`i from Georgia in 1942, will talk about WWII Honolulu and his experiences with discrimination.

Alphonso Braggs, current president of the Hawai`i chapter of the NAACP, a national civil rights organization. He will discuss why there is a need today for an active civil rights organization in Hawai`i and its cooperation with other civil rights groups in Hawai`i such as the Japanese American Civil Liberties Union.

Marie Smith, past president of the National AARP, who lived on Maui for 30 years, will discuss her experiences.

Wally "Famous" Amos, successful cookie entrepreneur, will talk about his experiences in Hawai`i over the past 30 years. He'll also discuss how Hawai`i has shaped his work with literacy programs.

THE EXPERTS

A panel of scholars is acting as advisers for the film. They include:

Kathryn W. Takara, PhD., Professor of interdisciplinary studies at the University of Hawai`i-Manoa.

Elisha Joy White, PhD., Professor of ethnic studies at University of Hawai`i-Manoa

Section III
President Barack H. Obama

Chapter 12

44th President of the United States

President Barack H. Obama

Chapter 13

Barack Obama Early Beginnings in Hawai`i

In chapters 12-19, we glimpse into the life of a boy who would grow up to be a President. We read with fascination about Hawai`i born President Barack Obama, his chronological speeches beginning with the announcement of his candidacy to run for President of the United States and concluding with his acceptance of the Nobel Peace Prize October 2009 after serving less than ten months in office.

Barack Obama was born in Honolulu, Hawai`i, on August 4, 1961.

The name "Barack" means "one who is blessed." And when Barack was young his family and friends called this blessed young boy "Barry" for short.

His father, Barack Obama, Sr., was from Kenya, and his mother, Ann Dunham, was from Kansas. His parents met at the University of Honolulu when they were students (his father was attending on scholarship).

Barack's parents separated when he was two years old and then divorced when he was four, and his father eventually returned to Kenya. His mother later married another foreign student, Lolo Soetoro, who was from Indonesia; and in 1967, Barack moved with his new stepfather and mother to Jakarta, where he lived from age six to ten.

When Barack was ten, he returned to Honolulu and lived with his grandparents, who took over parenting duties. While in Honolulu, Barack attended the renowned Punahou School until he graduated in 1979.

During this period, Barack was able to see his biological father, who returned to Honolulu for a brief visit in 1971. Sadly, that would be their last meeting as his father died in an automobile accident in 1982. (Barack would lose his mother to cancer 1995.)

After his 1979 high school graduation, Barack moved to Los Angeles to attend Occidental College. He studied there for two years and then transferred to Columbia University in New York City, where he majored in Political Science and received his Bachelor of Arts degree in 1983.

After graduation, Barack worked in New York at Business International Corporation and New York Public Interest Research Group before returning to Chicago, where he became a community organizer with a church-based group which worked to improve living conditions in poor neighborhoods.

He entered Harvard Law School in 1988, where he was elected the first African-American president of the Harvard Law Review in its 104-year history. He went on to receive his J.D. degree from Harvard in 1991 with magna cum laude honors.

He then returned to Chicago, directed a voter registration drive, and soon became a civil rights attorney and a lecturer on constitutional law; and in 1992, married the love of his life, Michelle.

It was in Chicago in 1995 that Barack released his first best-selling book: "Dreams from My Father." He was offered the book contract shortly after becoming the president of the Harvard Law Review. The book is a compelling memoir of his life.

Barack's political career began with his election to the Illinois Senate in 1996, where he would serve from 1997 to 2004. In 2000, he ran an unsuccessful campaign for a seat in the House of Representatives, but would go on to run for the U.S. Senate a few years later.

While Barack was running for U.S. Senate, he was presented with the opportunity of a lifetime: to give the keynote address at the 2004 Democratic National Convention in Boston. And it was at that convention that Barack gave one of the most inspiring and moving political speeches ever delivered, and by the time the speech was over, Barack became a political heavyweight and an instant celebrity.

Barack went on to win his U.S. Senate race in a landslide, capturing 70% of the votes. And, riding a wave of strong popularity published his second best-selling book in 2006, "The Audacity of Hope," which expanded on the issues he touched on in his 2004 DNC speech.

On February 10, 2007, Barack Obama announced his candidacy for president of the United States.

But of all of Barack's achievements, nothing has made him prouder than becoming a father to his two wonderful girls: Malia (born 1999), and Sasha (born 2001).

President Barack Obama
FAMOUS SPEECHES

Chapter 14

2004 Democratic National Convention Keynote Address

Thank you so much. Thank you. Thank you. Thank you so much. Thank you so much. Thank you. Thank you. Thank you, Dick Durbin. You make us all proud.

On behalf of the great state of Illinois, crossroads of a nation, Land of Lincoln, let me express my deepest gratitude for the privilege of addressing this convention.

Tonight is a particular honor for me because, let's face it, my presence on this stage is pretty unlikely. My father was a foreign student, born and raised in a small village in Kenya. He grew up herding goats, went to school in a tin-roof shack. His father -- my grandfather -- was a cook, a domestic servant to the British.

My grandfather had larger dreams for his son. Through hard work and perseverance my father got a scholarship to study in a magical place, America, which shone as a beacon of freedom and opportunity to so many who had come before.

While studying here, my father met my mother. She was born in a town on the other side of the world, in Kansas. Her father worked on oil rigs and farms through most of the Depression. The day after Pearl Harbor my grandfather signed up for duty; joined Patton's army, marched across Europe. Back home, my grandmother raised a baby and went to work on a bomber assembly line. After the war, they studied on the G.I. Bill, bought a house through F.H.A., and later moved west all the way to Hawaii in search of opportunity.

They, too, had big dreams for their daughter. A common dream, born of two continents.

My parents shared not only an improbable love, they shared an abiding faith in the possibilities of this nation. They would give me an African name, Barack, or "blessed," believing that in a tolerant America your name is no barrier to success. They imagined -- They imagined me going to the best schools in the land, even though they weren't rich, because in a generous America you don't have to be rich to achieve your potential.

They're both passed away now. And yet, I know that on this night they look down on me with great pride.

They stand here -- And I stand here today, grateful for the diversity of my heritage, aware that my parents' dreams live on in my two precious daughters. I stand here knowing that my story is part of the larger American story, that I owe a debt to all of those who came before me, and that, in no other country on earth, is my story even possible. Tonight, we gather to affirm the greatness of our Nation -- not because of the height of our skyscrapers, or the power of our military, or the size of our economy. Our pride is based on a very simple premise, summed up in a declaration made over two hundred years ago:

We hold these truths to be self-evident, that all men are created equal, that they are endowed by their Creator with certain inalienable rights, that among these are Life, Liberty and the pursuit of Happiness.

That is the true genius of America, a faith -- a faith in simple dreams, an insistence on small miracles; that we can tuck in our children at night and know that they are fed and clothed and safe from harm; that we can say what we think, write what we think, without hearing a sudden knock on the door; that we can have an idea and start our own business without paying a bribe; that we can participate in the political process without fear of retribution, and that our votes will be counted -- at least most of the time.

This year, in this election we are called to reaffirm our values and our commitments, to hold them against a hard reality and see how we're measuring up to the legacy of our forbearers and the promise of future generations.

Fellow Americans, Democrats, Republicans, Independents, I say to you tonight: We have more work to do -- more work to do for the workers I met in Galesburg, Illinois, who are losing their union jobs at the Maytag plant that's moving to Mexico, and now are having to compete with their own children for jobs that pay seven bucks an hour; more to do for the father that I met who was losing his job and choking back the tears, wondering how he would pay 4500 dollars a month for the drugs his son needs without the health benefits that he counted on; more to do for the young woman in East St. Louis, and thousands more like her, who has the grades, has the drive, has the will, but doesn't have the money to go to college.

Now, don't get me wrong. The people I meet -- in small towns and big cities, in diners and office parks -- they don't expect government to solve all their problems. They know they have to work hard to get ahead, and they want to. Go into the collar counties around Chicago, and people will tell you they don't want their tax money wasted, by a welfare agency or by the Pentagon. Go in -- Go into any inner city neighborhood, and folks will tell you that government alone can't teach our kids to learn; they know that parents have to teach, that children can't achieve unless we raise their expectations and turn off the television sets and eradicate the slander that says a black youth with a book is acting white. They know those things.

People don't expect -- People don't expect government to solve all their problems. But they sense, deep in their bones, that with just a slight change in priorities, we can make sure that every child in America has a decent shot at life, and that the doors of opportunity remain open to all.

They know we can do better, and they want that choice.

In this election, we offer that choice. Our Party has chosen a man to lead us who embodies the best this country has to offer. And that man is John Kerry.

John Kerry understands the ideals of community, faith, and service because they've defined his life. From his heroic service to Vietnam, to his years as a prosecutor and lieutenant governor, through two decades in the United States Senate, he's devoted himself to this country. Again and again, we've seen him make tough choices when easier ones were available.

His values and his record affirm what is best in us. John Kerry believes in an America where hard work is rewarded; so instead of offering tax breaks to companies shipping jobs overseas, he offers them to companies creating jobs here at home.

John Kerry believes in an America where all Americans can afford the same health coverage our politicians in Washington have for themselves.

John Kerry believes in energy independence, so we aren't held hostage to the profits of oil companies, or the sabotage of foreign oil fields.

John Kerry believes in the Constitutional freedoms that have made our country the envy of the world, and he will never sacrifice our basic liberties, nor use faith as a wedge to divide us.

John Kerry believes that in a dangerous world war must be an option sometimes, but it should never be the first option.

You know, a while back -- a while back I met a young man named Shamus in a V.F.W. Hall in East Moline,

Illinois. He was a good-looking kid -- six two, six three, clear eyed, with an easy smile. He told me he'd joined the Marines and was heading to Iraq the following week. And as I listened to him explain why he'd enlisted, the absolute faith he had in our country and its leaders, his devotion to duty and service, I thought this young man was all that any of us might ever hope for in a child, But then I asked myself, "Are we serving Shamus as well as he is serving us?"

I thought of the 900 men and women -- sons and daughters, husbands and wives, friends and neighbors, who won't be returning to their own hometowns. I thought of the families I've met who were struggling to get by without a loved one's full income, or whose loved ones had returned with a limb missing or nerves shattered, but still lacked long-term health benefits because they were Reservists.

When we send our young men and women into harm's way, we have a solemn obligation not to fudge the numbers or shade the truth about why they're going, to care for their families while they're gone, to tend to the soldiers upon their return, and to never ever go to war without enough troops to win the war, secure the peace, and earn the respect of the world.

Now -- Now let me be clear. Let me be clear. We have real enemies in the world. These enemies must be found. They must be pursued. And they must be defeated. John Kerry knows this. And just as Lieutenant Kerry did not hesitate to risk his life to protect the men who served with him in Vietnam, President Kerry will not hesitate one moment to use our military might to keep America safe and secure.

John Kerry believes in America. And he knows that it's not enough for just some of us to prosper -- for alongside our famous individualism, there's another ingredient in the American saga, a belief that we're all connected as one people. If there is a child on the south side of Chicago who can't read, that matters to me, even if it's not my child. If there is a senior citizen somewhere who can't pay for their prescription drugs, and having to choose between medicine and the rent, that makes my life poorer, even if it's not my grandparent. If there's an Arab American family being rounded up without benefit of an attorney or due process that threatens my civil liberties.

It is that fundamental belief -- It is that fundamental belief: I am my brother's keeper. I am my sister's keeper that makes this country work. It's what allows us to pursue our individual dreams and yet still come together as one American family. E pluribus Unum: "Out of many, one."

Now even as we speak, there are those who are preparing to divide us -- the spin masters, the negative ad peddlers who embrace the politics of "anything goes." Well, I say to them tonight, there is not a liberal America and a conservative America -- there is the United States of America. There is not a Black America and a White America and Latino America and Asian America -- there's the United States of America.

The pundits, the pundits like to slice-and-dice our country into Red States and Blue States; Red States for Republicans, Blue States for Democrats. But I've got news for them, too. We worship an "awesome God" in the Blue States, and we don't like federal agents poking around in our libraries in the Red States. We coach Little League in the Blue States and yes, we've got some gay friends in the Red States. There are patriots who opposed the war in Iraq and there are patriots who supported the war in Iraq. We are one people, all of us pledging allegiance to the stars and stripes, all of us defending the United States of America.

In the end -- In the end -- In the end, that's what this election is about. Do we participate in a politics of cynicism or do we participate in a politics of hope?

John Kerry calls on us to hope. John Edwards calls on us to hope.

I'm not talking about blind optimism here -- the almost willful ignorance that thinks unemployment will go away if we just don't think about it, or the health care crisis will solve itself if we just ignore it. That's not what I'm talking about. I'm talking about something more substantial. It's the hope of slaves sitting around a fire singing freedom songs; the hope of immigrants setting out for distant shores; the hope of a young naval lieutenant bravely patrolling the Mekong Delta; the hope of a mill worker's son who dares to defy the odds; the hope of a skinny kid with a funny name who believes that America has a place for him, too.

Hope -- Hope in the face of difficulty. Hope in the face of uncertainty. The audacity of hope!

In the end, that is God's greatest gift to us, the bedrock of this nation; a belief in things not seen, a belief that there are better days ahead.

I believe that we can give our middle class relief and provide working families with a road to opportunity.

I believe we can provide jobs to the jobless, homes to the homeless, and reclaim young people in cities across America from violence and despair.

I believe that we have a righteous wind at our backs and that as we stand on the crossroads of history, we can make the right choices, and meet the challenges that face us.

America! Tonight, if you feel the same energy that I do, if you feel the same urgency that I do, if you feel the same passion that I do, if you feel the same hopefulness that I do -- if we do what we must do, then I have no doubt that all across the country, from Florida to Oregon, from Washington to Maine, the people will rise up in November, and John Kerry will be sworn in as President, and John Edwards will be sworn in as Vice President, and this country will reclaim its promise, and out of this long political darkness a brighter day will come.

Thank you very much everybody. God bless you. Thank you.

Chapter 15

Official Announcement of Candidacy for President of The United States

BARACK OBAMA
Delivered February 10, 2007 Chicago, Illinois

Hello Springfield! ...Look at all of you. Look at all of you. Goodness. Thank you so much. Thank you so much. Giving all praise and honor to God for bringing us here today. Thank you so much. I am -- I am so grateful to see all of you. You guys are still cheering back there?

Let me -- Let me begin by saying thanks to all you who've traveled, from far and wide, to brave the cold today. I know it's a little chilly -- but I'm fired up.

You know, we all made this journey for a reason. It's humbling to see a crowd like this, but in my heart I know you didn't just come here for me. You...came here because you believe in what this country can be. In the face of war, you believe there can be peace. In the face of despair, you believe there can be hope. In the face of a politics that shut you out, that's told you to settle, that's divided us for too long, you believe that we can be one people, reaching for what's possible, building that more perfect union. The journey we're on today. But let me tell you how I came to be here. As most of you know, I'm not a native of this great state. I -- I moved to Illinois over two decades ago. I was a young man then, just a year out of college. I knew no one in Chicago when I arrived, was without money or family connections. But a group of churches had offered me a job as a community organizer for the grand sum of 13,000 dollars a year. And I accepted the job, sight unseen, motivated then by a single, simple, powerful idea: that I might play a small part in building a better America.

My work took me to some of Chicago's poorest neighborhoods. I joined with pastors and lay-people to deal with communities that had been ravaged by plant closings. I saw that the problems people faced weren't simply local in nature, that the decisions to close a steel mill was made by distant executives, that the lack of textbooks and computers in a school could be traced to skewed priorities of politicians a thousand miles away, and that when a child turns to violence -- I came to realize that -- there's a hole in that boy's heart that no government alone can fill.

It was in these neighborhoods that I received the best education that I ever had, and where I learned the meaning of my Christian faith.

After three years of this work, I went to law school, because I wanted to understand how the law should work for those in need. I became a civil rights lawyer, and taught constitutional law, and after a time, I came to understand that our cherished rights of liberty and equality depend on the active participation of an awakened electorate. It was with these ideas in mind that I arrived in this capital city as a state Senator.

It -- It was here, in Springfield, where I saw all that is America converge -- farmers and teachers, businessmen and laborers, all of them with a story to tell, all of them seeking a seat at the table, all of them clamoring to be heard. I made lasting friendships here, friends that I see here in the audience today. It was here -- It was here where we learned to disagree without being disagreeable; that it's possible to compromise so long as you know those principles that can never be compromised; and that so long as we're willing to listen to each other, we can assume the best in people instead of the worst.

That's why we were able to reform a death penalty system that was broken; that's why we were able to give health insurance to children in need; that's why we made the tax system right here in Springfield more fair and just for working families; and that's why we passed ethics reform that the cynics said could never, ever be passed.

It was here, in Springfield, where North, South, East, and West come together that I was reminded of the essential decency of the American people -- where I came to believe that through this decency, we can build a more hopeful America. And that is why, in the shadow of the Old State Capitol, where Lincoln once called on a house divided to stand together, where common hopes and common dreams still live, I stand before you today to announce my candidacy for President of the United States of America.

Now -- Now, listen, I -- I... -- thank you, thank you, thank you, thank you. Look, I -- I...recognize that there is a certain presumptuousness in this, a certain audacity, to this announcement. I know that I haven't spent a lot of time learning the ways of Washington. But I've been there long enough to know that the ways of Washington must change.

The genius of our Founders is that they designed a system of government that can be changed. And we should take heart, because we've changed this country before. In the face of tyranny, a band of patriots brought an empire to its knees. In the face of secession, we unified a nation and set the captives free. In the face of Depression, we put people back to work and lifted millions out of poverty. We welcomed immigrants to our shores. We opened railroads to the west. We landed a man on the moon. And we heard a King's call to let "justice roll down like waters, and righteousness like a mightly stream."

We've done this before: Each and every time, a new generation has risen up and done what's needed to be done. Today we are called once more, and it is time for our generation to answer that call. For that is our unyielding faith -- that in -- in the face of impossible odds, people who love their country can change it.

That's what Abraham Lincoln understood. He had his doubts. He had his defeats. He had his skeptics. He had his setbacks. But through his will and his words, he moved a nation and helped free a people. It's because of the millions who rallied to his cause that we're no longer divided, North and South, slave and free. It's because men and women of every race, from every walk of life, continued to march for freedom long after Lincoln was laid to rest, that today we have the chance to face the challenges of this millennium together, as one people -- as Americans.

All of us know what those challenges are today: a war with no end, a dependence on oil that threatens our future, schools where too many children aren't learning, and families struggling paycheck to paycheck despite working as hard as they can. We know the challenges. We've heard them. We've talked about them for years.

What's stopped us from meeting these challenges is not the absence of sound policies and sensible plans. What has stopped us is the failure of leadership, the smallness -- the smallness of our politics -- the ease with which we're distracted by the petty and trivial, our chronic avoidance of tough decisions, and our preference for scoring cheap political points instead of rolling up our sleeves and building a working consensus to tackle the big problems of America.

For the past six years we've been told that our mounting debts don't matter. We've been told that the anxiety Americans feel about rising health care costs and stagnant wages are an illusion. We've been told that climate change is a hoax. We've been told that tough talk and an ill-conceived war can replace diplomacy, and strategy, and foresight. And when all else fails, when Katrina happens, or the death toll in Iraq mounts, we've been told that our crises are somebody else's fault. We're distracted from our real failures, and told to blame the other Party, or gay people, or immigrants.

As people have looked away in disillusionment and frustration, we know what's filled the void: the cynics, the lobbyists, the special interests -- who've turned our government into a game only they can afford to play. They write the checks and you get stuck with the bill. They get the access while you get to write a letter. They think they own this government, but we're here today to take it back. The time for that kind of politics is over. It is through. It's time to turn the page -- right here and right now.

Now look --

[Audience chants "Obama...Obama...Obama"]

Okay. Alright. Thank you. Thank you. Thank you.

Look, look, we have made some progress already. I was proud to help lead the fight in Congress that led to the most sweeping ethics reforms since Watergate. But Washington has a long way to go, and it won't be easy. That's why we'll have to set priorities. We'll have to make hard choices. And although government will play a crucial role in bringing about the changes that we need, more money and programs alone will not get us to where we need to go. Each of us, in our own lives, will have to accept responsibility -- for instilling an ethic of achievement in our children, for adapting to a more competitive economy, for strengthening our communities, and sharing some measure of sacrifice.

So let us begin. Let us begin this hard work together. Let us transform this nation. Let us be the generation that reshapes our economy to compete in the digital age. Let's set high standards for our schools and give them the resources they need to succeed. Let's recruit a new army of teachers, and give them better pay and more support in exchange for more accountability. Let's make college more affordable, and let's invest in scientific research, and let's lay down broadband lines through the heart of inner cities and rural towns all across America. We can do that, and as our economy changes, let's be the generation that ensures our nation's workers are sharing in our prosperity. Let's protect the hard-earned benefits their companies have promised. Let's make it possible for hardworking Americans to save for retirement. Let's allow our unions and their organizers to lift up this country's middle-class again. We can do that.

Let's be the generation that ends poverty in America. Every single person willing to work should be able to get job training that leads to a job, and earn a living wage that can pay the bills, and afford child care so their kids can have a safe place to go when they work. We can do this.

Let's be the generation that finally, after all these years, tackles our health care crisis. We can control costs by focusing on prevention, by providing better treatment to the chronically ill, and using technology to cut the bureaucracy. Let's be the generation that says right here, right now: We will have universal health care in America by the end of the next President's first term. We can do that.

Let's be the generation that finally frees America from the tyranny of oil. We can harness homegrown, alternative fuels like ethanol and spur the production of more fuel-efficient cars. We can set up a system for capping greenhouse gases. We can turn this crisis of global warming into a moment of opportunity for innovation, and job creation, and an incentive for businesses that will serve as a model for the world. Let's be the generation that makes future generations proud of what we did here.

Most of all, let's be the generation that never forgets what happened on that September day and confront the terrorists with everything we've got. Politics doesn't have to divide us on this anymore; we can work together to keep our country safe. I've worked with the Republican Senator Dick Lugar to pass a law that will secure and destroy some of the world's deadliest weapons. We can work together to track down terrorists with a stronger military. We can tighten the net around their finances. We can improve our intelligence capabilities and finally get homeland security right. But let's also understand that ultimate victory against our enemies will only come by rebuilding our alliances and exporting those ideals that bring hope and opportunity to millions of people around the globe.

We can do those things, but all of this cannot come to pass until we bring an end to this war in Iraq. Most of you know -- Most of you know that I opposed this war from the start. I thought it was a tragic mistake. Today we grieve for the families who have lost loved ones, the hearts that have been broken, and the young lives that could have been. America, it is time to start bringing our troops home. It's time -- It's time to admit that no amount of

American lives can resolve the political disagreement that lies at the heart of someone else's civil war. That's why I have a plan that will bring our combat troops home by March of 2008. Let the Iraqis know -- Letting the Iraqis know that we will not be there forever is our last, best hope to pressure the Sunni and Shia to come to the table and find peace.

There's one other thing that it's not too late to get right about this war, and that is the homecoming of the men and women, our veterans, who have sacrificed the most. Let us honor their courage by providing the care they need and rebuilding the military they love. Let us be the generation that begins that work.

I know there are those who don't believe we can do all these things. I understand the skepticism. After all, every four years, candidates from both Parties make similar promises, and I expect this year will be no different. All of us running for President will travel around the country offering ten-point plans and making grand speeches; all of us will trumpet those qualities we believe make us uniquely qualified to lead this country. But too many times, after the election is over, and the confetti is swept away, all those promises fade from memory, and the lobbyists and special interests move in, and people turn away, disappointed as before, left to struggle on their own.

That's why this campaign can't only be about me. It must be about us. It must be about what we can do together. This campaign must be the occasion, the vehicle, of your hopes, and your dreams. It will take your time, your energy, and your advice to push us forward when we're doing right, and let us know when we're not. This campaign has to be about reclaiming the meaning of citizenship, restoring our sense of common purpose, and realizing that few obstacles can withstand the power of millions of voices calling for change.

By ourselves, this change will not happen. Divided, we are bound to fail. But the life of a tall, gangly, self-made Springfield lawyer tells us that a different future is possible.

He tells us that there is power in words.

He tells us that there's power in conviction.

That beneath all the differences of race and region, faith and station, we are one people.

He tells us that there's power in hope.

As Lincoln organized the forces arrayed against slavery, he was heard to say this: "Of strange, discordant, and even hostile elements, we gathered from the four winds, and formed and fought to battle through."[1]

That is our purpose here today. That is why I am in this race -- not just to hold an office, but to gather with you to transform a nation. I want -- I want to win that next battle -- for justice and opportunity. I want to win that next battle -- for better schools, and better jobs, and better health care for all. I want us to take up the unfinished business of perfecting our union, and building a better America.

And if you will join with me in this improbable quest, if you feel destiny calling, and see as I see, the future of endless possibility stretching out before us; if you sense, as I sense, that the time is now to shake off our slumber, and slough off our fears, and make good on the debt we owe past and future generations, then I am ready to take up the cause, and march with you, and work with you -- today.

Together we can finish the work that needs to be done, and usher in a new birth of freedom on this Earth.

Thank you very much everybody -- let's get to work! I love you. Thank you.

Chapter 16

A More Perfect Union

Barack Obama
Delivered 18 March 2008, Philadelphia, PA

Thank you so much. Thank you. Thank you. Thank you so much. Thank you. Thank you. Let me begin by thanking Harris Wofford for his contributions to this country. In so many different ways, he exemplifies what we mean by the word "citizen." And so we are very grateful to him for all the work he has done; and I'm thankful for the gracious and thoughtful introduction.

"We the people, in order to form a more perfect union." Two hundred and twenty one years ago, in a hall that still stands across the street, a group of men gathered and, with these simple words, launched America's improbable experiment in democracy. Farmers and scholars, statesmen and patriots who had traveled across the ocean to escape tyranny and persecution finally made real their Declaration of Independence at a Philadelphia convention that lasted through the spring of 1787.

The document they produced was eventually signed, but ultimately unfinished. It was stained by this nation's original sin of slavery, a question that divided the colonies and brought the convention to a stalemate until the founders chose to allow the slave trade to continue for at least 20 more years, and to leave any final resolution to future generations. Of course, the answer to the slavery question was already embedded within our Constitution -- A Constitution that had at its very core the ideal of equal citizenship under the law; a Constitution that promised its people liberty and justice, and a union that could be and should be perfected over time.

And yet words on a parchment would not be enough to deliver slaves from bondage, or provide men and women of every color and creed their full rights and obligations as citizens of the United States. What would be needed were Americans in successive generations who were willing to do their part -- through protests and struggles, on the streets and in the courts, through a civil war and civil disobedience, and always at great risk -- to narrow that gap between the promise of our ideals and the reality of their time.

This was one of the tasks we set forth at the beginning of this presidential campaign: to continue the long march of those who came before us, a march for a more just, more equal, more free, more caring, and more prosperous America. I chose to run for President at this moment in history because I believe deeply that we cannot solve the challenges of our time unless we solve them together, unless we perfect our union by understanding that we may have different stories, but we hold common hopes; that we may not look the same and may not have come from the same place, but we all want to move in the same direction: towards a better future for our children and our grandchildren. And this belief comes from my unyielding faith in the decency and generosity of the American people. But it also comes from my own story.

I'm the son of a black man from Kenya and a white woman from Kansas. I was raised with the help of a white grandfather who survived a Depression to serve in Patton's army during World War II, and a white grandmother who worked on a bomber assembly line at Fort Leavenworth while he was overseas. I've gone to some of the best schools in America and I've lived in one of the world's poorest nations. I am married to a black American who carries within her the blood of slaves and slave owners, an inheritance we pass on to our two precious daughters. I have brothers, sisters, nieces, nephews, uncles, and cousins of every race and every hue scattered across three continents. And for as long as I live, I will never forget that in no other country on earth is my story even possible. It's a story that hasn't made me the most conventional of candidates. But it is a story that has seared into my genetic makeup the idea that this nation is more than the sum of its parts -- that out of many, we are truly one.

Now throughout the first year of this campaign, against all predictions to the contrary, we saw how hungry the American people were for this message of unity. Despite the temptation to view my candidacy through a purely racial lens, we won commanding victories in states with some of the whitest populations in the country. In South Carolina, where the Confederate flag still flies, we built a powerful coalition of African Americans and white Americans. This is not to say that race has not been an issue in this campaign. At various stages in the campaign, some commentators have deemed me either "too black" or "not black enough." We saw racial tensions bubble to the surface during the week before the South Carolina primary. The press has scoured every single exit poll for the latest evidence of racial polarization, not just in terms of white and black, but black and brown as well.

And yet, it's only been in the last couple of weeks that the discussion of race in this campaign has taken a particularly divisive turn. On one end of the spectrum, we've heard the implication that my candidacy is somehow an exercise in affirmative action; that it's based solely on the desire of wild and wide-eyed liberals to purchase racial reconciliation on the cheap. On the other end, we've heard my former pastor, Jeremiah Wright, use incendiary language to express views that have the potential not only to widen the racial divide, but views that denigrate both the greatness and the goodness of our nation and that rightly offend white and black alike.

Now I've already condemned, in unequivocal terms, the statements of Reverend Wright that have caused such controversy, and in some cases, pain. For some, nagging questions remain: Did I know him to be an occasionally fierce critic of American domestic and foreign policy? Of course. Did I ever hear him make remarks that could be considered controversial while I sat in the church? Yes. Did I strongly disagree with many of his political views? Absolutely, just as I'm sure many of you have heard remarks from your pastors, priests, or rabbis with which you strongly disagree.

But the remarks that have caused this recent firestorm weren't simply controversial. They weren't simply a religious leader's efforts to speak out against perceived injustice. Instead, they expressed a profoundly distorted view of this country, a view that sees white racism as endemic and that elevates what is wrong with America above all that we know is right with America; a view that sees the conflicts in the Middle East as rooted primarily in the actions of stalwart allies like Israel instead of emanating from the perverse and hateful ideologies of radical Islam.

As such, Reverend Wright's comments were not only wrong but divisive, divisive at a time when we need unity; racially charged at a time when we need to come together to solve a set of monumental problems: two wars, a terrorist threat, a falling economy, a chronic health care crisis, and potentially devastating climate change -- problems that are neither black or white or Latino or Asian, but rather problems that confront us all.

Given my background, my politics, and my professed values and ideals, there will no doubt be those for whom my statements of condemnation are not enough. Why associate myself with Reverend Wright in the first place, they may ask? Why not join another church? And I confess that if all that I knew of Reverend Wright were the snippets of those sermons that have run in an endless loop on the television sets and YouTube, if Trinity United Church of Christ conformed to the caricatures being peddled by some commentators, there is no doubt that I would react in much the same way.

But the truth is, that isn't all that I know of the man. The man I met more than twenty years ago is a man who helped introduce me to my Christian faith, a man who spoke to me about our obligations to love one another, to care for the sick and lift up the poor. He is a man who served his country as a United States Marine, and who has studied and lectured at some of the finest universities and seminaries in the country, and who over 30 years has led a church that serves the community by doing God's work here on Earth -- by housing the homeless, ministering to the needy, providing day care services and scholarships and prison ministries, and reaching out to those suffering from HIV/AIDS.

In my first book, *Dreams From My Father*, I described the experience of my first service at Trinity, and it goes as follows:

People began to shout, to rise from their seats and clap and cry out, a forceful wind carrying the reverend's voice up to the rafters.

And in that single note -- hope -- I heard something else; at the foot of that cross, inside the thousands of churches across the city, I imagined the stories of ordinary black people merging with the stories of David and Goliath, Moses and Pharaoh, the Christians in the lion's den, Ezekiel's field of dry bones.

Those stories of survival and freedom and hope became our stories, my story. The blood that spilled was our blood; the tears our tears; until this black church, on this bright day, seemed once more a vessel carrying the story of a people into future generations and into a larger world. Our trials and triumphs became at once unique and universal, black and more than black. In chronicling our journey, the stories and songs gave us a meaning to reclaim memories that we didn't need to feel shame about -- memories that all people might study and cherish and with which we could start to rebuild.

That has been my experience at Trinity. Like other predominantly black churches across the country, Trinity embodies the black community in its entirety -- the doctor and the welfare mom, the model student and the former gang-banger. Like other black churches, Trinity's services are full of raucous laughter and sometimes bawdy humor. They are full of dancing and clapping and screaming and shouting that may seem jarring to the untrained ear. The church contains in full the kindness and cruelty, the fierce intelligence and the shocking ignorance, the struggles and successes, the love and, yes, the bitterness and biases that make up the black experience in America.

And this helps explain, And this helps explain, perhaps, my relationship with Reverend Wright. As imperfect as he may be, he has been like family to me. He strengthens my faith, officiated my wedding, and baptized my children. Not once in my conversations with him have I heard him talk about any ethnic group in derogatory terms or treat whites with whom he interacted with anything but courtesy and respect. He contains within him the contradictions -- the good and the bad -- of the community that he has served diligently for so many years.

I can no more disown him than I can disown the black community. I can no more disown him than I can disown my white grandmother, a woman who helped raise me, a woman who sacrificed again and again for me, a woman who loves me as much as she loves anything in this world, but a woman who once confessed her fear of black men who passed her by on the street, and who on more than one occasion has uttered racial or ethnic stereotypes that made me cringe.

These people are part of me. And they are part of America, this country that I love.

Now, some will see this as an attempt to justify or excuse comments that are simply inexcusable. I can assure you it is not. And I suppose the politically safe thing to do would be to move on from this episode and just hope that it fades into the woodwork. We can dismiss Reverend Wright as a crank or a demagogue, just as some have dismissed Geraldine Ferraro in the aftermath of her recent statements as harboring some deep -- deep-seated bias.

But race is an issue that I believe this nation cannot afford to ignore right now. We would be making the same mistake that Reverend Wright made in his offending sermons about America: to simplify and stereotype and amplify the negative to the point that it distorts reality. The fact is that the comments that have been made and the issues that have surfaced over the last few weeks reflect the complexities of race in this country that we've never really worked through, a part of our union that we have not yet made perfect. And if we walk away now, if we simply retreat into our respective corners, we will never be able to come together and solve challenges like health care or education or the need to find good jobs for every American.

Understanding -- Understanding this reality requires a reminder of how we arrived at this point. As William Faulkner once wrote, "The past isn't dead and buried. In fact, it isn't even past." We do not need to recite here the history of racial injustice in this country. But we do need to remind ourselves that so many of the disparities that exist between the African-American community and the larger American community today can be traced directly to inequalities passed on from an earlier generation that suffered under the brutal legacy of slavery and Jim Crow. Segregated schools were, and are, inferior schools. We still haven't fixed them, 50 years after Brown versus Board of Education. And the inferior education they provided, then and now, helps explain the pervasive achievement gap between today's black and white students.

Legalized discrimination, where blacks were prevented, often through violence, from owning property, or loans were not granted to African-American business owners, or black homeowners could not access FHA mortgages, or blacks were excluded from unions, or the police force, or the fire department meant that black families could not amass any meaningful wealth to bequeath to future generations. That history helps explain the wealth and income gap between blacks and whites and the concentrated pockets of poverty that persist in so many of today's urban and rural communities. A lack of economic opportunity among black men and the shame and frustration that came from not being able to provide for one's family contributed to the erosion of black families, a problem that welfare policies for many years may have worsened. And the lack of basic services in so many urban black neighborhoods -- parks for kids to play in, police walking the beat, regular garbage pick-up, building code enforcement -- all helped create a cycle of violence, blight, and neglect that continues to haunt us.

This is the reality in which Reverend Wright and other African-Americans of his generation grew up. They came of age in the late '50s and early '60s, a time when segregation was still the law of the land and opportunity was systematically constricted. What's remarkable is not how many failed in the face of discrimination, but how many men and women overcame the odds, how many were able to make a way out of no way for those like me who would come after them.

But for all those who scratched and clawed their way to get a piece of the American Dream, there were many who didn't make it -- those who were ultimately defeated, in one way or another, by discrimination. That legacy of defeat was passed on to future generations -- those young men and increasingly young women who we see standing on street corners or languishing in our prisons, without hope or prospects for the future. Even for those blacks who did make it, questions of race, and racism, continue to define their world view in fundamental ways. For the men and women of Reverend Wright's generation, the memories of humiliation and doubt and fear have not gone away, nor has the anger and the bitterness of those years.

That anger may not get expressed in public, in front of white co-workers or white friends, but it does find voice in the barbershop or the beauty shop or around the kitchen table. At times, that anger is exploited by politicians to gin up votes along racial lines or to make up for a politician's own failings. And occasionally it finds voice in the church on Sunday morning, in the pulpit and in the pews. The fact that so many people are surprised to hear that anger in some of Reverend Wright's sermons simply reminds us of that old truism that the most segregated hour of American life occurs on Sunday morning.

That -- That anger is not always productive. Indeed, all too often it distracts attention from solving real problems. It keeps us from squarely facing our own complicity within the African-American community in our own condition. It prevents the African-American community from forging the alliances it needs to bring about real change. But the anger is real; it is powerful, and to simply wish it away, to condemn it without understanding its roots only serves to widen the chasm of misunderstanding that exists between the races.

In fact, a similar anger exists within segments of the white community. Most working and middle-class white Americans don't feel that they've been particularly privileged by their race. Their experience is the immigrant experience. As far as they're concerned, no one handed them anything; they built it from scratch. They've worked hard all their lives, many times only to see their jobs shipped overseas or their pensions dumped after a lifetime of labor. They are anxious about their futures, and they feel their dreams slipping away. And in an era of stagnant wages and global competition, opportunity comes to be seen as a zero sum game, in which your dreams come at my expense. So when they are told to bus their children to a school across town, when they hear that an African American is getting an advantage in landing a good job or a spot in a good college because of an injustice that they themselves never committed, when they're told that their fears about crime in urban neighborhoods are somehow prejudice, resentment builds over time.

Like the anger within the black community, these resentments aren't always expressed in polite company. But they have helped shape the political landscape for at least a generation. Anger over welfare and affirmative action helped forge the Reagan Coalition. Politicians routinely exploited fears of crime for their own electoral ends. Talk show hosts and conservative commentators built entire careers unmasking bogus claims of racism while dismissing legitimate discussions of racial injustice and inequality as mere political correctness or reverse racism. And just as black anger often proved counterproductive, so have these white resentments distracted attention from the real culprits of the middle class squeeze: a corporate culture rife with inside dealing, questionable accounting practices, and short-term greed; a Washington dominated by lobbyists and special interests; economic policies that favor the few over the many. And yet, to wish away the resentments of white Americans, to label them as misguided or even racist without recognizing they are grounded in legitimate concerns, this, too, widens the racial divide and blocks the path to understanding.

This is where we are right now.

It's a racial stalemate we've been stuck in for years. And contrary to the claims of some of my critics, black and white, I have never been so naive as to believe that we can get beyond our racial divisions in a single election cycle or with a single candidate, particularly -- particularly a candidacy as imperfect as my own. But I have asserted a firm conviction, a conviction rooted in my faith in God and my faith in the American people, that, working together, we can move beyond some of our old racial wounds and that, in fact, we have no choice -- we have no choice if we are to continue on the path of a more perfect union.

For the African-American community, that path means embracing the burdens of our past without becoming victims of our past. It means continuing to insist on a full measure of justice in every aspect of American life. But it also means binding our particular grievances, for better health care and better schools and better jobs, to the larger aspirations of all Americans -- the white woman struggling to break the glass ceiling, the white man who's been laid off, the immigrant trying to feed his family. And it means also taking full responsibility for our own lives -- by demanding more from our fathers, and spending more time with our children, and reading to them, and teaching them that while they may face challenges and discrimination in their own lives, they must never succumb to despair or cynicism. They must always believe -- They must always believe that they can write their own destiny.

Ironically, this quintessentially American -- and, yes, conservative -- notion of self-help found frequent expression in Reverend Wright's sermons. But what my former pastor too often failed to understand is that embarking on a program of self-help also requires a belief that society can change. The profound mistake of Reverend Wright's sermons is not that he spoke about racism in our society. It's that he spoke as if our society was static, as if no progress had been made, as if this country -- a country that has made it possible for one of his own members to run for the highest office in the land and build a coalition of white and black, Latino, Asian, rich, poor, young and old -- is still irrevocably bound to a tragic past. What we know, what we have seen, is that America can change. America can change. That is true genius of this nation. What we have already achieved gives us hope -- the audacity to hope -- for what we can and must achieve tomorrow.

Now, in the white community, the path to a more perfect union means acknowledging that what ails the African-American community does not just exist in the minds of black people; that the legacy of discrimination -- and current incidents of discrimination, while less overt than in the past -- that these things are real and must be addressed. Not just with words, but with deeds -- by investing in our schools and our communities; by enforcing our civil rights laws and ensuring fairness in our criminal justice system; by providing this generation with ladders of opportunity that were unavailable for previous generations. It requires all Americans to realize that your dreams do not have to come at the expense of my dreams, that investing in the health, welfare, and education of black and brown and white children will ultimately help all of America prosper.

In the end, then, what is called for is nothing more and nothing less than what all the world's great religions demand: that we do unto others as we would have them do unto us. Let us be our brother's keeper, Scripture tells us. Let us be our sister's keeper. Let us find that common stake we all have in one another, and let our politics reflect that spirit as well.

For we have a choice in this country. We can accept a politics that breeds division and conflict and cynicism. We can tackle race only as spectacle, as we did in the O.J. trial; or in the wake of tragedy, as we did in the aftermath of Katrina; or as fodder for the nightly news. We can play Reverend Wright's sermons on every channel every day and talk about them from now until the election, and make the only question in this campaign whether or not the American people think that I somehow believe or sympathize with his most offensive words. We can pounce on some gaffe by a Hillary supporter as evidence that she's playing the race card; or we can speculate on whether white men will all flock to John McCain in the general election regardless of his policies. We can do that. But if we do, I can tell you that in the next election, we'll be talking about some other distraction, and then another one, and then another one. And nothing will change.

That is one option.

Or, at this moment, in this election, we can come together and say, "Not this time." This time we want to talk about the crumbling schools that are stealing the future of black children and white children and Asian children and Hispanic children and Native-American children. This time we want to reject the cynicism that tells us that these kids can't learn; that those kids who don't look like us are somebody else's problem. The children of America are not "those kids," -- they are our kids, and we will not let them fall behind in a 21st-century economy. Not this time. This time we want to talk about how the lines in the emergency room are filled with whites and blacks and Hispanics who do not have health care, who don't have the power on their own to overcome the special interests in Washington, but who can take them on if we do it together.

This time we want to talk about the shuttered mills that once provided a decent life for men and women of every race, and the homes for sale that once belonged to Americans from every religion, every region, and every walk of life. This time we want to talk about the fact that the real problem is not that someone who doesn't look like you might take your job; it's that the corporation you work for will ship it overseas for nothing more than a profit. This time -- This time we want to talk about the men and women of every color and creed who serve together, and fight together, and bleed together under the same proud flag. We want to talk about how to bring them home from a war that should've never been authorized and should've never been waged. And we want to talk about how we'll show our patriotism by caring for them, and their families, and giving them the benefits that they have earned.

I would not be running for President if I didn't believe with all my heart that this is what the vast majority of Americans want for this country. This union may never be perfect, but generation after generation has shown that it can always be perfected. And today, whenever I find myself feeling doubtful or cynical about this possibility, what gives me the most hope is the next generation -- the young people whose attitudes and beliefs and openness to change have already made history in this election.

There's one story in particular that I'd like to leave you with today, a story I told when I had the great honor of speaking on Dr. King's birthday at his home church, Ebenezer Baptist, in Atlanta. There's a young, 23-year-old woman, a white woman named Ashley Baia, who organized for our campaign in Florence, South Carolina. She'd been working to organize a mostly African-American community since the beginning of this campaign, and one day she was at a roundtable discussion where everyone went around telling their story and why they were there. And Ashley said that when she was 9 years old, her mother got cancer. And because she had to miss days of work, she was let go and lost her health care. They had to file for bankruptcy, and that's when Ashley decided that she had to do something to help her mom.

She knew that food was one of their most expensive costs, and so Ashley convinced her mother that what she really liked and really wanted to eat more than anything else was mustard and relish sandwiches -- because that was the cheapest way to eat. That's the mind of a 9 year old. She did this for a year until her mom got better. And so Ashley told everyone at the roundtable that the reason she had joined our campaign was so that she could help the millions of other children in the country who want and need to help their parents too.

Now, Ashley might have made a different choice. Perhaps somebody told her along the way that the source of her mother's problems were blacks who were on welfare and too lazy to work, or Hispanics who were coming into the country illegally. But she didn't. She sought out allies in her fight against injustice. Anyway, Ashley finishes her story and then goes around the room and asks everyone else why they're supporting the campaign. They all have different stories and different reasons. Many bring up a specific issue. And finally they come to this elderly black man who's been sitting there quietly the entire time. And Ashley asks him why he's there. And he doesn't bring up a specific issue. He does not say *health care* or *the economy*. He does not say *education* or *the war*. He does not say that he was there because of Barack Obama. He simply says to everyone in the room, "I am here because of Ashley." "I'm here because of Ashley." Now, by itself, that single moment of recognition between that young white girl and that old black man is not enough. It is not enough to give health care to the sick, or jobs to the jobless, or education to our children. But it is where we start. It is where our union grows stronger. And as so many generations have come to realize over the course of the 221 years since a band of patriots signed that document right here in Philadelphia that is where perfection begins. Thank you very much, everyone. Thank you.

Chapter 17

The American Promise

Barack Obama
Democratic National Convention, August 28, 2008 Denver, Colorado

To Chairman Dean and my great friend Dick Durbin; and to all my fellow citizens of this great nation;

With profound gratitude and great humility, I accept your nomination for the presidency of the United States.

Let me express my thanks to the historic slate of candidates who accompanied me on this journey, and especially the one who traveled the farthest - a champion for working Americans and an inspiration to my daughters and to yours -- Hillary Rodham Clinton. To President Clinton, who last night made the case for change as only he can make it; to Ted Kennedy, who embodies the spirit of service; and to the next Vice President of the United States, Joe Biden, I thank you. I am grateful to finish this journey with one of the finest statesmen of our time, a man at ease with everyone from world leaders to the conductors on the Amtrak train he still takes home every night.

To the love of my life, our next First Lady, Michelle Obama, and to Sasha and Malia - I love you so much, and I'm so proud of all of you.

Four years ago, I stood before you and told you my story - of the brief union between a young man from Kenya and a young woman from Kansas who weren't well-off or well-known, but shared a belief that in America, their son could achieve whatever he put his mind to.

It is that promise that has always set this country apart - that through hard work and sacrifice, each of us can pursue our individual dreams but still come together as one American family, to ensure that the next generation can pursue their dreams as well.

That's why I stand here tonight. Because for two hundred and thirty two years, at each moment when that promise was in jeopardy, ordinary men and women - students and soldiers, farmers and teachers, nurses and janitors -- found the courage to keep it alive.

We meet at one of those defining moments - a moment when our nation is at war, our economy is in turmoil, and the American promise has been threatened once more.

Tonight, more Americans are out of work and more are working harder for less. More of you have lost your homes and even more are watching your home values plummet. More of you have cars you can't afford to drive, credit card bills you can't afford to pay, and tuition that's beyond your reach.

These challenges are not all of government's making. But the failure to respond is a direct result of a broken politics in Washington and the failed policies of George W. Bush.

America, we are better than these last eight years. We are a better country than this.

This country is more decent than one where a woman in Ohio, on the brink of retirement, finds herself one illness away from disaster after a lifetime of hard work.

This country is more generous than one where a man in Indiana has to pack up the equipment he's worked on for twenty years and watch it shipped off to China, and then chokes up as he explains how he felt like a failure when he went home to tell his family the news.

We are more compassionate than a government that lets veterans sleep on our streets and families slide into poverty; that sits on its hands while a major American city drowns before our eyes.

Tonight, I say to the American people, to Democrats and Republicans and Independents across this great land - enough! This moment - this election - is our chance to keep, in the 21st century, the American promise alive. Because next week, in Minnesota, the same party that brought you two terms of George Bush and Dick Cheney will ask this country for a third. And we are here because we love this country too much to let the next four years look like the last eight. On November 4th, we must stand up and say: "Eight is enough."

Now let there be no doubt. The Republican nominee, John McCain, has worn the uniform of our country with bravery and distinction, and for that we owe him our gratitude and respect. And next week, we'll also hear about those occasions when he's broken with his party as evidence that he can deliver the change that we need.

But the record's clear: John McCain has voted with George Bush ninety percent of the time. Senator McCain likes to talk about judgment, but really, what does it say about your judgment when you think George Bush has been right more than ninety percent of the time? I don't know about you, but I'm not ready to take a ten percent chance on change.

The truth is, on issue after issue that would make a difference in your lives - on health care and education and the economy - Senator McCain has been anything but independent. He said that our economy has made "great progress" under this President. He said that the fundamentals of the economy are strong. And when one of his chief advisors - the man who wrote his economic plan - was talking about the anxiety Americans are feeling, he said that we were just suffering from a "mental recession," and that we've become, and I quote, "a nation of whiners."

A nation of whiners? Tell that to the proud auto workers at a Michigan plant who, after they found out it was closing, kept showing up every day and working as hard as ever, because they knew there were people who counted on the brakes that they made. Tell that to the military families who shoulder their burdens silently as they watch their loved ones leave for their third or fourth or fifth tour of duty. These are not whiners. They work hard and give back and keep going without complaint. These are the Americans that I know.

Now, I don't believe that Senator McCain doesn't care what's going on in the lives of Americans. I just think he doesn't know. Why else would he define middle-class as someone making under five million dollars a year? How else could he propose hundreds of billions in tax breaks for big corporations and oil companies but not one penny of tax relief to more than one hundred million Americans? How else could he offer a health care plan that would actually tax people's benefits, or an education plan that would do nothing to help families pay for college, or a plan that would privatize Social Security and gamble your retirement?

It's not because John McCain doesn't care. It's because John McCain doesn't get it.

For over two decades, he's subscribed to that old, discredited Republican philosophy - give more and more to those with the most and hope that prosperity trickles down to everyone else. In Washington, they call this the Ownership Society, but what it really means is - you're on your own. Out of work? Tough luck. No health care? The market will fix it. Born into poverty? Pull yourself up by your own bootstraps - even if you don't have boots. You're on your own.

Well it's time for them to own their failure. It's time for us to change America.

You see, we Democrats have a very different measure of what constitutes progress in this country.

We measure progress by how many people can find a job that pays the mortgage; whether you can put a little extra money away at the end of each month so you can someday watch your child receive her college diploma. We measure progress in the 23 million new jobs that were created when Bill Clinton was President - when the average American family saw its income go up $7,500 instead of down $2,000 like it has under George Bush.

We measure the strength of our economy not by the number of billionaires we have or the profits of the

Fortune 500, but by whether someone with a good idea can take a risk and start a new business, or whether the waitress who lives on tips can take a day off to look after a sick kid without losing her job - an economy that honors the dignity of work.

The fundamentals we use to measure economic strength are whether we are living up to that fundamental promise that has made this country great - a promise that is the only reason I am standing here tonight.

Because in the faces of those young veterans who come back from Iraq and Afghanistan, I see my grandfather, who signed up after Pearl Harbor, marched in Patton's Army, and was rewarded by a grateful nation with the chance to go to college on the GI Bill.

In the face of that young student who sleeps just three hours before working the night shift, I think about my mom, who raised my sister and me on her own while she worked and earned her degree; who once turned to food stamps but was still able to send us to the best schools in the country with the help of student loans and scholarships.

When I listen to another worker tell me that his factory has shut down, I remember all those men and women on the South Side of Chicago who I stood by and fought for two decades ago after the local steel plant closed.

And when I hear a woman talk about the difficulties of starting her own business, I think about my grandmother, who worked her way up from the secretarial pool to middle-management, despite years of being passed over for promotions because she was a woman. She's the one who taught me about hard work. She's the one who put off buying a new car or a new dress for herself so that I could have a better life. She poured everything she had into me. And although she can no longer travel, I know that she's watching tonight, and that tonight is her night as well.

I don't know what kind of lives John McCain thinks that celebrities lead, but this has been mine. These are my heroes. Theirs are the stories that shaped me. And it is on their behalf that I intend to win this election and keep our promise alive as President of the United States.

What is that promise?

It's a promise that says each of us has the freedom to make of our own lives what we will, but that we also have the obligation to treat each other with dignity and respect.

It's a promise that says the market should reward drive and innovation and generate growth, but that businesses should live up to their responsibilities to create American jobs, look out for American workers, and play by the rules of the road.

Ours is a promise that says government cannot solve all our problems, but what it should do is that which we cannot do for ourselves - protect us from harm and provide every child a decent education; keep our water clean and our toys safe; invest in new schools and new roads and new science and technology.

Our government should work for us, not against us. It should help us, not hurt us. It should ensure opportunity not just for those with the most money and influence, but for every American who's willing to work.

That's the promise of America - the idea that we are responsible for ourselves, but that we also rise or fall as one nation; the fundamental belief that I am my brother's keeper; I am my sister's keeper.

That's the promise we need to keep. That's the change we need right now. So let me spell out exactly what that change would mean if I am President.

Change means a tax code that doesn't reward the lobbyists who wrote it, but the American workers and small businesses who deserve it.

Unlike John McCain, I will stop giving tax breaks to corporations that ship jobs overseas, and I will start giving them to companies that create good jobs right here in America.

I will eliminate capital gains taxes for the small businesses and the start-ups that will create the high-wage, high-tech jobs of tomorrow.

I will cut taxes - cut taxes - for 95% of all working families. Because in an economy like this, the last thing we should do is raise taxes on the middle-class.

And for the sake of our economy, our security, and the future of our planet, I will set a clear goal as President: in ten years, we will finally end our dependence on oil from the Middle East.

Washington's been talking about our oil addiction for the last thirty years, and John McCain has been there for twenty-six of them. In that time, he's said no to higher fuel-efficiency standards for cars, no to investments in renewable energy, no to renewable fuels. And today, we import triple the amount of oil as the day that Senator McCain took office.

Now is the time to end this addiction, and to understand that drilling is a stop-gap measure, not a long-term solution. Not even close.

As President, I will tap our natural gas reserves, invest in clean coal technology, and find ways to safely harness nuclear power. I'll help our auto companies re-tool, so that the fuel-efficient cars of the future are built right here in America. I'll make it easier for the American people to afford these new cars. And I'll invest 150 billion dollars over the next decade in affordable, renewable sources of energy - wind power and solar power and the next generation of bio fuels; an investment that will lead to new industries and five million new jobs that pay well and can't ever be outsourced.

America, now is not the time for small plans.

Now is the time to finally meet our moral obligation to provide every child a world-class education, because it will take nothing less to compete in the global economy. Michelle and I are only here tonight because we were given a chance at an education. And I will not settle for an America where some kids don't have that chance. I'll invest in early childhood education. I'll recruit an army of new teachers, and pay them higher salaries and give them more support. And in exchange, I'll ask for higher standards and more accountability. And we will keep our promise to every young American - if you commit to serving your community or your country, we will make sure you can afford a college education.

Now is the time to finally keep the promise of affordable, accessible health care for every single American. If you have health care, my plan will lower your premiums. If you don't, you'll be able to get the same kind of coverage that members of Congress give themselves. And as someone who watched my mother argue with insurance companies while she lay in bed dying of cancer, I will make certain those companies stop discriminating against those who are sick and need care the most.

Now is the time to help families with paid sick days and better family leave, because nobody in America should have to choose between keeping their jobs and caring for a sick child or ailing parent.

Now is the time to change our bankruptcy laws, so that your pensions are protected ahead of CEO bonuses; and the time to protect Social Security for future generations.

And now is the time to keep the promise of equal pay for an equal day's work, because I want my daughters to have exactly the same opportunities as your sons.

Now, many of these plans will cost money, which is why I've laid out how I'll pay for every dime - by closing corporate loopholes and tax havens that don't help America grow. But I will also go through the federal budget, line by line, eliminating programs that no longer work and making the ones we do need work better and cost less - because we cannot meet twenty-first century challenges with a twentieth century bureaucracy.

And Democrats, we must also admit that fulfilling America's promise will require more than just money. It will require a renewed sense of responsibility from each of us to recover what John F. Kennedy called our "intellectual and moral strength." Yes, government must lead on energy independence, but each of us must do our part to make our homes and businesses more efficient. Yes, we must provide more ladders to success for young men who fall into lives of crime and despair. But we must also admit that programs alone can't replace parents; that government can't turn off the television and make a child do her homework; that fathers must take more responsibility for providing the love and guidance their children need.

Individual responsibility and mutual responsibility - that's the essence of America's promise.

And just as we keep our promise to the next generation here at home, so must we keep America's promise abroad. If John McCain wants to have a debate about who has the temperament, and judgment, to serve as the next Commander-in-Chief, that's a debate I'm ready to have.

For while Senator McCain was turning his sights to Iraq just days after 9/11, I stood up and opposed this war, knowing that it would distract us from the real threats we face. When John McCain said we could just "muddle through" in Afghanistan, I argued for more resources and more troops to finish the fight against the terrorists who actually attacked us on 9/11, and made clear that we must take out Osama bin Laden and his lieutenants if we have them in our sights. John McCain likes to say that he'll follow bin Laden to the Gates of Hell - but he won't even go to the cave where he lives.

And today, as my call for a time frame to remove our troops from Iraq has been echoed by the Iraqi government and even the Bush Administration, even after we learned that Iraq has a $79 billion surplus while we're wallowing in deficits, John McCain stands alone in his stubborn refusal to end a misguided war.

That's not the judgment we need. That won't keep America safe. We need a President who can face the threats of the future, not keep grasping at the ideas of the past.

You don't defeat a terrorist network that operates in eighty countries by occupying Iraq. You don't protect Israel and deter Iran just by talking tough in Washington. You can't truly stand up for Georgia when you've strained our oldest alliances. If John McCain wants to follow George Bush with more tough talk and bad strategy, that is his choice - but it is not the change we need.

We are the party of Roosevelt. We are the party of Kennedy. So don't tell me that Democrats won't defend this country. Don't tell me that Democrats won't keep us safe. The Bush-McCain foreign policy has squandered the legacy that generations of Americans -- Democrats and Republicans - have built, and we are here to restore that legacy.

As Commander-in-Chief, I will never hesitate to defend this nation, but I will only send our troops into harm's way with a clear mission and a sacred commitment to give them the equipment they need in battle and the care and benefits they deserve when they come home.

I will end this war in Iraq responsibly, and finish the fight against al Qaeda and the Taliban in Afghanistan. I will rebuild our military to meet future conflicts. But I will also renew the tough, direct diplomacy that can prevent

Iran from obtaining nuclear weapons and curb Russian aggression. I will build new partnerships to defeat the threats of the 21st century: terrorism and nuclear proliferation; poverty and genocide; climate change and disease. And I will restore our moral standing, so that America is once again that last, best hope for all who are called to the cause of freedom, who long for lives of peace, and who yearn for a better future.

These are the policies I will pursue. And in the weeks ahead, I look forward to debating them with John McCain.

But what I will not do is suggest that the Senator takes his positions for political purposes. Because one of the things that we have to change in our politics is the idea that people cannot disagree without challenging each other's character and patriotism.

The times are too serious, the stakes are too high for this same partisan playbook. So let us agree that patriotism has no party. I love this country, and so do you, and so does John McCain. The men and women who serve in our battlefields may be Democrats and Republicans and Independents, but they have fought together and bled together and some died together under the same proud flag. They have not served a Red America or a Blue America - they have served the United States of America.

So I've got news for you, John McCain. We all put our country first.

America, our work will not be easy. The challenges we face require tough choices, and Democrats as well as Republicans will need to cast off the worn-out ideas and politics of the past. For part of what has been lost these past eight years can't just be measured by lost wages or bigger trade deficits. What has also been lost is our sense of common purpose - our sense of higher purpose. And that's what we have to restore.

We may not agree on abortion, but surely we can agree on reducing the number of unwanted pregnancies in this country. The reality of gun ownership may be different for hunters in rural Ohio than for those plagued by gang-violence in Cleveland, but don't tell me we can't uphold the Second Amendment while keeping AK-47s out of the hands of criminals. I know there are differences on same-sex marriage, but surely we can agree that our gay and lesbian brothers and sisters deserve to visit the person they love in the hospital and to live lives free of discrimination. Passions fly on immigration, but I don't know anyone who benefits when a mother is separated from her infant child or an employer undercuts American wages by hiring illegal workers. This too is part of America's promise - the promise of a democracy where we can find the strength and grace to bridge divides and unite in common effort.

I know there are those who dismiss such beliefs as happy talk. They claim that our insistence on something larger, something firmer and more honest in our public life is just a Trojan Horse for higher taxes and the abandonment of traditional values. And that's to be expected. Because if you don't have any fresh ideas, then you use stale tactics to scare the voters. If you don't have a record to run on, then you paint your opponent as someone people should run from.

You make a big election about small things.

And you know what - it's worked before. Because it feeds into the cynicism we all have about government. When Washington doesn't work, all its promises seem empty. If your hopes have been dashed again and again, then it's best to stop hoping, and settle for what you already know.

I get it. I realize that I am not the likeliest candidate for this office. I don't fit the typical pedigree, and I haven't spent my career in the halls of Washington.

But I stand before you tonight because all across America something is stirring. What the nay-sayers don't understand is that this election has never been about me. It's been about you.

For eighteen long months, you have stood up, one by one, and said enough to the politics of the past. You understand that in this election, the greatest risk we can take is to try the same old politics with the same old players and expect a different result. You have shown what history teaches us - that at defining moments like this one, the change we need doesn't come from Washington. Change comes to Washington. Change happens because the American people demand it - because they rise up and insist on new ideas and new leadership, a new politics for a new time.

America, this is one of those moments.

I believe that as hard as it will be, the change we need is coming. Because I've seen it. Because I've lived it. I've seen it in Illinois, when we provided health care to more children and moved more families from welfare to work. I've seen it in Washington, when we worked across party lines to open up government and hold lobbyists more accountable, to give better care for our veterans and keep nuclear weapons out of terrorist hands.

And I've seen it in this campaign. In the young people who voted for the first time, and in those who got involved again after a very long time. In the Republicans who never thought they'd pick up a Democratic ballot, but did. I've seen it in the workers who would rather cut their hours back a day than see their friends lose their jobs, in the soldiers who re-enlist after losing a limb, in the good neighbors who take a stranger in when a hurricane strikes and the floodwaters rise.

This country of ours has more wealth than any nation, but that's not what makes us rich. We have the most powerful military on Earth, but that's not what makes us strong. Our universities and our culture are the envy of the world, but that's not what keeps the world coming to our shores.

Instead, it is that American spirit - that American promise - that pushes us forward even when the path is uncertain; that binds us together in spite of our differences; that makes us fix our eye not on what is seen, but what is unseen, that better place around the bend.

That promise is our greatest inheritance. It's a promise I make to my daughters when I tuck them in at night, and a promise that you make to yours - a promise that has led immigrants to cross oceans and pioneers to travel west; a promise that led workers to picket lines, and women to reach for the ballot.

And it is that promise that forty five years ago today, brought Americans from every corner of this land to stand together on a Mall in Washington, before Lincoln's Memorial, and hear a young preacher from Georgia speak of his dream.

The men and women who gathered there could've heard many things. They could've heard words of anger and discord. They could've been told to succumb to the fear and frustration of so many dreams deferred.

But what the people heard instead - people of every creed and color, from every walk of life - is that in America, our destiny is inextricably linked. That together, our dreams can be one.

"We cannot walk alone," the preacher cried. "And as we walk, we must make the pledge that we shall always march ahead. We cannot turn back."

America, we cannot turn back. Not with so much work to be done. Not with so many children to educate, and so many veterans to care for. Not with an economy to fix and cities to rebuild and farms to save. Not with so many families to protect and so many lives to mend. America, we cannot turn back. We cannot walk alone. At this moment, in this election, we must pledge once more to march into the future. Let us keep that promise - that American promise - and in the words of Scripture hold firmly, without wavering, to the hope that we confess.

Thank you, God Bless you, and God Bless the United States of America.

Chapter 18

President-Elect Victory Speech

Barack Obama
Delivered 4 November 2008, Grant Park, Chicago, Illinois

Hello, Chicago.

If there is anyone out there who still doubts that America is a place where all things are possible; who still wonders if the dream of our founders is alive in our time; who still questions the power of our democracy, tonight is your answer.

It's the answer told by lines that stretched around schools and churches in numbers this nation has never seen; by people who waited three hours and four hours, many for the very first time in their lives, because they believed that this time must be different; that their voices could be that difference.

It's the answer spoken by young and old, rich and poor, Democrat and Republican, black, white, Hispanic, Asian, Native American, gay, straight, disabled and not disabled -- Americans who sent a message to the world that we have never been just a collection of individuals or a collection of Red States and Blue States: we are, and always will be, the United States of America!

It's the answer that -- that led those who have been told for so long by so many to be cynical, and fearful, and doubtful about what we can achieve to put their hands on the arc of history and bend it once more toward the hope of a better day.

It's been a long time coming, but tonight, because of what we did on this day, in this election, at this defining moment, change has come to America.

A little bit earlier this evening, I received an extraordinarily gracious call from Senator McCain. Senator McCain fought long and hard in this campaign, and he's fought even longer and harder for the country that he loves. He has endured sacrifices for America that most of us cannot begin to imagine. We are better off for the service rendered by this brave and selfless leader. I congratulate him; I congratulate Governor Palin for all that they've achieved, and I look forward to working with them to renew this nation's promise in the months ahead.

I want to thank my partner in this journey, a man who campaigned from his heart and spoke for the men and women he grew up with on the streets of Scranton and rode with on the train home to Delaware, the Vice President-elect of the United States, Joe Biden.

And I would not be standing here tonight without the unyielding support of my best friend for the last 16 years, the rock of our family, the love of my life, the nation's next First Lady: Michelle Obama. Sasha and Malia, I love you both more than you can imagine, and you have earned the new puppy that's coming with us to the White House. And while she's no longer with us, I know my grandmother's watching, along with the family that made me who I am. I miss them tonight, and I know that my debt to them is beyond measure. To my sister Maya, my sister Alma, all my other brothers and sisters -- thank you so much for the support that you've given me. I am grateful to them.

And to my campaign manager, David Plouffe -- the unsung hero of this campaign, who built the best -- the best political campaign, I think, in the history of the United States of America. To my chief strategist David Axelrod -- who's been a partner with me every step of the way. To the best campaign team ever assembled in the history of politics -- you made this happen, and I am forever grateful for what you've sacrificed to get it done.

But above all, I will never forget who this victory truly belongs to. It belongs to you. It belongs to you. I was never the likeliest candidate for this office. We didn't start with much money or many endorsements. Our campaign was not hatched in the halls of Washington. It began in the back yards of Des Moines and the living rooms of Concord and the front porches of Charleston. It was built by working men and women who dug into what little savings they had to give 5 dollars and 10 dollars and 20 dollars to the cause. It grew strength from the young people who rejected the myth of their generation's apathy, who left their homes and their families for jobs that offered little pay and less sleep. It drew strength from the not-so-young people who braved the bitter cold and scorching heat to knock on doors of perfect strangers, and from the millions of Americans who volunteered and organized and proved that more than two centuries later a government of the people, by the people, and for the people has not perished from the Earth. This is your victory.

And I know you didn't do this just to win an election. And I know you didn't do it for me. You did it because you understand the enormity of the task that lies ahead. For even as we celebrate tonight, we know the challenges that tomorrow will bring are the greatest of our lifetime: two wars, a planet in peril, the worst financial crisis in a century. Even as we stand here tonight, we know there are brave Americans waking up in the deserts of Iraq and the mountains of Afghanistan to risk their lives for us. There are mothers and fathers who will lie awake after the children fall asleep and wonder how they'll make the mortgage or pay their doctors' bills or save enough for their child's college education. There's new energy to harness, new jobs to be created, new schools to build, and threats to meet, alliances to repair.

The road ahead will be long. Our climb will be steep. We may not get there in one year or even in one term. But, America, I have never been more hopeful than I am tonight that we will get there. I promise you, we as a people will get there.

There will be setbacks and false starts. There are many who won't agree with every decision or policy I make as President. And we know the government can't solve every problem. But I will always be honest with you about the challenges we face. I will listen to you, especially when we disagree. And, above all, I will ask you to join in the work of remaking this nation, the only way it's been done in America for 221 years -- block by block, brick by brick, calloused hand by calloused hand. What began 21 months ago in the depths of winter cannot end on this autumn night.

This victory alone is not the change we seek. It is only the chance for us to make that change. And that cannot happen if we go back to the way things were. It can't happen without you, without a new spirit of service, a new spirit of sacrifice. So let us summon a new spirit of patriotism, of responsibility, where each of us resolves to pitch in and work harder and look after not only ourselves but each other. Let us remember that, if this financial crisis taught us anything, it's that we cannot have a thriving Wall Street while Main Street suffers. In this country, we rise or fall as one nation, as one people. Let's resist the temptation to fall back on the same partisanship and pettiness and immaturity that has poisoned our politics for so long.

Let's remember that it was a man from this state who first carried the banner of the Republican Party to the White House, a Party founded on the values of self-reliance and individual liberty and national unity. Those are values that we all share. And while the Democratic Party has won a great victory tonight, we do so with a measure of humility and determination to heal the divides that have held back our progress. As Lincoln said to a nation far more divided than ours: "We are not enemies but friends...." "Though passion may have strained, it must not break our bonds of affection."[1]

And to those Americans who -- whose support I have yet to earn, I may not have won your vote tonight, but I hear your voices. I need your help. And I will be your President, too.

And to all those watching tonight from beyond our shores, from parliaments and palaces, to those who are huddled around radios in the forgotten corners of the world, our stories are singular, but our destiny is shared, and a new dawn of American leadership is at hand.

To those -- To those who would tear the world down: We will defeat you. To those who seek peace and security: We support you. And to all those who have wondered if America's beacon still burns as bright: Tonight we've proved once more that the true strength of our nation comes not from the might of our arms or the scale of our wealth, but from the enduring power of our ideals: democracy, liberty, opportunity, and unyielding hope.

That's the true genius of America: that America can change. Our union can be perfected. What we've already achieved gives us hope for what we can and must achieve tomorrow.

This election had many firsts and many stories that will be told for generations. But one that's on my mind tonight's about a woman who cast her ballot in Atlanta. She's a lot like the millions of others who stood in line to make their voice heard in this election except for one thing: Ann Nixon Cooper is 106 years old.

She was born just a generation past slavery; a time when there were no cars on the road or planes in the sky; when someone like her couldn't vote for two reasons: because she was a woman and because of the color of her skin.

And tonight, I think about all that she's seen throughout her century in America -- the heartache and the hope; the struggle and the progress; the times we were told that we can't, and the people who pressed on with that American creed: Yes we can.

At a time when women's voices were silenced and their hopes dismissed, she lived to see them stand up and speak out and reach for the ballot: Yes we can.

ANN N. COOPER

When there was despair in the dust bowl and depression across the land, she saw a nation conquer fear itself with a New Deal, new jobs, a new sense of common purpose: Yes we can.

When the bombs fell on our harbor and tyranny threatened the world, she was there to witness a generation rise to greatness and a democracy was saved: Yes we can.

She was there for the buses in Montgomery, the hoses in Birmingham, a bridge in Selma, and a preacher from Atlanta who told a people that "we shall overcome": Yes we can.

A man touched down on the moon, a wall came down in Berlin, a world was connected by our own science and imagination.

And this year, in this election, she touched her finger to a screen, and cast her vote, because after 106 years in America, through the best of times and the darkest of hours, she knows how America can change: Yes we can.

America, we have come so far. We have seen so much. But there is so much more to do. So tonight, let us ask ourselves -- if our children should live to see the next century; if my daughters should be so lucky to live as long as Ann Nixon Cooper, what change will they see? What progress will we have made?

This is our chance to answer that call. This is our moment. This is our time, to put our people back to work and open doors of opportunity for our kids; to restore prosperity and promote the cause of peace; to reclaim the American dream and reaffirm that fundamental truth, that, out of many, we are one;[2] that while we breathe, we hope. And where we are met with cynicism and doubt and those who tell us that we can't, we will respond with that timeless creed that sums up the spirit of a people: Yes, we can.

Thank you. God bless you. And may God bless the United States of America.

Chapter 19

Inaugural Address

President Barack Obama

My fellow citizens:

I stand here today humbled by the task before us, grateful for the trust you have bestowed, mindful of the sacrifices borne by our ancestors. I thank President Bush for his service to our nation, as well as the generosity and cooperation he has shown throughout this transition.

Forty-four Americans have now taken the presidential oath. The words have been spoken during rising tides of prosperity and the still waters of peace. Yet, every so often the oath is taken amidst gathering clouds and raging storms. At these moments, America has carried on not simply because of the skill or vision of those in high office, but because we the people have remained faithful to the ideals of our forebears, and true to our founding documents.

So it has been. So it must be with this generation of Americans.

That we are in the midst of crisis is now well understood. Our nation is at war, against a far-reaching network of violence and hatred. Our economy is badly weakened, a consequence of greed and irresponsibility on the part of some, but also our collective failure to make hard choices and prepare the nation for a new age. Homes have been lost; jobs shed; businesses shuttered. Our health care is too costly; our schools fail too many; and each day brings further evidence that the ways we use energy strengthen our adversaries and threaten our planet.

These are the indicators of crisis, subject to data and statistics. Less measurable but no less profound is a sapping of confidence across our land a nagging fear that America's decline is inevitable, and that the next generation must lower its sights.

Today I say to you that the challenges we face are real. They are serious and they are many. They will not be met easily or in a short span of time. But know this, America they will be met.

On this day, we gather because we have chosen hope over fear, unity of purpose over conflict and discord.

On this day, we come to proclaim an end to the petty grievances and false promises, the recriminations and worn out dogmas, that for far too long have strangled our politics.

We remain a young nation, but in the words of Scripture, the time has come to set aside childish things. The time has come to reaffirm our enduring spirit; to choose our better history; to carry forward that precious gift, that noble idea, passed on from generation to generation: the God-given promise that all are equal, all are free and all deserve a chance to pursue their full measure of happiness.

In reaffirming the greatness of our nation, we understand that greatness is never a given. It must be earned. Our journey has never been one of shortcuts or settling for less. It has not been the path for the faint-hearted for those who prefer leisure over work, or seek only the pleasures of riches and fame. Rather, it has been the risk-takers, the doers, the makers of things some celebrated but more often men and women obscure in their labor, who have carried us up the long, rugged path towards prosperity and freedom.

For us, they packed up their few worldly possessions and traveled across oceans in search of a new life.

For us, they toiled in sweatshops and settled the West; endured the lash of the whip and plowed the hard earth.

For us, they fought and died, in places like Concord and Gettysburg; Normandy and Khe Sanh.

Time and again these men and women struggled and sacrificed and worked till their hands were raw so that we might live a better life. They saw America as bigger than the sum of our individual ambitions; greater than all the differences of birth or wealth or faction.

This is the journey we continue today. We remain the most prosperous, powerful nation on Earth. Our workers are no less productive than when this crisis began. Our minds are no less inventive, our goods and services no less needed than they were last week or last month or last year. Our capacity remains undiminished. But our time of standing pat, of protecting narrow interests and putting off unpleasant decisions that time has surely passed. Starting today, we must pick ourselves up, dust ourselves off, and begin again the work of remaking America.

For everywhere we look, there is work to be done. The state of the economy calls for action, bold and swift, and we will act not only to create new jobs, but to lay a new foundation for growth. We will build the roads and bridges, the electric grids and digital lines that feed our commerce and bind us together. We will restore science to its rightful place, and wield technology's wonders to raise health care's quality and lower its cost. We will harness the sun and the winds and the soil to fuel our cars and run our factories. And we will transform our schools and colleges and universities to meet the demands of a new age. All this we can do. All this we will do.

Now, there are some who question the scale of our ambitions who suggest that our system cannot tolerate too many big plans. Their memories are short. For they have forgotten what this country has already done; what free men and women can achieve when imagination is joined to common purpose, and necessity to courage.

What the cynics fail to understand is that the ground has shifted beneath them that the stale political arguments that have consumed us for so long no longer apply. The question we ask today is not whether our government is too big or too small, but whether it works whether it helps families find jobs at a decent wage, care they can afford, a retirement that is dignified. Where the answer is yes, we intend to move forward. Where the answer is no, programs will end. Those of us who manage the public's dollars will be held to account to spend wisely, reform bad habits, and do our business in the light of day because only then can we restore the vital trust between a people and their government.

Nor is the question before us whether the market is a force for good or ill. Its power to generate wealth and expand freedom is unmatched, but this crisis has reminded us that without a watchful eye, the market can spin out of control and that a nation cannot prosper long when it favors only the prosperous. The success of our economy has always depended not just on the size of our gross domestic product, but on the reach of our prosperity; on our ability to extend opportunity to every willing heart not out of charity, but because it is the surest route to our common good.

As for our common defense, we reject as false the choice between our safety and our ideals. Our founding fathers ... our found fathers, faced with perils we can scarcely imagine, drafted a charter to assure the rule of law and the rights of man, a charter expanded by the blood of generations. Those ideals still light the world, and we will not give them up for expedience's sake. And so to all the other peoples and governments who are watching today, from the grandest capitals to the small village where my father was born: know that America is a friend of each nation and every man, woman, and child who seeks a future of peace and dignity, and that we are ready to lead once more.

Recall that earlier generations faced down fascism and communism not just with missiles and tanks, but with sturdy alliances and enduring convictions. They understood that our power alone cannot protect us, nor does it entitle us to do as we please. Instead, they knew that our power grows through its prudent use; our security emanates from the justness of our cause, the force of our example, the tempering qualities of humility and restraint.

We are the keepers of this legacy. Guided by these principles once more, we can meet those new threats that demand even greater effort even greater cooperation and understanding between nations. We will begin to responsibly leave Iraq to its people, and forge a hard-earned peace in Afghanistan. With old friends and former foes, we will work tirelessly to lessen the nuclear threat, and roll back the specter of a warming planet. We will not apologize for our way of life, nor will we waver in its defense, and for those who seek to advance their aims by inducing terror and slaughtering innocents, we say to you now that our spirit is stronger and cannot be broken; you cannot outlast us, and we will defeat you.

For we know that our patchwork heritage is a strength, not a weakness. We are a nation of Christians and Muslims, Jews and Hindus and non-believers. We are shaped by every language and culture, drawn from every end of this Earth; and because we have tasted the bitter swill of civil war and segregation, and emerged from that dark chapter stronger and more united, we cannot help but believe that the old hatreds shall someday pass; that the lines of tribe shall soon dissolve; that as the world grows smaller, our common humanity shall reveal itself; and that America must play its role in ushering in a new era of peace.

To the Muslim world, we seek a new way forward, based on mutual interest and mutual respect. To those leaders around the globe who seek to sow conflict, or blame their society's ills on the West know that your people will judge you on what you can build, not what you destroy. To those who cling to power through corruption and deceit and the silencing of dissent, know that you are on the wrong side of history; but that we will extend a hand if you are willing to unclench your fist.

To the people of poor nations, we pledge to work alongside you to make your farms flourish and let clean waters flow; to nourish starved bodies and feed hungry minds. And to those nations like ours that enjoy relative plenty, we say we can no longer afford indifference to the suffering outside our borders; nor can we consume the world's resources without regard to effect. For the world has changed, and we must change with it.

As we consider the road that unfolds before us, we remember with humble gratitude those brave Americans who, at this very hour, patrol far-off deserts and distant mountains. They have something to tell us, just as the fallen heroes who lie in Arlington whisper through the ages. We honor them not only because they are guardians of our liberty, but because they embody the spirit of service; a willingness to find meaning in something greater than themselves. And yet, at this moment a moment that will define a generation it is precisely this spirit that must inhabit us all.

For as much as government can do and must do, it is ultimately the faith and determination of the American people upon which this nation relies. It is the kindness to take in a stranger when the levees break, the selflessness of workers who would rather cut their hours than see a friend lose their job which sees us through our darkest hours. It is the firefighter's courage to storm a stairway filled with smoke, but also a parent's willingness to nurture a child, that finally decides our fate.

Our challenges may be new. The instruments with which we meet them may be new. But those values upon which our success depends hard work and honesty, courage and fair play, tolerance and curiosity, loyalty and patriotism these things are old. These things are true. They have been the quiet force of progress throughout our history. What is demanded then is a return to these truths. What is required of us now is a new era of responsibility a recognition, on the part of every American, that we have duties to ourselves, our nation, and the world, duties that we do not grudgingly accept but rather seize gladly, firm in the knowledge that there is nothing so satisfying to the spirit, so defining of our character, than giving our all to a difficult task.

This is the price and the promise of citizenship.

This is the source of our confidence the knowledge that God calls on us to shape an uncertain destiny.

This is the meaning of our liberty and our creed why men and women and children of every race and every faith can join in celebration across this magnificent Mall, and why a man whose father less than sixty years ago might not have been served at a local restaurant can now stand before you to take a most sacred oath.

So let us mark this day with remembrance, of who we are and how far we have traveled. In the year of America's birth, in the coldest of months, a small band of patriots huddled by dying campfires on the shores of an icy river. The capital was abandoned. The enemy was advancing. The snow was stained with blood. At a moment when the outcome of our revolution was most in doubt, the father of our nation ordered these words be read to the people:

"Let it be told to the future world ... that in the depth of winter, when nothing but hope and virtue could survive...that the city and the country, alarmed at one common danger, came forth to meet (it)."

America, in the face of our common dangers, in this winter of our hardship, let us remember these timeless words. With hope and virtue, let us brave once more the icy currents, and endure what storms may come. Let it be said by our children's children that when we were tested we refused to let this journey end, that we did not turn back nor did we falter; and with eyes fixed on the horizon and God's grace upon us, we carried forth that great gift of freedom and delivered it safely to future generations.

Thank you. God bless you. And God bless the United States of America.

Barack's Lifetime

A young Barack Obama playing in the ocean in the 1960s

A young Barack Obama, with baseball bat, in the 1960s

A young Barack Obama on a tricycle in Hawai`i in the 1960s

Barack Obama, Sr. and Ann Dunham, Barack's parents, in Hawai`i in 1972.

Barack Obama plays basketball at Punahou School in Hawai`i, 1979.

A young Barack Obama with his grandfather.

Barack Obama at Harvard Law School, where he was the first black president of the Harvard Law Review

Barack Obama's yearbook picture from 1979.

Barack Obama in New York City.

Barack Obama with his grandparents, New York City, 1980s.

Barack and Michelle Obama at their wedding in October, 1992.

Barack Obama with his youngest daughter Sasha.

Barack and Michelle Obama, with daughters Malia and Sasha, waiting for the
results of his senate bid on election night 2004

Barack and Michelle spending Christmas in Hawai`i.

Barack Obama's Harvard Law School graduation year picture, 1991.

Barack Obama's Sr

Barack Obama Sr

In 1992, Barack Obama went form Harvard Law School back to Chicago, where he ran a voter registration drive.

Barack Obama in 1970, at age 9, with mother Ann Dunham, step-father Lolo and sister Maya, age 1.

Barack Obama and his father during his visit to Hawai`i in 1972.

A young Barack Obama with his mother, Ann Dunham.

Barack Obama at his high school graduation in 1979.

Barack Obama after his high school graduation in 1979, with his grandparents.

Inauguration Day

Barack & Michelle Obama

Election Night Win

Inauguration Day

Eastern State Ball of the Obamas

Inauguration Day

Swearing In Ceremony

Obamas Dance

Inauguration Ball

Inauguration Ball

Email received on Friday, Oct 9, 2009 from Barack Obama America on his winning the prestigious Nobel Peace Prize.

Ayin –

This morning, Michelle and I awoke to some surprising and humbling news. At 6 a.m., we received word that I'd been awarded the Nobel Peace Prize for 2009.

To be honest, I do not feel that I deserve to be in the company of so many of the transformative figures who've been honored by this prize -- men and women who've inspired me and inspired the entire world through their courageous pursuit of peace.

But I also know that throughout history the Nobel Peace Prize has not just been used to honor specific achievement; it's also been used as a means to give momentum to a set of causes.

That is why I've said that I will accept this award as a call to action, a call for all nations and all peoples to confront the common challenges of the 21st century. These challenges won't all be met during my presidency, or even my lifetime. But I know these challenges can be met so long as it's recognized that they will not be met by one person or one nation alone.

This award -- and the call to action that comes with it -- does not belong simply to me or my administration; it belongs to all people around the world who have fought for justice and for peace. And most of all, it belongs to you, the men and women of America, who have dared to hope and have worked so hard to make our world a little better.

So today we humbly recommit to the important work that we've begun together. I'm grateful that you've stood with me thus far, and I'm honored to continue our vital work in the years to come.

Thank you,
President Barack Obama

Section IV
Contemporary Hawai`i

Chapter 20

Who's Who In Hawai`i

"In chapter 20, readers can enjoy the biographies of some of the many African Americans who have made significant contributions to Hawai`i, past and present."

MarshaRose Joyner is energetic, imaginative and creative. MarshaRose is an interesting combination of an activist, capitalist and "tree-hugger." I was exhausted spending the day with this non-stop, high energy, radio producer, democrat, wife, mother and grandmother. "I see my role in life as a grain of sand" she told me. "A grain of sand?" I asked, to which she replied, "You know . . . to make a truly beautiful pearl there must be a grain of sand in the oyster," as she stopped long enough to pick a flower. "To make a truly beautiful world, there must be people like me…the irritants that keep everything growing." We walked along in silence. Born into a family whose fight for Black equality and justice goes back more than 100 years, her great-granduncle, John Oliver, born a slave, became an attorney, and was on the grand jury that indicted Jefferson Davis, President of the Confederate States (May, 1866). Grandfather Dr. Jacob B. Oliver (also born a slave), a distinguished black physician in Brazil, Indiana, was twice named Minister to Liberia, by President Woodrow Wilson.

The Murphy-Oliver family, of which Joyner is the oldest of the fourth generation, has owned *Afro-American Newspapers* for 107 years, at one time the largest chain of Black owned newspapers in the world. MarshaRose's father, Marshall Kelvin Hood, now deceased, was a part of a family whose leadership and influence included City Council people, judges, professors, educators, doctors, ministers and independent business people in Indiana, Illinois, Michigan and Africa. "There has never been a time in my life when I have not been a part of a cause", Marsha said. "The newspaper was always championing the cause of Civil Rights, which has afforded me the opportunity to know most of the great Black leaders and martyrs of our time." She went on to add, "My mother Dr. Elizabeth Murphy Oliver, was awarded the Black Marylanders of Distinction Award along with 91 other awards for her continued work on behalf of the African American community."

For more than 40 years of living in Hawai`i and being a part of the Pacific-Asia indigenous community, she has come to know, admire, and respect some of the great Human Rights leaders, not only in , but around the world. Having met most of the Heads of State from around the Pacific and in the United Nations, Joyner says, "Being involved in the indigenous community gives me a perspective into the world that western culture does not provide, and has fostered a greater appreciation for my own culture and its roots."

Arriving in Honolulu

October 1946, at the Presidio in California and the warm sun is shining. It is never warm in October in Baltimore nor does the sun shine. We had orders, so we boarded the USS Admiral Hass with hundreds of other dependents bound for the week long voyage to Hawai`i. Once we entered Pearl Harbor, a sassy little tugboat, with the harbormaster waving to us, scooted alongside. I grinned so wide my face hurt. He came on board to take over for the Captain, as is the custom in all ports of call, barking order to the crew . . . passing through the narrow opening at Hospital Point, picking gingerly amid the wreckage left over from the December 7th bombing . . .expertly bringing us to the dock.

Later, when we arrived at our hotel, my heart sank. Surely, this shabby hotel was not the Royal Hawaiian Hotel that I had dreamed of. This place, naval jumpers hanging from clothes lines on the lanais and bobbed wire fencing rolled along the beach, was the beginning of a nightmare with white men peering down on us like animals in the zoo. Standing in line, which is a military tradition as we had learned, we waited to register at the front desk. When our turn came, the clerk choked hard trying to clear his throat, while turning a strange color of pink. "May I help you Madame" he intoned. "Yes, we are here to register, we have orders," Mama replied pushing the papers forward. "Yes Madame I understand. But you and your daughter cannot stay here." I could hear Mama's heart break. "But we have orders".... Mama's voice moved up an octave. The decibel level dropped completely in the hotel lobby. Everyone held their breaths this was 1946 and martial law was a fresh memory. Martial law, a policy that was written long before December 7th, was a part of the belief that the threat was from within (everyone looked like Japanese to them). It began within hours of the bombing of Pearl Harbor and many local Japanese were herded into "re-location camps."

Governor Joseph Poindexter (a FDR appointee) requested that General Walter Short, Commanding General of the Army in Hawai`i, take control of the territorial government. "I know Madame, but this hotel is for whites only". By this time my beautiful mother with skin like brown velvet, had turned into an enormous grizzly bear. Bearing her teeth and red fingernails, I heard her say, "You aren't worth a damn! We have orders and I want to see some one in charge." I wrapped my self into the folds of her skirt, trying to disappear.

This significantly unpleasant exchange went on for what seemed like an eternity. When Mama took on a fight like this, there were always casualties, and she was not one of them. The tall, solid, brown skinned Hawaiian bellman dressed in the hotel uniform, dropped his head in unqualified embarrassment; he couldn't stay there either. I thought we had left segregation behind in Baltimore. Soon, and not soon enough, the one and only Admiral Chester Nimitz appeared pouring his own kind of snake oil on the troubled waters. We were whisked off in a staff car, to a guesthouse at Schofield Barracks for the night. Riding in silence, Mama, thoroughly overcome with exhaustion, put her head back on the seat, and was soon asleep. Finally we entered into the old wooden town of Wahiawa and drove around Lake Wilson. This had been a three hour drive! The guesthouse at Schofield Barracks was home of the 'colored' 25th infantry. When all was said and done, Mama and Admiral Nimitz went on to become good friends.

In spite of segregation and Jim Crow, she had come from wealth and privilege. Mama's father, Dr. Jacob Oliver was the only doctor in the little town of Brazil, Indiana. The comfort and service of the Pullman cars and the ship had suited her perfectly. So I held her hand with the knowingness that only a child has, and assured her we would get through this.

Peter Hose, or the "Hula Cop for several years, at the corner of Fort and Merchant Streets," had become one of Honolulu's most beloved traffic control cops, guiding cars and pedestrians through this intersection. The first African American officer in the Honolulu Police Department, Hose delighted Honolulu citizens with his smooth graceful movements and always well natured attitude. The first traffic light was dedicated to him. There is a small plaque also dedicated to Peter Hose. It reads "Honolulu's Most Courteous Traffic Cop Who Smiled His Way into the Hearts of the People."

The next day we left for Guam. On the final approach to Guam, everything was flat looking like tinker toys. azzoomm. . azzoom we roared to a stop. There was Daddy. He was more handsome than I had remembered, so tall with straight broad shoulders. His rugged good looks and the Army uniform worked well, complimenting his complexion. Spending more than a year out there in the tropical sun, he was a beautiful tan, instead of that pale, washed out, nothing color. Thank goodness, he could no longer be mistaken for white. This color thing is always a problem in America. But this was Saipan, hopefully. Daddy saluted and so did I.

Uncle Ernest announced that while this was Saipan, henceforth, it was to be known as "Hood's Island," and indeed it was. Ernest was the company commander. In the Army, the 'colored' outfit was the Ordinance, the white company was The Corp of Engineers. Their combined job was to clean up the islands after the war. "The white officers were getting out of here so fast that I was left with the command," said Uncle Ernest. A year before, a white officer had called Uncle Ernest, and with a smirk in his voice said, "I have a "boy" down here who says he is your little brother." I looked at Daddy who stood an imposing six feet tall and Uncle Ernest, who was slightly built with refined features like his mother, whose family was from India. The sun had also turned Ernest a golden brown. "His name is Marshall Hood, is that him?" "Yes, it is." Uncle Ernest replied. To which the other officer asked, still a bit hesitant, "What if I send him to you and make him your First Sergeant?" uncle Ernest replied, "Thank you sir". It was done.

The daily clearing of the island including the shoreline, hilltops and the bay of debris, and spent ammunition and removing hundreds of dead bodies from caves was a huge chore. However, Daddy "and company" found a wrecked PT boat on the Navy's side of the Island, and by hook and crook they towed it over to the Army's side of the Island. Armed with Daddy's "want list," Uncle Ernest managed to get from the Navy every little piece, part and paint needed for them to put the boat in operating condition. Soon we had a working boat. While Daddy loved every minute of creating this boat, Mama had many hours of jokes about Daddy's homemade PT boat.

The native people, the Chamorros, unknown, but for their ethnic place names (Guam, Saipan, Rota, and Tinian), reflected both the beauty and the tragedy of those places. The tragedy! Within a two square mile area near Lake Susupe was life in the compound, constructed by The Navy for the Natives. It was primitive and only the bare necessities were provided. Weathered boards, tattered tents and battered tin sheets from the bombed out sugar refinery provided the only shelter from the weather. Each hut *(han)* accommodated from 20 to 55 people. After the fighting, families were released from Camp Susupe during the day to cultivate vegetables, since food was scarce. They had to return in the evening. In September, 1946, just before we arrived, the camps housed 13,954 Japanese, 1,411 Koreans, 2,966 Chamorros and 1,025 Carolinians.

As is the custom on the many Islands of the Pacific, the military lived on the very best parts of the Island. Most of the Pacific Islands have been alternately coveted and neglected by most of the major world powers and were often the basis for disputes among them. Men and nations have been interested in the islands for a variety of reasons, such as religious, economic, strategic, and very often the periods of interest brought more misery to the inhabitants of the islands than the periods of neglect. The compound became a playground for me, a home away from home.

Everyday, I would awake with the sun and the sounds of geckoes. My nanny, Bill and I would go to Camp Susupe. Since the compound was off limits to the GIs, we would hide the jeep in the thick foliage, climb over the fence, and drop down behind their supply of fresh water. Bill was eighteen years old, loved the pretty girls, and they liked him. So, while he dallied with the girls, I played with the native children. In spite of our language difference, the fenced in children became my friends. At the end of the day, Bill and I would retrace our steps and proceed home. By the end of summer, we went back to the cold weather in Baltimore, back to segregation, back to America, and to my parent's divorce.

Like all middle class girls, regardless of race, I was sent off to Boarding School in Cornwells Heights, Pennsylvania. It was the next stop after leaving MainLine Philadelphia on the Pennsylvania Railroad line. A huge sign on the lavish lawns of the Italian Villa, announced "Holy Providence Convent for Negroes and Indians," (again, The Sisters of the Blessed Sacrament) While the nuns were a challenge, they were never a bore. It was a great education, I learned about the "Great Books" (imagine, *Alice in Wonderland* was not among them) I learned to listen to European classical music, and I enjoyed the luxury of handspun oriental carpets on the walls and on the highly polished hardwood floors. I walked the corridors lined with art works that would rival any museum. I learned to ride an Arabian stallion with an English saddle, and of course, I set a perfect table, baked bread, and cleaned the stables. I learned nothing about being a 'Negro' or an 'Indian.'

MarshaRose Joyner Returns to Saipan

As an 8-year-old girl at the close of World War II, MarshaRose Joyner, daughter of a military father stationed on Saipan, has fond memories of climbing the fence around the Camp Susupe Detention Center, and sneaking in to play with the Chamorro children living within the compound.

On Jan. 19, 2009, Joyner returned to Saipan for the first time since 1949, to deliver a special keynote address for the third annual Martin Luther King (MLK) Day Commemoration organized by Saipan's African American Cultural Preservation Committee Inc., with support from the Northern Marianas Council for the Humanities.

"We're privileged and honored to have Ms. Joyner return to Saipan and share her story with us for MLK day," said Joe Hill, AACPC committee president. "As people who actually lived during those times get harder to find, it's rare to find individual servicemen who were stationed here to tell their story, rarer still to find entire families. So to have the perspective of a civilian dependent who is also African-American, and who actually spent time inside the camp, is quite unique."

Having lived and experienced her memorable U.S. to Pacific Island journey during the "Jim Crow" era in the U.S., where white racism was law, she was witness to, and victim of, one brand of prejudice and segregation. On Saipan, she witnessed another form of segregation and discrimination at Camp Susupe. She went on to become an activist, accumulating honors and accomplishments. She then returned to Hawai`i in 1970, where she currently resides (an excerpt from her memoirs will be available online). She is an advocate of indigenous rights and is currently Project Director for the Pacific Justice and Reconciliation Center.

Andre' Wooten. After obtaining a B.A. in world history at Reed College in 1971, and graduating from the University of Washington Law School in 1975, Attorney Andre' Wooten went to work for KCTS Channel 9 TV, the educational public television station in Seattle, where he film documentaries and community affairs news programs.

Andre' Wooten practiced law as a deputy Corporation Counsel for the City of Seattle from 1976-1980; he taught Afro-American History and Constitutional Law for the University of Washington Black Studies Department from 1978-1980.

In 1985, Andre' Wooten established a litigation practice in Civil Rights, Criminal Defense, Personal Injury and Real Estate law in Honolulu. He is former president of the African American Lawyers Association of Hawai`i which he founded in 1987. He lobbied the legislature for the appointment of a black judge.

In 1988, as president of the Afro-American Association of Hawai`i, he helped form a community coalition which successfully lobbied the Hawai`i State legislature for passage of the Martin Luther King, Jr. State holiday. Since 1988, Andre' has published numerous articles as history editor of the *Afro-* and later in the *Mahogany* newspapers of Honolulu. He has lectured in various colleges and universities in Hawai`i, and has appeared many times in television programs in Honolulu discussing civil rights issues and facts related to the historical impact of the international African diaspora.

In 1995, Andre and his wife, Daphne, formed *"A RIPE IDEA,"* Amen Rasta I Production Enterprises, a company which creates, produces, and distributes educational African history and music videos world wide, beginning with the Nile Valley civilizations of Nubia, KMT-Egypt, Kush and the Sudan. www.amenrasta.com. He expanded his videos and CD's to include the African Diaspora; West Africa, South Africa, Brazil in South America, Fiji and the South Pacific, the Caribbean and Jamaica, that reflect his on- site research in these places.

Wooten was inspired by his step-father and mentor, former Seattle criminal defense lawyer, judge and legislator, Charles M. Stokes, who was elected to the Black Lawyers "Hall of Fame" of the National Bar Association in 1992. A small park was named for Stokes in Seattle.

Song For My Father, written by Wooten's sister *Essence* editor, Stephanie Stokes Oliver, tells the story of his career in law and politics.

Since moving to in 1980, Wooten has also taught in the public high schools of the Big Island and lectured on African and American history, law and politics at the University of Hawai`i, Chaminade University, Wayland Baptist College, Kaneohe Marine Core Base, Schofield Army Barracks, Pearl Harbor Naval Base and to numerous community groups.

Professionally, Wooten's successes are noteworthy.

In December 2002, a Hawai`i Federal Jury awarded Wooten's client, Umar Rahsaan $1,055,000.00 in damages, the largest civil rights violation award for a black person in Hawai`i history. In 2005, Wooten settled a discrimination case for ***Chadd Eaglin vs. University of Hawai`i Medical School***. The University of Hawai`i Medical School had never admitted a first year African American male student and had only graduated one black male student in 30 years. The University of Hawai`i had twice passed over this qualified Afro-Hawaiian male candidate, for both regular admissions and for "special Affirmative Action" admission. In April 2006, Wooten won a $1,095,000 medical malpractice verdict against Queens Hospital and a surgeon in a wrongful death case. In 2006, Wooten settled a case of John *MacAllister vs. University of Hawai`i At Diamond Head Community College,* involving discrimination against a black U.S. Army veteran in V.A. contracted educational services.

Wooten has real estate business interests in Hawai`i, Washington, Texas and Jamaica. His hobbies include surfing the seven seas, archeology, music, dance, photography, writing and adventure. Www.attyandrewooten.com

Daphne Barbee-Wooten and Andre' Wooten

AmenRastaCom

Andre & Daphne Essence

Andre & Amenophis III

Andre & Daphne

Andre' Wooten

Andre' with T-Shirt of His Father

CIMG

Daphne Mandela

Andfre' Wooten

Maya & Daphne

TransPacific

TransPacificHoward

Andre' Wooten

Daphne Barbee-Wooten, Esq.

WOOTEN ROOTS

Andre' Wooten was born in Seattle. His father moved there from Texas. His mother who was from Alabama. His father's people had been brought into Texas in 1840, through the port of Galveston, from South Carolina. They were marched about 200 miles north with about 200 other blacks and sold at the Crockette town square. After the Civil War, they started farming in a small black community called Fodice, Texas.

By 1900 Wooten's great-grand parents had acquired 500 acres of good farming land which they left to their four sons. His grandfather went to Prairie View on a football scholarship in 1910, served in WWI, had twelve children and left them each 125 acres of Texas land. His brothers did the same but did not have as many kids. Today, 160 years later, Wooten and his brothers share ownership in that old plantation.

In an interview, Wooten said, "My father was a Tuskegee Air man, who met my mom in Seattle while working as an aircraft mechanic after the war. The Air Force used his face on recruiting posters in June 2002 in *Sports Illustrated*, ESPN, *Air Force Magazine*, and others. My father took a job painting bridges when I was born, took a fall, and died when I was 4 months old. Mom and I wound up in the projects. She went back to school, got her teaching credentials, and taught grade school for 35 years. In 1950 when I was two, mom married Charles Stokes, one of the few black lawyers in Seattle. He was a criminal defense lawyer, a legislator and a judge, who also started the first black bank, Liberty, and the first soul radio station in Seattle, KZAM.

On the military, Wooten said, "Hawai`i is the major military base in the Pacific for the U.S. Empire. At least 40% of over 100,000 soldiers, sailors, air men and marines, and their families are black. But since they do not vote here, they do not get counted in the census as permanent residents. But their legal cases go through the Hawai`i Federal and State court system, where they do not sit on juries. African-Americans have lived in Hawai`i for over 200 years."

Daphne Barbee-Wooten received her Juris Doctor from the University of Washington. In addition to her J.D., she has a Certificate in International Law from the Peace Palace, The Hague, Netherlands. She obtained her B.A. Degree in Philosophy from the University of Wisconsin, at Madison. In Seattle, Washington, she worked as a legal intern for Northwest Labor & Employment Law Office, and prepared the *Antonio v. Ward's Cove* case for trial, a disparate impact law suit by Filipino cannery workers against segregation, discrimination, and disparate terms and conditions in the Alaskan canneries. From 1979 to June 1980 she worked at the Office of Women's Rights and Office of Human Rights, City of Seattle, conducting settlement agreements and fact finding conferences. She also conducted workshops on sexual harassment.

In 1981, Daphne became a Hawai`i State Public Defender, gaining a vast amount of litigation experience. In 1984, she opened her own law practice in Honolulu, specializing in the general practice of law, with an emphasis on labor, appellate law, employment discrimination and criminal law. In 1989, she was appointed as one of the original founding members of the Hawai`i Civil Rights Commissions, and served in this position until 1995.

In November 1998, she was hired by the EEOC Honolulu Office as the senior trial attorney. She was the first attorney hired for the Honolulu office, where she litigated class action civil rights cases in Hawai`i, Saipan, and Guam.

In April 2001, Daphne returned to private practice, specializing in civil rights. Her memberships include the Hawai`i State Bar Association, the Afro-American Lawyers Association of , the Board of Bar Examiners (1993 - present), the National Employment Lawyers Association, and the National Association of Women Lawyers.

Her publications include: Women Lawyers "*Our Rights, Our Lives*" a hand book, contributing writer, co-editor for 3rd Edition, December 1996; *Essence Magazine,* African Americans in, April 1994, *Bar Journal,* " 's First Black Lawyer" February 2004," Civil Rights Commission" August 1993, "Spreading the Aloha of Civil Rights", *Bar Journal*, November 1999, *Go Girl, A Black Woman's Guide to Travel and Adventure,* August 1999, contributing writer about Nanny Town, Jamaica. "*They Followed the Trade Winds: African Americans in Hawai`i,*UH Press 2004, "The Politics of Change: Law and African Americans in Twentieth-Century", *Bar Journal*, The Lawgiver: George Marion Johnson, J.D., LLD, (February 2005).

Her video projects include: Reclaiming Our African Heritage, Parts 1-6; "Temples of Nubia; Queens of Ancient KMT; Basil Bunting, A Centenary Celebration, 2002 Civil Rights Seminar in, 2004 Blacks in, Botswana and Bafoking and other projects which air on Olelo, community television."

Daphne has given numerous speeches, appeared on various television programs: Kapuna Network, Harambee, Afro American Lawyers Association Law Talk, and Legally Speaking: You and the Law, and participated in many panel discussions on civil rights and discrimination. She travels extensively in her free time.

John Stan Rippy was born and raised in Philadelphia, one of twelve children. John was a pioneer in his family. He was the first to purchase a new house. He was the first to own two businesses in Philadelphia. One of his establishments held the longest name in Pennsylvania; 'Peter Piper Picked A Peck of Pickled Peppers Lounge'. John has been a contractor for more than 21years. John grew tired of Philadelphia. When he was stationed in the Marines and the Navy, he had a desire to visit Hawai`i.

John arrived in Hawai`i with his wife Lorraine Nole Rippy in 1976 on the island of O`ahu. They moved to Maui in1977. John was employed with an insurance company, then went on to become a Grand Diamond Winner in sales, and later District Manager for Maui County. By using the tools of his mentor W.Clements Stone, he opened his own company, *This Is The House That Jack Built*, a successful solar energy company.

John also owned Rippy's handyman services. He became politically active and met and became friends with Mr. Molina of Molina's Bar & Rooms, never imagining that one day, he would own Mr. Molina's Bar. In 1994, John became the first African American to obtain a liquor license in Maui County.

Due to his community-minded sense of responsibility, he began to make improvements in Wailuku Town where he lives and works. John began to help the town out the best way he could. Soon he became an extremely successful businessman which he attributes to hard work and to Mr. Molina who gave him and his wife an opportunity to grow and thrive. Mr. Molina also sold the Rippy's their first house and suggested that they not move to the Big Island as they had planned. He reminded them that they, too, belong on Maui. They remained on Maui helping the community. John credits W.Clements Stone and Mr. Molina for his success and commitment to help people, to give back to the community, and at the end of the day, to give thanks to God.

Saying thank you at the end of everyday, a practice which he does daily deep within his heart, he promised to share his positive mental attitude with people regarding personal growth and development using the story of little engines that open big doors.

Lorrraine Nole Rippy is a cosmetologist who was born in South Philadelphia (also known as little Italy). She began styling hair at age seven, braiding the neighborhood kids' hair. Her mother, the late Esterine Nole, said to her one day, "Looks like you like what you're doing, it's time to get a license." Lorraine acquired her business license at age 16. She attended Bok Technical Vocational H.S., specializing in cosmetology and hair styling. She would eventually teach others how to style hair. Lorraine has worked with the Ebony Fashion Fair Modeling Shows, and styled hair for Universal Pictures actors and actresses. Lorraine has also worked with noted actors such as Sidney Potier, the Joyous Lake Production Company, Judge Stout, and others.

On Maui, Lorraine was the first African American cosmologist to open her own hair salon, named "Pampering At Lorraine's." She chose "Pampering at Lorraine," because "mom pampered me, spoiled me, and I wanted to do the same for people and teach them how to take care of their own hair." She says, "It took me all night to come up with that name." Lorraine's television commercial produced headlines and was shown on the local channel 2 news attracting folks from all over, including the U.S.A. mainland.

Lorraine became a fashion celebrity hair stylist, sought by many well known celebrities as well as local residents, and she continues to be in demand to this day. Lorraine often used the old press and curl, which was a cultural fixture of Black hair. She now engages in braiding hair, applying weaves, extensions, relaxing hair, and curling. There were no black hair dressers on Maui until Lorraine arrived more than 30 years ago. She continues to be the only licensed professional black hair stylist and cosmetologist on the island. Lorraine created new hair styles, often leaving those in her chair looking and feeling good about themselves. Customers would be asked, "Who did your hair," and more clients would flock to Lorraine to get their hair done. In 2004, Lorraine downsized her salon, when her mother became ill. She cared for her until her mother's transition in February 2005. Lorraine still maintains her client list and continues to do hair a couple of days each week. She says she will never stop doing hair, "until God needs his hair done and his wings fluffed."

Kelly Covington is a singer, songwriter, musician and actress. Kelly arrived in the Hawaiian Islands in 1982 from Long Island, New York. She was raised in a musical family. Her father, Glen Covington was a jazz musician and vocalist who toured with his trio across the United States, Canada and the Caribbean. Kelly's parents were born and raised in the South. Kelly attended Fisk University and toured with the world renowned "Jubilee Singers." After college she worked on the road and recorded with several artists. Kelly continues to lend her vocal talents and background vocal arranging skills to many island artists. She released her first Jazz CD entitled *"Quiet Mind and Body"* and is currently about to release her second CD *"Jazz at the Spa."*

Career highlights include writing and recording with Grammy award winning producers and musicians Narada Michael Walden and "American Idol" judge Randy Jackson. On Maui, Kelly has been a staple in the corporate convention circuit with her band "Raw Silk" performing in Hotel resorts, restaurants, night clubs private estates, and theater. Kelly Covington is a world class seasoned performer and is considered Maui's best.

George & Terri Rainey arrived in the Hawaiian Islands in February, 1988. The Raineys connected with the community and began to support activities in the African American community. As time went on, they extended themselves to various other cultures, always representing their ancestors, and they began to make their mark. They became well known as "Rainey & Rainey." Rainey & Rainey created the Nubian Pageant Systems (NPS) program in 1994, and produced Nubian Pageant Family pageants in Hawai`i annually. This African Cultural Pageant System helped raise the consciousness level of the local community and highlighted the importance of African World Her/History, teaching about African peoples' contributions to the world. The Nubian Pageant Systems' pageants comprise three pageants: Women, Men and Children, from age four years old to adulthood. NPS enhances and develops its contestants' self-esteem and confidence, along with valuable life skills, and builds role model individuals.

In addition, the pageant family performs community service utilizing their learned skills such as public speaking, emceeing and/or talents. NPS expanded and was honored to receive its New York State Franchise License in 2000. NPS is still based out of Honolulu, Hawai`i, and has centers in New York and Nova Scotia, Canada.

George Rainey served as State Commissioner for two terms, from 1990 to 1998, in the Department of Commerce & Consumer Affairs (Consumer Advisory Council). George also taught computer science and world history at the Halawa Prison. George served as the first President of the Martin Luther King Jr. Holiday Coalition and Terri served as a public relations Coordinator while working in the local tourist industry. The Raineys served as grand marshals for the 2006 Dr. Martin Luther King, Jr. Day Parade.

Martin Charles Hennessey. (Marty Dread), named after Dr. Martin Luther King, Jr., was born in the Bronx, New York in 1969. When Marty was eight years old, his father passed away and his mother moved the family to Maui, Hawai'i. The change from concrete jungle to botanical jungle was great, but Marty was quick to adapt to the laid-back ways of his new island home. Marty's life was again changed forever in 1981 when he was exposed to the music of Bob Marley. Marty was hooked on reggae music. He began singing with local bands. After graduating from Maui High School, Marty was selected by the Youth Ambassadors of America to travel to the Soviet Union to assist in the creation of a mural, "Maui to Moscow", a gift of peace from the children of Maui to the children of Moscow. The following year, Marty and his new reggae band performed before an international audience at "Moscow meets Maui", a concert on Maui that honored the Soviet students who Marty had befriended while in Russia. In 1992, Marty Dread released his first smash hit, "Wicked Wahine" which skyrocketed to the top of the an charts. In 1994, Marty launched his own record label, Five Corners Music, with the release of "Versatile Roots," which included a duet with Kris Kristofferson. Kristofferson was so impressed with Marty that he offered to lend a hand in the studio, resulting in the song, "Reggae Blues." In 1996, three of Marty's songs were featured in the international motion picture release, "Maui Heat." In 1997, Marty released his first live album, "Marty Dread Live." In 2000, Marty released his fifth album, "*Keiki* Reggae" (aka Reggae for Children) with music tracks that included school children from throughout Maui County. Marty Dread released a collection of hits from the first ten years of his recording career, plus six previously unreleased songs, and continues to tour far and wide. With music and purpose, Marty Dread is poised for the future as Maui's premier Reggae Ambassador.

Nara Boone's singing career began at age 14 with Marty Dread's reggae band, "Culture Shock." Having no formal training, Nara attended Scripps College in Claremont, California studying voice while immersing herself in concert, chamber, madrigal and gospel choirs. She also took private classes as a mezzo soprano, and studied Hip-Hop and R&B collaborations. On Maui, Nara has performed with several club and convention bands and has sung on recordings for artists from Hawai`i, California and Canada. Currently, Nara is the lead vocalist for the theatrical performance "*Ulalena*" playing in Lahaina, Maui. Nara continues to hone her skills using the vocal technique called Speech Level Singing.

Lawrence Taylor had a career in telecommunications that took him around the world and eventually brought him to his new found home in Maui in 2000. A native of Michigan, Lawrence spent 23 adult years in northern and southern California, searching for his Shangri-la.

Lawrence has worked in Maui's art and real estate industries and has written for most of Maui's local newspapers. He is currently working on his second book, "*Moon Over Maui*", a romantic mystery, providing an inside look into Maui's art industry and the enjoyable lifestyle on Maui. When posed with the question by mainlanders "What do you do for vacation?" Lawrence smiles and says, "I go to another island, of course!"

Lawrence says, "Maui is one of the two most spiritual places I have been on this earth, the other is Bali. I think if you asked those of us who have migrated to Maui, we would likely agree that this island has healing properties that are indescribable. We would also agree that if your mind, heart or spirit does not agree with Maui, the island will chew you up and spit you out! Maui is also home to so many 'shipwrecks', those people who come here for a holiday but never go home, their spirits have been called and they know it on arrival. Maui draws so many who are in need of healing or very conscious of their spiritual path."

"In the near decade that Maui has been home to me, I have seen but a fraction of its beauty. From caves to crater and waterfalls to beaches, there is abundant natural beauty on this island that will keep the adventurer in awe for years. Fortunately, there are many more places not found in the best tourist guide books, as these locations could not support the trampling that comes with such exposure to the entire outside world. However, that won't prevent me from taking an appreciative person to such spots, blindfolded albeit! Hopefully, we will learn to protect our precious environment and balance the wonderment with preservation."

Lawrence credits his parents, Charles and LeClaire Taylor for the lifestyle he enjoys today. Charles Taylor, who died in 2007, was a Tuskegee Airman, engineer and mathematician. Charles and LeClaire both earned Master degrees from the University of Michigan and taught in public schools to meet the growing need for committed educators. They moved to Hawai`i in 1996 where his mother, LeClaire Taylor, continues to enjoy the ocean and sunsets on West Maui."

Today, Lawrence makes West Maui his home and spends much of his time exploring Maui's diverse beauty from the crater of Haleakala to the caves of Hana.

Earl 'Sundance' Shepperd arrived in Maui in 1987. He is a singer, composer, and percussionist. He began his musical exploration in New York City, soaking up the sounds of Harlem R&B and Spanish Harlem Salsa. He has studied West African music and percussion. Partial releases have been aired on ABC, NBC, and UPN television. He has performed around the island extensively. Sundance regularly performs at the African opening libations here on the island, and at African American functions, contributing a dynamic ritual call to the ancestors. Sundance continues to absorb the multi-cultural musically diverse melting pot of the Pacific.

Terry Moore is a Los Angeles native and has lived on Maui for more than eight years. Before coming to the islands, her varied background included nearly a decade as a location manager of films, commercials and photo shoots in the Chicago area. A huge patron of the arts, today Terry feels honored to lend her support to powerful cultural enrichment projects and to the many talented artists.

Kenyavani 'Pema Wangmo' Gilman Pema Wangmo was born 68 years ago in Boston, where she met her husband, photographer Robert Gilman. They have lived in Maui since 1971. She has a son, Matthew Gilman, and a granddaughter, Hokuoka'ale Gilman. In an interview, Pema explained her names, the first of two names was Kenyavani, reflecting her African roots, and the second was Pema Wangmo. Kenyavani refers to the African place where God dwells and speaks. One of her teachers translated it as "big mouth." At the time she was nettled, but she now believes the name indicated "another way to serve." Being of service has been always important to me." Kenya Wangmo translates to powerful lotus woman. She switched from using Kenya to Pema, pronounced pay-mah, at the urging of colleagues. The lotus is a flower that shows its beauty, not the mud in which it is rooted.

Her internal exploration began as a youngster fascinated by different religions. She was particularly struck by a quote attributed to St. Francis of Assisi, "Be still and know that I am God. Let me be an instrument of thy peace."

Robert and Pema traveled to California. Robert wanted to continue to Hawai`i. Pema didn't think much of the idea. Later, she listened to "the quiet, still voice" that she said each of us has in our heads. It told her "maybe we should go." On O`ahu, the Gilmans decided they wanted less city and more country. In the late 1960s, Maui was very much country, and Pema found a path through the open spaces. "Maui is a very magical place. All the important teachers come here."

Out of curiosity, Pema went with a friend to see Swami Muktananda, her first teacher for ten years. He was followed by another teacher, Kalu Rinpoche, "a beautiful old man, who emanated what Buddhists call stillness. It has elements of love and compassion." In Haiku, Pema met Jamgon Konetrul Rinpoche and found herself making "a formal declaration of Buddhism." For the last seven years, her current teacher and mentor has been Anam Thubten Rinpoche. He travels regularly to Maui but is currently based in Santa Clara, California. His lessons and counsel flow across the Internet. "Anam Thubten is teaching an emerging school of American Buddhism that adapts Eastern philosophy to the West mind-set," Pema said. "The path is simplified to be better understood and practiced by Westerners."

After 30 years of study and practice, Pema was ordained and/or certified, by Anam Thubten as one of a small number of Western Tibetan Buddhist Dharma teachers. Pema said the essence of what she has learned and teaches is "to clear away the confusion and to slow down inside, to be in the moment, and to not rehash the past or fret about the future."

She said, "the calm and insight that meditation has brought to my life has supported me in my work as an advocate for victims of domestic violence and helps me remain compassionate and caring without carrying the weight of others' problems."

Pema Wangmo Gilman opened a window for a *pa'akiki* (this-worlder). The practice of meditation "leads to ways of giving up self-cherishing and promotes peaceful awareness, a feeling of love and compassion, and an open heart."

She enjoys gardening, orchids, reading, gourmet cooking, and works for women's rights, environmental protection, indigenous people's sovereignty, and the campaign against world hunger.

Diana L. Drake better known as Dee, was born in Cleveland, Ohio, and moved to San Francisco in 1976. She relocated to Maui in 1989. She is employed by the Hawai`i State Public Library System and encourages the public to learn about black history. Her interests include ceramic, painting, tennis, and golf, and of course reading good books.

Deborah Taylor was born in the Bronx, New York, and moved to Maui in 1995. Taylor retired from the military after serving fifteen years active duty in the Navy and six years in the Air National Guard. Her son, Terence Taylor, currently is serving in the Navy. Deborah currently is employed with the Department of Corrections since 1997 and has moved through the ranks to Captain. Deborah is the first African American woman to hold such a high ranking position in the Department of Corrections in Maui County. Deborah or says, she does her best and focuses on helping the inmates to not come back to prison. She joined the Correction Department to help make a difference in people's lives.

Sodengi Camille Orimaladi Mills was born in Philadelphia, PA, and has lived in Maui for more than ten years. She holds a B.A. in Communication Science and a Masters of Education in Deaf Education. Sodengi is currently employed with the Hawai`i State Department of Education, and has taught special education for the past eleven years.

Sodengi is also a resident West African dance instructor who has taught and performed West African Dance for ten years, including interpretive dance poetry for 18 years. As an artist Sodengi pours her love, knowledge, experience and culture into her classes. She encourages others to participate and reciprocate. She enjoys watching her students develop as dancers connected with West African Culture, leading them to experience a Rites of Passage, so that they too may guide the next participants through their own rites.

Sodengi became inspired to learn about the politics that drives public education. She participated as a Delegate for Hawai`i State Representative Assembly through the Hawai`i State Teachers Association (HSTA). Sodengi attended two National Education Association (NEA) Conventions as a Delegate for the Representative Assembly for Hawai`i State (Summer 2008 and 2009). "What an experience to be among educators working hard to offer and improve and/or enhance public education," Sodengi says.

Sodengi has presented two New Business Items (NBIs) at the state level (extended school year application process) and at the national level (effective school cleanliness). Both NBIs passed. She states, "What an encouragement to me, my state and fellow states, to have our missions - to give to/work for public education in a way that supports our students for their future successes - emerging and taking effect." Sodengi currently serves on the HSTA Elections Committee and is a Grievance Representative (Union Rep.) at Wailuku Elementary School where she teaches.

Sodengi met her husband, Wahkimba and his son, Lionel, in Maui (1999). They married in St Thomas, Virgin Islands (2003). Wahkimba, born in St. Kitts, British Virgin Island is an organic farmer and has farmed for 16 years on Maui. He enjoys fishing, landscaping and carpentry. Lionel twelve years old attends Haleakala's Waldorf School and enjoys playing basketball, volley ball, track-n-field, and soccer. Sodengi says, "It's a blessed life in paradise."

Arid T. Chappell's career in the arts began in North Carolina in the seventh grade when he drew a sketch of an eagle. Enrolled in a special class for gifted students, his work caught the eye of his teacher. By age 14, New York City became his inspirational focus and he drew his insights from the world of glamour and bright lights from the Big Apple. After graduating from the prestigious school of American Business and Fashion Institute, Arid began traveling from Paris to London, New York City, to Switzerland. Channeling his creative energy, Arid came to the conclusion that opportunity is an open field and abundance is everywhere present. He then moved to Maui and became engaged in film and television. He filmed and produced several television shows, airing throughout the Hawaiian Islands. His recent film, "Front Street" screened at the New York International Independent Film & Video Festival in 2000 garnering acclaim. Arid was then tapped to create a fashionable chair by Maggie Coulombe on Maui, where stars, models, tourists, and locals flock to wear couture clothing. Clients have included former Miss America Vanessa Williams, Lindsey Lohan, Hale Berry, Loretta Devine, Paris Hilton, Desperate Housewife star Terri Hatcher, and other celebrities.

Patricia Henderson moved to Hawai`i in 2008. She was raised in California. By age two, she had her sights on Hollywood. By age six she was already taking dance and piano lessons. Soon, she joined the late Eartha Kitt Troop in Watts and earned a scholarship to the Gene Marrinaccio school of Ballet in Hollywood. Performing in high school musicals prepared her for a professional career as a singer, dancer, and actress.

Patricia worked with Helen Reddy, Ann Margret, The Beach Boys, and Rick Nelson. Her passion for singing landed her in the recording studio where she expanded her talents as musician, producer, and songwriter for the groups 'Krystal' and 'The Emotions' who went on to record a number one hit. Patricia went into television as production manager where her work earned her an "Emmy Award" with 'The Simpsons'. Then the visual artist within her was awakened and she turned to focused on the canvas, yielding a sold out gallery showing her artwork. Patricia's art, like her life, embraces all mediums, blending color, texture, and movement. Currently, Patricia has combined her singing talent with her spiritual commitment in a vanguard meditation method called, 'Resonation' where everyone can find their song. Stay tuned to this healing modality now sweeping the globe.

Rodney Potter, born in Dayton Ohio, first visited Hawai`i at age eleven with his family in 1962. His grandfather owned a Café in Southern California where his mother worked. A customer gave his mother a ukulele at age 13 which Rodney still treasurers. His mother had a deep love for Hawai`i and promised herself that one day she would visit Hawai`i. That day came in 1962 when Rodney was eleven years old and his family visited four islands in two weeks at an astounding cost of $600.00 per person. Rodney grew up listening to Hawaiian music in his home.

His mother, born in 1913, had achieved her goal by planting the seed of Hawai`i in Rodney as a young boy. Thus it was not surprising that Rodney would decide that he wanted to live in Hawai`i. She would go on to instill many positive determining factors in Rodney's life that would play an important role in raising his own children. Rodney made several trips to Hawai`i from Southern California before actually living here. He spent two years on the Big Island and two years on Kauai, before settling in Maui in 1988.

Upon his arrival on Maui, Rodney was looking through the classified ads, when his eyes fell upon a construction related job. He was told that he needed to have skills and the stomach for this job, which later turned out to be working with toilets. A year later, Rodney was offered the opportunity to purchase the company. Today, Rainbow Rentals provides the cleanest, highest-quality portable toilets available on the island of Maui. Rainbow Rentals provides services for companies, construction sites, special events, businesses, weddings, concerts, luau, graduations, government, fairs, and golf tournaments. Rainbow Rentals is one of four similar companies on Maui and is the largest company on the island to provide this type of service. Rodney has given back to the community while creating jobs and hiring ten to twelve employees.

Rodney Potter was an early member of the African American Heritage Foundation of Maui in the early 1990s, and served as the group's treasurer. Rodney continues to support African American events on the island.

Rodney has two sons, ages eleven and thirteen. Using the wisdom his mother inspired in him, Rodney has made a conscious decision to demonstrate responsible awareness in his life by being a positive role model for his children. He is making a difference. Rodney says, "Life is short as you get older." Questions arises such as, "What am I doing? Am I making a difference?" Rodney Potter is making a difference in his life, his sons' lives, and helping others in his community.

Bryant Neal was born in Helena, Arkansas on February 19, 1957. He graduated from Hendrix College with a BA in Theatre Arts and a minor in Business in 1979. In an interview, he said, "After graduation I lived and worked in the U. S. and British Virgin Islands where I first experienced and fell in love with the island life style. After leaving the Virgin Islands, I lived and worked at the Keystone Ski Resort in Dillon, Colorado, followed by a season working as a technical director for a small community theatre; then I spent a season traveling and working with a children's theatre company.

I moved to Maui, Hawai`i during the summer of 1982 and was hired immediately as a salesperson with the jewelry company Maui Divers of Hawai`i . During my eight year tenure, I worked as a regional sales manager and was instrumental in creating and implementing a comprehensive sales training program that is still being used to this date by the multi-million dollar company. I married my college sweetheart, Debbie, in 1987, and our daughter Olivia was born on January 30, 1991.

In 1990, I changed careers and began working with Lahaina Printsellers Ltd. as a sales manager. During the next ten years I rose to become Vice President and partner with the firm as well, and I started a separate business called A & B Imports.

In 1996, when my daughter Olivia was five years old and attending school without an after school program or an art and music program, I created the non-profit organization Arts Education for Children Group to fill the niche. Over the past twelve years, the organization has offered art, music and cultural enrichment for thousands of Maui's youth and adults."

Founded in 1996, Arts Education For Children Group (AECG) is a nonprofit organization dedicated to providing opportunities for artistic and cultural enrichment for the people of Maui. Additionally, AECG is committed to improving the quality of education in our schools by restoring music programs and raising public awareness about the importance of music participation.

He continued, "In 1997 I worked with Ayin Adams at Ka`ahumanu Center Stage playing her son in Langston Hughes' *Mother to Son*, and again, under Ayin's direction, I played the role of Rev. Dr. Martin Luther King Jr., the first African American produced stage production on Maui. Reciting the "I Have A Dream" speech has led to the production of an annual concert and a variety of Black History Month activities on the island. Together, Ayin Adams and I worked to create the Martin Luther King Jr. *Stone of Hope monument* in 2006. I am a member of the Lahaina Rotary and African Americans On Maui Association."

J'aime Martinique Ka'iminaniloa Kawaioneokekai Sisson is of an, Native American and French Creole ancestry. J'aime comes from a long family legacy of *Kahu*, (priest/minister) and Polynesian dancers all the way back to the island of Molokai. She is a professional hula and Tahitian dancer. She was raised under the traditional Hawaiian values and cultural disciplines. J'aime is currently attending the University of Hawai`i, Hilo with a double major in Hawaiian Studies and Psychology. Her mission and service to humanity is to bring together the Sacred Dance of Hula and Psychology as a form of Alternative Dance Therapy,

Adesina Ogunelese is a vegetarian gourmet chef and yoga instructor. She enjoys sharing her knowledge of African culture and has conducted talks on Juneteenth and Black History Month on Maui. Adesina grew up in Philadelphia, PA. attended West Philadelphia High School and Penn State University.

With her many skills, in the 1990s Adesina introduced and produced Reggae music to San Diego. She helped organized and produced the first reggae radio show, the first reggae boat rides, and publicity for Bob Marley, Peter Tosh, and Angilique Kidjo. The Bob Marley Birthday Celebration Concert drew an attendance of 10,000 people. Adesina was a charter and co-founding member of the World Beat Center in San Diego which was the first non-profit African American Cultural Center in the City, with a mission to heal the world through music, art, dance technology and culture.

Adesina became a certified Kripalu Yoga instructor in 1994 and traveled to Ghana with the International Black Yoga Teachers Association to teach Yoga. Later on Maui, she started a vegetarian catering company called *Quiche Me Quick*. Adesina wrote her first cookbook and produced a Yoga CD in 2004. She is currently writing her second cookbook called *"Optimal Health through Conscious Eating."*

Cherisse Nicole is a resident of Maui for five years. She moved from California following an inspiring vacation to the islands. As a behavior specialist Cherisse works with autism spectrum children which she says is intense and fulfilling job. Cherisse also discovered an outlet for another of her passions, fashion. Cherisse modeled as a teenager. The fashion world had been a long-standing part of her lifestyle, but Maui seemed an unlikely place for high-end fashion. She began working with local Maui designer Maggie Coulombe and stylist Arid Chappell, rekindling a part of the L.A. lifestyle long left behind. Inspired by the island lifestyle, and her work, Cherisse founded her own company, *VIP Style*, which focuses on personal styling and shopping services for high-end clients and visitors. "I help connect them to the best products and clothing from real designers and artists who live here," says Cherisse, who has translated her head turning fashion sense into a business. "I enjoy putting looks together for special events and seeing women looking and feeling their best." For Cherisse, moving to Maui was like a calling that was meant to be. "People say the islands have a healing power with energy that gives new life and inspires you to dream bigger dreams and fulfill them. I feel like I've come home though I have never been here before." *VIP Style,* plans to expand to O`ahu.

Shirley Jean Davenport was born in Greenville, North Carolina, to a family of share croppers. As the fifth eldest child of ten, life was a challenge, and Shirley took the challenge from the cotton fields all the way to the field of social work. Shirley had a military career in the United States Navy after graduating from High School. She arrived in Hawai`i in 1981, fell in love with and married her husband, Calvin Jerome Davenport from Philadelphia in 1984. Calvin also enjoyed a lustrous career with the military. Shirley fell in love with the island because it held many similarities to life in North Carolina. On the Leeward Coast of O`ahu, Waianae, she says, "We can be poor or rich. We love God and the land as we appreciate the crystal blue ocean and the moderate sea breezes." Shirley spent more than twenty-seven years of her life in Hawai`i working mostly in the visitor and convention business. The last ten years, she has spent working in the mental health field while enrolled at school full time to earn an Associate Degree in Liberal Arts, a Bachelor Degree in Psychology and a Master's Degree in Social Work.

Jewel McDonald moved to Chicago, Illinois at age five with her family. She move to Honolulu in 1975. Jewel earned her B.A. degree in Human Development from the University of Hawai`i at Manoa. As a successful entrepreneur and business woman, she owned and managed Jewel's Beauty Supplies successfully for 14 years. Today she owns Cap's Get Away Travel and Notary www.capsgetawaytravel.com. Jewel has survived three open heart surgeries (valve replacements) stemming from rheumatic fever she contracted as a child. In 1985 she became a charter and founding member of the African American Association of Hawai`i. Currently, she serves as President. Jewel is one of the leaders in Hawaii's Black Community. Her organizational affiliations are: Board of Directors for NAACP Chapter (Membership Chair), the Honolulu African American Acting Ensemble (Drama Student), the YMCA Nu'uanu Branch (Board of Directors), the Martin Luther King Coalition (Board of Directors Chair), the Food Bank volunteer, the Screen Actors Guild, a Democratic Party Member (Precinct President), and a Muscular Dystrophy volunteer.

Mahealani Uchiyama has been a student of dance since her early childhood. She was raised within the discipline of the classical hula tradition. Mahealani holds a B.A. in Dance Ethnology and a M.A. in Pacific Islands Studies from the University of Hawai'i. She has studied extensively with one of Hawaii's most honored hula masters, Joseph Kamoha'i Kaha'ulelio. She has performed with numerous multi-cultural dance ensembles, and is the founder and director of the Mahea Uchiyama Center for International Dance (M.U.C.I.D.) and of the award-winning KaUaTuahine Polynesian Dance Company (Halau KaUaTuahine). M.U.C.I.D. opened in 1993 to provide an environment where students of all ages and abilities can take part in a holistic multicultural dance experience through traditional training, lectures, demonstrations, performance opportunities and workshops with master teachers. Mahealani Uchiyama has been a teacher of Polynesian music and dance for over 25 years. She has served numerous times as an adjudicator for the San Francisco Ethnic Dance Festival. She has taught Hawaiian language at Stanford University and has performed with numerous an, Tahitian, and Caribbean dance ensembles. As the director of the KaUaTuahine Polynesian Dance Company, Mahealani and her dancers have performed in such venues as San Francisco Palace of Fine Arts, Te Papa Tongarewa (the National Museum of New Zealand, Aotearoa), and the Grand Heiva in Tahiti, French Polynesia.

She has also won numerous awards in dance, chant, singing and drumming from competitions throughout California and Hawai`i, including the King Kamehameha Hula and Chant Competition in Honolulu.

Mahealani Uchiyama has produced a series of instructional and performance DVDs, CDs and manuals on the art of Hawaiian and Tahitian dance. Of these, the CD "Tatau", a collection of Tahitian music and drumming, has been received with high acclaim in Tahiti, French Polynesia. She was also the Executive Producer of the documentary "Black Pearl", a film which documents her Halau KaUaTuahine's first tour to Tahiti. "Black Pearl" won top honors in the 2002 Berkeley Film Festival and was featured on KHET Hawai'i Public Television on May 17th, 2003. Her latest CD, "A Walk by the Sea" is the winner of the Hawai'i Music Award for "Best World Music" of 2007.

Mahealani, is also a priestess of Ifa (a religion from West Africa), and approaches dance as a manifestation of the human spirit. She encourages her students and her audiences to explore and celebrate their cultural differences and common humanity.

Wanda Yates worked for the Police Department in Pasadena, California, before arriving in Maui in 1982 when she moved to Pukalani. When she was a young girl in the Midwest, she would take her allowances and buy Hawaiian records, not knowing anything about Hawai`i. Her Spirit would draw her to Hawai`i in later years. Looking back, Wanda recalls her longing for this place, a place of quiet peacefulness and tranquility. With her youngest son by her side stepping off the aircraft, she knew this place was home. She loved it. She camped on the beach. The locals found her a house and car within two weeks, and everything fell together. Wanda recalls filling out applications for employment and remembers that there was no ethnic group listed to reflect her culture. The forms read Indian, Eskimos, Islanders. Wanda sent the application home for folks to see and told them, "I have arrived."

Judy D. Harrison moved to Honolulu from Toronto, Canada in 1978. She became a licensed real estate agent in 1990 and a certified paralegal in 1996 to enhance her career in real estate. Her notary commission was issued in 2005 and is current. Judy has worked in both sales and property management over the years, as well as working in office positions assisting attorneys, mortgage companies and as a sales representative for Kona coffee and sundry items.

She has extensive knowledge in civil litigation proceedings, including foreclosures and Chapter 7 bankruptcy, and that knowledge has really helped her in the representation of both buyers and sellers. Judy has lived on several islands and is extremely familiar with Oahu, Maui, and the Big Island.

Yoellah Yuhudah was born and raised on the south side of Chicago, Illinois. Raised in the style of a large island family, Yoellah grew up with many uncles and aunts who shared the family value of love. Her mother died when she was 12, and she was reared by her grandparents who provided holistic approaches to life. After graduating from high school, she received her AA degree in Theater. She received her M.A. in 1988 and became a Nurse's Assistant. She also attended Kapiolani Community College where she earned her phlebotomy certificate. Presently, she is a graduate candidate for her BA in Ceramics at the University of Hawai`i. Yoellah's spiritual quests lead her to live in Dimona Israel for five years with the group called The Hebrew Israelites. For the past 19 years, Hawai`i has been her residence, and she is presently living on Maui. Her two sons and grandson live on the island of O`ahu. Her interest takes on a broad span of creative outlets focusing on ceramics and glass making. In the past, she has also been a dancer, gospel singer, and a self learned acupuncturist. Her jobs in early life were a bus driver for the Chicago Transit Authority, an art teacher in Dimona, Israel, and more recently she has been working toward being a lamp maker and an aspiring teacher of ceramics. Yoellah wants to live a simple life and achieve all of her dreams through her art work.

Leah Tunkara was born in Manhattan, New York, and raised in San Francisco. She made her home in Maui for more than 28 years. Leah is a multifaceted talented artist who is inspiring, motivating as a teacher, and always enhancing her life as well as others. Leah is a member of the Screen Actor's Guild and the American Federation of Television and Radio. She has been a TV Host, coach, writer, director, photographer, dance instructor, editor, and filmmaker. Leah is a world class traveler who began traveling professionally on assignment at the age of 14. She has traveled to Canada, London, the Bahamas, France, the Netherlands, Jamaica, and around Europe as the personal assistant to the late recording artist Nina Simone. In 1980, Leah graced the covers of *Waikiki Beach Press* becoming the first African American model to be so successful in Maui. Leah has appeared in a variety of television shows and films such as "Magnum P.I.", "Cheers", "Star Trek: The Next Generation" and various commercials. In 1995, Leah founded and launched Leilani Films, LT., Inc., in Paia. Utilizing her talents and skills from Broadway to Hollywood, Leah has gone on to produce, direct, write, and edit more than 50 films. She has enjoyed some screenings at the independent film festivals and programming on community access channels throughout the Hawaiian Islands.

Leah wrote *Let's Do Hollywood,* a resource guide book to assist aspiring actors, writers, and filmmakers. The book is a complete guide including celebrity phone numbers and much critical advice to help the novice. Leah taught *Let's Do Hollywood* at Maui Community College PACE Program. Leah Tunkara has skillfully and successfully integrated motherhood with a career in front of and behind the scenes. Her daughter, Chaka Ra has been nominated, chosen, and invited to be among the People To People Student Ambassador Program with former President George W. Bush serving as honorary chairman. Chaka Ra has represented the State of Hawai`i in the Miss Teen All America Pageant in 2002 (which Oscar Winner Halle Berry won as a teenager). Leah urges individuals to follow their dreams and stay on their paths of artistic expression and creativity.

Sandra Shawhan was born and raised in Kansas and graduated from the University of Kansas with a B.S. degree in Elementary Education. Sandra has been living in Maui County since 1966. When she arrived from Kansas, she went to the island of Moloka`i for her first teaching position. Sandra spent seventeen years on Moloka`i and moved to Maui in 1984 with her daughter.

In 1992, Sandra graduated from the University of Hawai`i with a Master's Degree in Educational Administration and began her administrative career, first becoming a Vice Principal, and later spending the next sixteen years as an Elementary School Principal. Sandra spent thirty-seven years with the Department of Education, State of Hawai`i , and retired on June 30, 2008. "I have been very fortunate in my life to live in a place as beautiful and as diverse as Hawai`i, and I am grateful for the opportunities given to me."

During her early years on Maui, Sandra joined a group of African Americans under the leadership of Dr.

Roberta Courier (who later formed the African American Heritage Foundation of Maui) often meeting at her home, holding rallies, and marches perpetuating Black culture and Black heritage. African Americans on Maui have always had some kind of organization, and Sandra has always participated in at least four annual cultural events: Dr. Martin Luther King Jr. March, Black History Month activities, Juneteenth, and Kwanzaa, and her efforts continue today.

Sandra has held various offices within the organization of the African American Heritage Foundation of Maui such as Vice-President, Secretary, and Committee Chairperson for Kwanzaa and Juneteenth. Sandra enjoys the cultural and educational events, and participates as often as she can because she believes the history of African Americans in America, and especially in Hawai`i, is rich and very important.

Lama Choyin Rangdrol is the only African American teacher of Buddhism recognized by the First Conference of Tibetan Buddhist Centers in North and South America that was convened by the Office of Tibet and attended by the Dalai Lama. Lama Rangdrol was honored as a special invited guest to the Dalai Lama's teachings on *World Peace Through Inner Peace* in Miami, Florida.

He was born in Bellevue hospital, New York, in America's oldest maternity ward founded in 1799. The hospital is also famous for its attempts to bring humane treatment to the mentally ill since 1826. His mother, a single parent social worker in Harlem, moved their small family to Los Angeles County, California in 1961 where she pursued a career as a counselor for women in prison, and retired with distinction.

Lama insulated himself from gangs that emerged in his neighborhood by his passion for music. By the end of middle school, he had won the John Phillips Sousa Award for Band and the American Legion Award for Music. As the player of several brass instruments, he was selected to tour with the Southern California Junior High School Honor Band. He first encountered Buddhism on a youth band tour to Japan, where he visited Osaka, Kyoto, and Tokyo, and camped at the base of Mount Fuji. After encountering a tremendous typhoon, he was evacuated to Buddhist temples around Japan for several weeks.

He spent his early twenties working full time as a licensed psychiatric technician to fund his education in art, which included the University of Redlands School of Music (BA), graduate work in Multicultural Theatre at Sacramento State University, and he received certificates of study from the National Shakespeare Company (New York) and the Royal Academy of Dramatic Art (London). He appeared in classical plays such as Euripides' *The Bacchae*, produced by the director of the National Theater of Greece while also taking time to tour Northern California farm country in productions of Luis Valdez's *Actos* for the United Farm Workers.

Lama Rangdrol pursued both his interest in psychology and the arts, working as a psychiatric technician and drama therapist in several departments of psychiatry, including the UCLA Neuropsychiatric Hospital, the USC University Hospital, and numerous acute psychiatric hospitals and clinics serving severely mentally ill, developmentally disabled and homeless populations. He has also served as a group home manager, a home health caregiver for paraplegic and hemiplegic stroke clients, and as director of independent and supportive living services for dually diagnosed individuals.

When his mother became critically ill with cancer, he moved back to Los Angeles, his hometown, to oversee her hospice care. It was during this time that he decided to share his classical arts education with the community by founding a school of performing arts. This was at the start of the Los Angeles break-dance movement, and he quickly found that the youth were more interested in breakin' than Shakespeare. He managed young talent appearing in both Breakin' 1 and 2 films and worked for the premiere retail phenomenon *For Breakers Only*, headquartered at the corner of Hollywood and Vine in Hollywood, California. Lama also worked to formally integrate Graffiti Art into the design of Los Angeles' Metro Transit System facilities and coordinated a Financial News Network (FNN) segment on the monetary and artistic value of graffiti Art from Los Angeles to Basquiat.

When David Wolper produced the 1984 Olympic Closing Ceremonies in Los Angeles, Lama Rangdrol responded to his call for break dancers by sending his performers and personally assisting in the production. This was the beginning of Lama's work in the entertainment industry, and he soon became employed by Radio City Music Hall Productions' west coast events.

Lama went on to support productions of large scale event ceremonies including the 1986 Statue of Liberty Centennial Celebration, the 1988 Beverly Hills 75th Diamond Jubilee, the 1992 Superbowl XXVII Halftime Show, and the 1994 World Cup Soccer opening and closing ceremonies. As a result he was able to support shows starring Lionel Richie, the late Michael Jackson, Whitney Houston, Kenny G and many others at the height of their careers as well as work with many corporate sponsors.

In 1995, he had a vision of the Tibetan Buddhist deity, Padmasambhava, and the lama who would be his first teacher. In Jungian style, he stepped away from his worldly successes to pursue the meaning of his vision by entering a Buddhist retreat at Pema Osel Ling in California, under the tutelage of Dzogchen lineage holder Lama Tharchin Rinpoche. He was given the Tibetan name "Choyin Rangdrol," "naturally liberating enlightenment." He remained in the seclusion of the forest for two years, immersed in the Dudjom Tersar lineage. During this time, he received teachings from other Dzogchen masters including Khenpo Orgyen Tinly Rinpoche (Khenpo Chozod), Tulku Thubten (Anam Thubten), Lama Nawang, Lama Gyaltsen, Lama Namkhar, Lama Yeshe Wangmo, and Thinley Norbu. He discovered a special connection with a lama, Khenpo Yurmed Tinly who didn't speak much English and affectionately referred to him as "Sasquatch."

In 1998, he became Khenpo Yurmed Tinly's private student and remained with him until the Khenpo's death in 2005. The Venerable Khenpo Gyurmed Trinley Rinpoche was a Dzogchen master, a Chöd-pa, monk, and a scholar in the Nyingma school of Tibetan Buddhism as well as being trained in the Kagyu, Shakya, and Gelugpa schools.

1998 was also the year Lama envisioned Rainbow Dharma as an emerging activity to include people of color in the American Buddhist community, a lingering issue that was subsequently covered by Buddhist magazines *Turning Wheel, Tricycle*, and *Shambhala Sun*. It also prompted major Buddhist organizations to create diversity components charged with addressing the needs of people of color within their own institutions.

Today, Lama Rangdrol is known for his clarity of insight and talent for easily communicating complex ideas. Lama Rangdrol has taught Buddhism to Tibetan, Zen, Vipassana, SGI, ecumenical, Christian, Yoruba, Astrologist, Interfaith, non-sectarian, and secular communities. Lama is the recipient of the Martin Luther King Jr. Community Service Award. The award was presented jointly by Buddhist and Christian organizations in the city of Oakland, California for his ground-breaking commentary on KPFA radio, the "Oakland Is" cable series, and his community work on Buddhist peace.

His work in the field of masculinity was also recognized through his essay in *What Makes a Man: 22 Writers Imagine the Future* edited by Rebecca Walker (Riverhead Books). Langdrol and Walker subsequently attended the International Conference on Masculinity, Tallin, Estonia.

He has authored five books, written two music albums, and his recent documentary, *Festival Cancel Due To Heavy Rains* won the Aloha Accolade Award for Excellence in Filmmaking at the Honolulu International Film Festival.

Through his achievements, Lama has helped to change forever the face of American Buddhism. His work to uncover and liberate racism in American Buddhism is considered by some as provocative and controversial, but Lama Rangdrol feels that we must liberate ourselves from all our cultural illusions, including race, in order to create a true refuge for sentient beings, including ones who don't necessarily think, act, or fit the conventional archetype or the American Buddhist norm.

His Buddhist activity is solely supported by his family and his dedicated students who have gained insight from his teachings and living example. His work is known in America's urban streets and prisons, the American Buddhist community, the Cambodian jungle, European city centers, and, according to Google tracking, his site has been visited by students and professors from over 450 universities in 100 countries including America's most prestigious institutions.

Lama Rangdrol is the father of a multiracial family including four children and three grandchildren. He lives in a retreat on the slope of a dormant volcano in the Hawaiian Islands.

Alphonso Braggs was born and raised in Wilmington, North Carolina and graduated from John T. Hoggard High School in 1978. Braggs became active in politics and community programs at an early age. He was elected to three consecutive terms on the Wilmington City Council (Youth Member) where he served as an administrative assistant to the council president and schools' director.

He served as newspaper editor while attending Williston High School, and he was on the year book staff and was a newspaper feature writer while attending John T. Hoggard High School. Braggs was inducted into the National Honor Society for the Quill and Scroll in 1978. He was a member of the Drama Club and performed with the Willis Richards Players, a local theatrical community group. A devout member the African Methodist Episcopal Zion Church, Braggs, served as Youth Council President and Junior Trustee at St Andrews AME Zion Church. Braggs also served as Wilmington District Youth Council President and Southeast Region Treasurer for the AME Zion Church.

Following high school, Braggs enlisted in the U.S. Navy and completed 26 years of honorable service before retiring in January 2004. At sea, he served on five nuclear submarines and completed ten arduous deployments throughout the Atlantic, Pacific, Indian, and Arctic Oceans. Mr. Braggs also completed an extended combat deployment to the Gulf. On shore duty, he was assigned as military secretary on the immediate staff of the Secretary of the Navy, Pentagon and as administrative assistant to the Deputy Chief of Staff at Headquarters, U.S. Pacific Submarine Force, at Pearl Harbor.

A long time member of the NAACP, Mr. Braggs joined the Honolulu Branch in 1998 and become president in 2004. In 2005 he was appointed Chair of the Pacific Rim Conference of the NAACP covering the areas of Japan, Korea, Guam, and Hawai`i. A committed civil and human rights activist, he serves on the Board of Directors for both the Japanese American Citizens League (JACL) and Street Beat, Inc., a non-profit homeless advocacy organization.

He is a charter member of the Blacks in Government Pacific Rim Chapter. He is the former president of the Navy and Marine Corps Black Heritage Association and former Co-chair for the Delegation, National Summit on Africa. He is the current host of the Olelo weekly community television show, "NAACP Today."

Following retirement, Braggs joined the private sector and worked with Angel Network Charities, Inc. as Operations Director until December 2006. In May, 2007, Braggs joined the staff of the U.S. Treasury Department, Internal Revenue Service Division.

Braggs holds a Bachelor of Science Degree in Business Management and working on his Master's of Business Administration. A proud father, he enjoys hiking, writing, coin collecting, and singing in his spare time.

Betty "Bala" Clayborne was born in St. Louis Missouri and is the author of an award-winning book, "*How to Remember Your Bliss: Transforming Your Life, Enhancing Your World.*" In 2007, she arrived in Kauai, and has dedicated her life to helping others discover their own true path to bliss, joy and fulfillment. A natural educator, Dr. Clayborne earned a Ph.D. in Human Development and went on to teach Developmental and Educational Psychology at the university level. In 1973 she was personally trained by Maharishi Mahesh Yogi in The Science of Creative Intelligence and The Transcendental Meditation Program. She also has studied other stress reduction and transformational technologies. In 1992 she received funding from the National Institutes of Health to support her research into Transcendental Meditation, hypertension and anger.

Dr. Clayborne currently teaches the Transcendental Meditation Program, and also is a practitioner in Jyoti Atman, a healing modality of the ancient science of Ayurvedic medicine. Dr. Clayborne is presently completing her second book, an inspiring and uplifting account of her two miraculous healings of ovarian cancer.

Gloria Purter moved to Kauai on Martin L King Jr. Day January 15th 2007, and calls her arrival, "My Freedom Day." Purter holds a B.A. in accounting from Cal State University.

Purter is passionate about connecting and working together to empowering our Black communities to grow strong, and to create positive solutions to challenges. Purter desires world peace and global prosperity. "If one man is hungry we all suffer for it. The human race must be about One Love. People of Color must be about One Love. Less we all perish."

As a recording artist and songwriter, Purter performs with the Pacific Sound Machine, a band that has been performing on Kauai for more than twenty years. Purter sings jazz, R&B, and reggae. Since living in Kauai, Purter says she has been blessed over and over again in her pursuit of a rewarding entertainment career. For Purter Kauai represents healing and new beginnings. She is currently working on her second album.

Gloria Purter is the Chief Executive Officer of the African Heritage Cultural Center on Kauai. The African Heritage Cultural Center of Kauai's mission is to educate, motivate and heal our community. The African Heritage Cultural Center of Kauai was born out of a need to be connected with black culture and a need to identify with the Hawaiian people whose roots stretch as far back as Africa. She believes Hawaiian culture is a heritage that is shared with my people. For more information, one can visit the African Heritage Cultural Center of Kauai at www.ahccok.org.

Jimmy L. French says he is "Weaving my way through paradise. The Army showed me the way to paradise in 1974, it was like a dream come true when my drill sergeant in basic training at Fort Polk, Louisiana, said to me that I was going to Hawai`i for my permanent duty station." After two years in the army, I was honorably discharged and enrolled in college on the Big Island. My love for the Big Island of began during military training in the mountains of Pohakaloa.

It was at Pohakaloa that Jimmy met Lesley Deliasantos, a Portuguese guy, in Paipakoi five miles out of Hilo. There he lived with his brothers, who weaved in their front yard where tourists and passerby took notice of their intricate and detailed weaving. Jimmy said, "I knew this was a chance for me to save a lost art and to be recognized for my work. I learned how to weave. I recalled earning twenty dollars for my first hat. I seized the opportunity, learning how to weave. I recalled earning twenty dollars for my first hat. I learned to weave birds, fish, roses, hats, and baskets for the tourists."

Jimmy continues, "Two years later, I continued to weave, often traveling around the Big Island, learning more about weaving and sharing this beautiful art. I also traveled back to South Carolina and Florida to demonstrate the art of weaving: weaving is a meditation for the mind and soul. These days I live on Kauai, I attend the coconut festival each year and help at the Stones Shop on Kauai. I teach weaving at the Kauai Products Fair in Kapa`a. When you come to Kauai, look for me, riding my bike, wearing my hats, and weaving my way through Paradise.

Khalil Yeamie Toure Shaheed, Jr., is from Omaha, Nebraska. Khalil moved to Kauai May 2008. After learning that he was of Choctaw heritage, Khalil began to study African American cultures around the world. Khalil produced his vision on youtube.com under the name Yeamie, in hopes of addressing indigenous issues from the perspective of the Black man. He then went on to successfully create www.1kblackmen.com. Khalil's founded the Black Men Investment Group, to bring about financial prosperity to communities. Currently, Khalil is documenting and conducting research on connections between Black Egyptians and Polynesian cultural similarities with African Countries.

Melissa B. Hall was raised in Northern California and moved to New York in her early twenties. I was accepted into Fashion Institute of Technology in Manhattan as a Textile Design/Surface Design Major in the mid 1980's. I worked in the Fashion Industry on Fashion Avenue as a Freelance Textile Designer for eight years. I returned to school, majoring in Education, and earned an A.A. in Liberal Arts from Eugene Hostos Community College in the Bronx, and a B.A. in Psychology.

I moved to Kauai in 2007, employed with the YWCA of Kauai as a Prevention Educator and Case Manager/Art Specialist. I conducted workshops and classes within the schools on Kauai regarding preventions on staying safe from Sexual Assault and Abuse. I established an educational series for Kauai Community College regarding *Dating Violence: Suicide and Effects Media has on Young Adults*.

Creatively, I penned a Puppet Show devised to inform small children on "*Good Touch, Bad Touch and Secret Touch*". For Sexual Assault Awareness month, I sponsored an Art Show "*Survivors*" through the Kauai's Society of Artist gallery space in Lihue. I am one of the founding members of the Kauai Suicide Task Force, and founding members of the African Heritage Culture Center of Kauai.

Sandra A. Simms retired Circuit Court Judge, State of, Mediator/Arbitrator, Adjunct Lecturer in Criminal Justice, at Chaminade University. Judge Sandra Simms was appointed to the First Circuit Court, Twelfth Division, in May 1994. Prior to her appointment to the Circuit she served on the District Court from November, 1991. She retired from the bench June 1, 2004.

Simms was born in Chicago, Illinois. She is a graduate of Hyde Park High School, and obtained a B. A. from the University of Illinois, at Chicago, with a major in Sociology and Political Science. She earned her Juris Doctor degree from DePaul University, College of Law in 1978.

After graduating from the University of Illinois, she was employed as a flight attendant for United Airlines from 1972-1977. She and her husband Hank, moved to Hawai'i in 1979 upon his transfer with United Airlines. From 1980 until March 1982, she was a law clerk to the Honorable Yoshimi Hayashi, and then Chief Judge for the then newly formed Intermediate Court of Appeals.

She served as Deputy Corporation Counsel for the City and County of Honolulu from 1982 until 1991. In that capacity, she served as legal counsel to a variety of city agencies and commissions, including, the Police Commission, Civil Service Commission, Liquor Commission Building, Public Works, Fire Department, and Family Support Division. She also served as a as Staff Attorney for the Department of the Attorney General's Office of Information Practices until she was appointed judge to the District Court of the First Circuit, in November, 1991, by Chief Justice Herman Lum, becoming the first African American female judge in the state of Hawai'i. In May, 1994, she was appointed by Governor John Waihee to the position of Circuit Court Judge for the First Judicial Circuit, State of Hawai`i. As a trial judge, she presided over matters involving domestic violence, restraining orders, civil proceedings and felony jury trials, a substantial number of which were extensively covered by the media.

Simms' is also a member of the distinguished panel of neturals for Dispute Prevention Resolution, a private alternative dispute resolution (ADR) firm in Honolulu, and she is a member of the Supreme Court's Appellate Mediation Conference. She has completed mediation training at the Center for ADR in Honolulu and the Strauss Institute at Pepperdine University. Most recently she was named Adjunct Lecturer in Criminal Justice Studies at Chaminade University in Honolulu.

She served on a number of judicial committees, contributing to the work of the Jury Innovations Committee, the Domestic Violence Backlog Reduction Project, and the District Court Civil Rules Committee among others.

She was a member of the Judiciary's Speakers Bureau, and gave numerous presentations to a variety of community organizations, schools and forums to assist them in understanding the judicial system. Among the programs she has participated in have been school career days, the Peoples' Law School, the High School Mock Trial Tournament, the William S. Richardson Law School Appellate Advocacy, and the Dr. Martin Luther King , Jr. Coalition.

She has been a speaker and/ or presenter for innumerable community organizations and functions, including the Rotary Club, Chaminade University, Soroptimist International, the NAACP, Delta Sigma Theta Sorority, Honolulu Black Nurses, Trinity Missionary Baptist Church, the University of SEED program, Honolulu Masons, Hawai'i Chapter of the Links, Inc., YWCA Leadership Luncheon, and the Girl Scout Council, and various military programs and forums.

Judge Simms is a member of the Hawai'i State Bar Association, the National Bar Association, the American Bar Association and is president of the Afro American Lawyers Association. She currently serves on the Hawai'i State Board of Bar Examiners which writes and administers the Bar exam for attorneys who want to practice law in the State of Hawai'i. She is a current member and former director of Hawai`i Women Lawyers. Active with the Judicial Council of the National Bar Association, she has also been a group facilitator for the National Judicial College in Reno, Nevada.

Simms' community and civic responsibilities include six years of service on Neighborhood Board #25 (1983-1990), and she has been on various public school committees when her children were students. She is president of Soroptimist International of Waikiki. She also serves as Vice President of the Board of Directors for Mental Health America of Hawai`i (formerly the Mental Health Association in Hawai`i) and chairs its' Resource Development Committee. She is president of the Hawai`i Chapter of The Links, Incorporated and Chair of the Elections Committee for the Western Area.

She is a member of Sewjourner Truth, a group of attorneys and judges who enjoy the art of quilting.

Kathryn Waddell Takara, Ph.D., was born and raised in Tuskegee, Alabama, has taught at the University of Hawai`i at Manoa for more than 31 years, first in the Ethnic Studies Department, and later in interdisciplinary studies. She has developed courses in African American politics, history and culture.

In 1971 she created the first "Black Studies" courses in Ethnic Studies at the University of Hawai`i, and has been the only African American lecturer and Assistant Professor of Ethnic Studies teaching "Black Studies" in the University of academic setting. She earned a B.A. in French from Tufts University (Jackson College), an M.A. in French from the University of California, Berkeley, and a Ph.D. in Political Science from the University of Hawai`i at Manoa, and has been a Fulbright Scholar twice.

Dr. Takara's many titles and accomplishments include those of scholar, poet, writer, researcher, social and community service activist, adviser, coordinator, mentor, mother, wife, and proud daughter of one of the oldest living Buffalo Soldiers, Dr. William Waddell, VMD.

She was the recipient of the Board of Regents Outstanding Teacher Award during the 1995-1996 school year. Dr. Takara's love for diverse cultures and languages and search for common ground found her traveling and teaching in China five times, once as a visiting professor at the University of Quindao (teaching American Cultural Studies and Conversational English), and a lecturer at Beijing University of Technology. She also gave lectures at the National Women's Federation in Beijing.

Dr. Takara has published three books: *Pacific Raven: Hawai`i Poems*, *New and Collected Poems* published by Ishmael Reed Publishing, and *Oral Histories of African Americans* (In Hawai`i). She has also published over 250 poems, several articles in refereed journals, chapters in books, a monograph, several encyclopedia entries, articles on the Internet, and book reviews. She has been featured and interviewed in newspaper articles, and often appears on local video and TV productions. Dr. Takara has invited, introduced and/or interviewed such prestigious African-American scholars such as Frank Marshall Davis, Dr. Barbara Christian, Ishmael Reed, Maya Angelou, Stokely Carmichael (Kwame Ture), Angela Davis, Alice Walker, Opal Palmer Adisa, Audre Lorde as well as many others.

Dr. Takara has also conducted oral histories and researched the experiences of many African Americans living in Hawai`i, lending a unique and intelligent perspective, analysis, and a voice to their heretofore little documented presence. Dr. Takara is without a doubt a prominent sojourner and a dedicated and leading pioneer in the small but vital African American community in the Hawaiian Islands.

Dr. Takara has read her poetry extensively in Honolulu, California, University of Texas at Austin, the Harlem Book Fair, Arkansas University, Tuskegee University, Beijing and Qingdao, China, Black Oak Books in Berkeley. She has been interviewed and read her poetry on many radio shows including KPFA in Berkeley. She has done several book tours in the past five years including Barnes & Noble Books in Hawai`i and the Bay Area, Border's Books & Music in Hawai`i, Cody's in Berkeley and the Pro Arts Gallery in Oakland, City Lights Books in San Francisco. She was invited to perform at the Texas Book Fair in Austin, and at Tribes and the Bowery Poetry Club in New York City.

Ishmael Reed says "It's hard to find a poet like Kathryn, she mixes things up. There are a lot of things particular to in her work, she moves in and out of cultures."

Her writing reflects her travels in Africa, China, Europe and her Alabama childhood growing up black in the Jim Crow South. In a five star customer review on amazon.com, writer Bill Danks says "Some jewels are obvious. They sparkle and shine and call all kinds of attention to themselves. Diamonds are a good example. Other jewels are more humble and quiet and perhaps a bit shy, but they can possess a deeper darker beauty of even greater value. Emeralds are of this type."

Poet Kathryn Waddell Takara is an emerald. …in addition to being a World Poet, she is also most decidedly a `world class poet' with an amazingly sensual gift of language honed and crafted to perfection over a lifetime of writing."

Currently, Kathryn Waddell Takara launched her writing career with the recently published poetry book, "Pacific Raven: Poems." Her forthcoming book, "Tourmalines: Beyond the Ebony Portal" will be released in 2010. www.kathrynwaddelltakara.com

Miles M. Jackson, PhD., retired professor and Dean Emeritus of the University of at Manoa. He served for twenty years in the School of Library and Information Studies, and was Dean from 1982 1995. He is a graduate of Virginia Union University and earned a Masters Degree from Drexel University's College of Information Studies, and a PhD. in Communication from Syracuse University. He began his career as a librarian/ information specialist with the Free Library of Philadelphia. Following a few years in Philadelphia he held positions as Head Librarian at Hampton University, 1958-1962; Territorial Librarian, American Samoa; Chief Librarian, Atlanta University Center; Associate Professor, State University of New York. He has over 50 articles in various professional publications and as a freelance writer he is an occasional contributor to the Honolulu *Advertiser*. Among the seven books written or edited are *Pacific Islands Studies*, (1986), *Publishing in the Pacific* (1985), *Linkages Over Space and Time* (1986), *And They Came* (2001), and *They Followed the Trade Winds: African Americans in* (2005). He writes a monthly column for *Mahogany*, covering people of color.

He has acted as a consultant to the People's Republic of China, Taiwan, Pakistan, India, Fiji, Papua, New Guinea, Australia, New Zealand, and Indonesia. In 1968- 1969 he was a Senior Fulbright Professor at the University of Tehran, Iran and received a Ford Foundation award for travel in East and West Africa. His work in Asia and the Pacific was for the United States Information Agency and U.S. State Department Specialists Program.

Ayin M. Adams, native New Yorker, began writing at age five selling her poetry on a street corner in Brooklyn New York for twenty-five cents. Ayin studied drama at the Performing Arts School, The Michael Sawyer's Studio, and learned the Stanislavski Method Acting Technique in New York City. Adams appeared in television commercials in the late 1960s. In the early 1970s, she made television appearances on such sitcoms as Different Strokes, Fish, Welcome Back Kotter, Zoom, and other TV and film performances.

Later, she starred in off Broadway productions, performing with such noted actors as James Earl Jones Sr., Glenn Thurman, the late Nell Carter, and others. Adams would go on to travel across the United States with her staged productions.

Adams appeared in numerous films. She received more acting and writing training in NYC at the Frank Silvera's Writer's Workshop, Ujamaa Black Theatre, and Shooting Star Performers. Ayin received her B.A. in Speech & Theatre at Lehman College in Bronx, N.Y. She earned her PhD in Human Services and her M.A. & PhD. in Metaphysics at the University of Metaphysics. Open-minded as Adams is, she is the perfect personification of the diversity within the global multicultural society we live in today!

In 1992, Adams moved to O'ahu Hawai`i, for five years, then sailed to Maui where she felt right at home amidst the beauty of nature. In Maui, she began to build a life full of new challenges, surpassing herself and boldly unfolding and spreading out to a path of constant growth towards inner depth and spirituality.

Adams is without the shadow of a doubt a gifted and prolific poet and author. Adams walks with an incredible determination. She walks from one achievement to another, creating a spiritual, positive, living vibration that is enchanting to everyone who meets her. The pure beauty of Maui became a source of spiritual creativeness, a fertile soil on which the poetic talent of Adams would bloom, not only as a poet, but also as a filmmaker, a playwright, a screenwriter, a performer, a teacher and a healer.

In 2005, Adams' book, *The Woods Deep Inside Me,* was published. In 2006, she wrote an autobiographical poetry book, *Walking Through my Fire*, in which she allows the readers to walk with her through her painful past, and to emerge in crowning glory. Then, in 2007, she wrote *Walking in Sappho's Garden* which was nominated as a GCLS Literary Awards Finalist. She wrote about 'Soul' poetry that touched her readers. She recorded a series of transformational transcendent CDs for healing on all levels; *Healing The Child Within, The High Cost of Unforgiveness, A New Day/A New You, The Tree of Life is You, How to Handle Pressure, and Relationships on a Spiritual Level;* www.ayinadams.com. In between all this, Adams wrote and published black plays, edited and published three volumes of poetry books by her young middle school students whom she passionately inspired to hit that enchanted road of poetry; *Climbing a Rainbow of Dreams, Butterfly Blossoms, From Dawn To Dusk*, and forthcoming in 2010 *Graffiti Dreams.*

She was chosen as 'Teacher of the Year 2008' by the International Peace Poem Awards Committee, In 2000, she was nominated Poet of The Year. Adams is the winner of the Pat Parker Poetry Award, the Audre Lorde Memorial Prose Prize Winner, the Award Winner for Literary Excellence 2001, and the Zora Neale Hurston/Richard Wright Award. She has been published in *Bum Rush The Page*, A Defjam Poetry Publication, Adams has been published in numerous magazines, e-zines, on-line publications, and *Women In The Moon Publication, Illiad Press*, and *Quiet Mountain Essays.* Her work has also been translated in French, Dutch, and German.

Today, Adams boldly challenges herself and has become one of the many voices that documents the history of her people, the African Americans, and their community in the Hawaiian Islands. What better time could she have chosen, now that one of Hawaii's own, Barack Obama, has been elected President of the United States and has been acclaimed as the 2009 recipient of the Nobel Peace Prize Winner. Adams has been digging into history, interviewing, and exploring all possible sources to create a work of value as complete as possible.

This book will become a 'must have' for all African American households, a history to discover with pride, the written proof of their Hawai`i past, their achievements, and their future. Adams offer the ultimate exposure of the spiritual richness and talents that African Americans have brought to this Diaspora.

AFRICAN AMERICAN ORGANIZATIONS IN HAWAI`I

According to research conducted by renowned scholar and noted black historian of African American Culture; Dr. Kathryn Waddell Takara, states that the earliest group(s) of African Americans formed around 1941 with the first black church, Trinity Baptist Church, in Honolulu. This list is a partial listing of groups in the Islands, more groups are continuing to form and give rise to the Black voice yearly.

Afro American Association of Hawai`i
African American Chamber of Commerce
African American Cultural Center of Kauai
African American Culture Clubs
African American Diversity Cultural Center
African American Education Center of Hawai`i
African American Heritage Foundation Of Maui
African American Lawyers Association
African Americans On Maui Association
African Heritage Culture Center
Alphas
Amen Rasta Wooten
Atlas
Black Doctors Association
Black Military
Black Ministers Alliance
Black Nurses Association
Black Repertory Theatre
Deltas
Eastern Stars
Harambe Connection
HOPE Harvest Our People's Energy
Hawai`i
Iota
Kappas Alpha Ii
Links, Inc.
Martin Luther King Jr. Holiday Coalition
Masons
NAACP
Nubian Pageant Systems
Omegas
Phi Beta Sigma
Prima or Aging
Shriners
Sigma Yamma Roe
Sisters 2 Sisters
Zeta Phi Beta

African American Diversity Cultural Center Hawai`i

The African American Diversity Cultural Center Hawai`i (**AADCCH**) was founded in 1997 as a museum repository to archive 200 years of African descent history in Hawai`i. The purpose is to share the collections by displaying and exhibiting artifacts, photographs, oral history to tell the story of African Americans past and present history in all its permutations: family life, civic contributions, inventions, medicine, architecture, politics, religion, law and arts that will educate the people in Hawai`i about the cultural heritage of black people in this country. Delores Guttman is the CEO and President. You may visit: www.aadcch.org

Purpose

The African American Diversity Cultural Center Hawai`i (AADCCH) was established as a museum repository to archive, document, collect, preserve maintain, and display 200 years of Black history in Hawai`i to share and provide the community with a better understanding about its cultural heritage.

Vision Statement

A venue to share our rich cultural heritage and values through quality education programs in collaboration with businesses to encourage participation and enhance cultural appreciation.

Mission Statement

Amalgamation of Ethnic Cultural Diversity and Community Collaboration

NAACP Names Its Leaders for 1947

The National Association for the Advancement of Colored People held its annual election of officers for the Honolulu chapter Sunday afternoon, January 5, at the Nuuanu Congregational church. Arthur Gilliam served as chairman of the election and reviewed the progress of the organization for the past year. gratification was expressed at the way cosmopolitan Hawai`i has responded to NAACP. The organization pledged cooperation along cultural lines. Fleming R. Waller was reelected President for 1947, James Neal, Vice President, and Mrs. Lucille Neal, secretary. E.L. Stafford succeeded Charles T. Mackey as treasurer. An executive committee of 19 was elected to guide NAACP for 1947.

Article in Star Bulletin Jan. 10, 1947

Planning Busy 1947 are these new Officers of NAACP:
Left to right, James Neal, Vice President,
Fleming R. Waller, President, Lucille Neal, Secretary,
and E.I. Stafford, Treasurer. Photo by Nelson

FOLK CHURCH TO OBSERVE 5TH BIRTHDAY

The Folk Church of Civilian Housing Area 3 will celebrate its 5th anniversary on Sunday, June 29, and on the same day will observe the 45th birthday of its pastor Ivory Washington Collins. The group which makes up the Folk Church has survived the changes occasioned by the war and the post-war period. The church was organized in 1941 and some of the original members still attend. The meeting place is at 942 17th St. CHA-3.

Members of this group have been active in helping their brethren throughout the Pacific Ocean area and have answered many calls for financial aid. The greater part of their financial assistance has gone and is still going to help liberate members of their race in Portuguese West Africa, where according to the custom of the country, children at the age of 6 are still being sold into slavery. Since the Folk Church was organized here its members have liberated more than 1,500 such children, Pastor Collins reports.

Note: Article appearing in the Honolulu Advertiser
June 1941. Church was founded in 1941

Chapter 21

Building The Stone of Hope

STONE OF HOPE MONUMENT: Dedicated to the Life, Legacy, and the work of Dr. Martin Luther King Jr.

Chapter 21 offers a unique look at the author's community involvement and the sacredness of building monuments and stones to represent African American Heritage in the islands, thus establishing a sense of belonging. Building the **Stone of Hope** commemorates the life work of Dr. Martin Luther King Jr. African Americans in Hawai`i, seek, like, Dr. King, to champion a movement that draws fully from the deep well of America's potential for freedom, opportunity, and justice. Dr. King's vision of America is captured in his message of hope and possibility for a future anchored in dignity, sensitivity, and mutual respect, a message that challenges each of us to recognize that America's true strength lies in its diversity of talents, thus, "…with this faith, we will be able to hew out of the mountain of despair, a **Stone of Hope**…"

Lynn Araki-Regan & Ayin Adams

Stone of Hope Ceremony; Folks Gathering with Mayor Alan Arakawa

Former Mayor Alan Arakawa, Ayin, Bryant, Rev. Alalani, Le'ohu Rider

Lynn Araki-Regan

Unveiling The Stone of Hope Monument

Funding for the Stone of Hope monument provided by former Mayor of Maui County, Alan Arakawa and Lynn Araki-Regan serving under Arakawa as Maui Economic Development Coordinator.

Lorraine Nole Rippy &
Andrew Valentine at Ceremony

Andrew Valentine

Lorraine Nole Rippy

Lorraine Nole Rippy

Ayin Adams
@ Ceremony

Stone of Hope Monument

Seated Caroline Ware, Lorraine Nole Rippy,
Mother Esterine Nole 2nd Row Ayin Adams,
Marie Smith, Sandra Shawhan, SaEeda King,
Standing Sodengi, Marie Watu, Ear Sundance,
Roland Vegas, and Mary Wagner.

Stone of Hope Monument

Wailuku County Historic Courthouse

OPENING CEREMONIES AT THE
STONE OF HOPE MONUMENT
DEDICATED TO DR. MARTIN LUTHER KING JR.

Hawaiian Kahuna Rev. Alalani, &
Rob At Opening Ceremonies

At Opening Ceremonies
Ayin, Omar, & Bryant

Preparing For Dr. King's
March Jan. 2009

Tiona & Father Sundance, Adesina Ogunelese, Omar,
Ayin, Bryant, Rev. Alalani, & Rob

Resting at Stone of Hope Monument,
photos of Queen Lili'uokalani, Dr. King & Family

Folks Gathering For The March

Rev. Alalani Hill, Ayin Adams, Bryant Neal, Earl Sundance,
Adesina Oguneles, Rev. Kedar St. John

Dr. King's March Begins

Ayin Adams, Earl Sundance, and Bryant Neal Marches with Banner

A Perfect Day in Paradise Maui, HI for a March

Group Marches past the County of Maui Government Buildings

March concludes at Café Marc
Auriel in downtown Wailuku

Blue Skies For A Dr. King March

Marching For Peace

Chapter 22

Cultural and Community Events

COMMUNITY EVENTS-DR. MARTIN LUTHER KING JR. HOLIDAY JAN. 2009

Chapter 22 depicts photos of community, love, joy, transformations and celebrations of black culture and education, sharing and giving, learning and a sense of responsibility and duty to our Oneness as humans on the islands revealing a group spirit.

Robert Digman   Bobbie Moore   Dwight Green   Abigail Robinson & Konjit Robinson

Toni & Lorenzo Allen   Kyra-Denise Kendall   Cassandra Prentice   Andrea Johnson

Earl Love Sr.   Earl Love Sr.   Ayin Adams

Sodengi Camille Orimaladi Mills (Performs African Dance) Sodengi Camille Orimaladi Mills (Performs African Dance)

Bryant Neal (Delivering Dr. King's I Have A Dream Speech)

Bryant Neal   Ayin Adams & Bryant Neal   Bobby Ingram (Singer)   Bobby Ingram & Earl Love

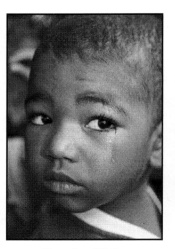

Bobby Ingram & Earl Love   Adisa Omar (Singer)   Brandon White   Leah Tunkara

Fulton Tshombe & Adisa Omar

Ayin Adams, Fulton Tshombe,
Queen Lili'uokalani & Dr. King (photo)

Sofia, Tenee, & Amazon   Naimu with sons Brandon & Alexander White

Brothers Embrace

Mother& Son

Jaime

Jaime

Jaime

Nara Boone

Brothers Ben Isaiah & Julian Marcus

Ed (Professor) Connor

Drummer; Elder Juan
"Windcloud" Montalvo

Earl Sundance: African Opening
Libation & The Pouring of Sacred
Water For Our Ancestors

Glen Lacy

Patricia Roberts

Bryant Neal

Glen Lacy

Patricia & Glen

Linda Spraggins

Stan

Brian Corley

Mother & Son

Alima, Amina & Brennan

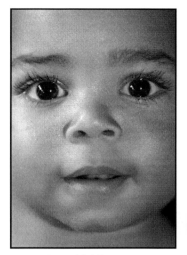
Beautiful Brennan

Jimi Winn

Sheries Hodges

Harold Hodges

Patricia & Glen
(African Dance & Drumming)

Queen Lili'uokalani

Dr. Martin Luther King Jr.

Sundance (Caught In A Moment)

Celebrating Dr. King &
President Barack Obama

Father & Son (Sundance & Tiona)

Banner Of Dr. MLK Jr. &
President Barack Obama

Lorraine Nole Rippy Celebrates
Dr. King & President Barack Obama

John Stan Rippy &
Lorraine Nole Rippy

John Stan Rippy

Devery Bailey

Devery Bailey

The Group:
The Black Experience

The Black Experience Group BBQ

Folks playing Spades

Donnie King

Shirley Davenport

Richard and Devin Griffin

Richard and Devin Griffin

Shirley Davenport

Shirley & Calvin Davenport

Black History Month Events

Playbill of 1st Black Play Ever
Presented in History Of Maui

Back Cover of Playbill depicting Black
Owned "Squeaky's Restaurant"

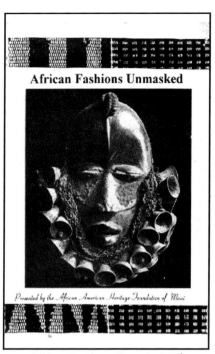

African Fashions Unmasked "1st
African American Fashion Show on Maui" 1994

African Americans Heritage Foundation of Maui "1st Officers" 1993

Bryant Neal

Bryant Neal & Adesina Ogunelese

Student reads poetry during Black History Month with Ayin

Ayin & Adesina

Ayin & Sodgeni Performs @ Maui Arts & Culture Center

Ayin Adams @ Wailuku Public Library Exhibit

Ayin performs dramatic reading

Earl Sundance & Playwright Ayin Adams
stands under Playbill @ Iao Theatre1

Rosaria Regina Torres

Mariah Small & Father David

Juneteenth Celebration

African Quilt Presentation with Wanda Yates.
(Sundance helps)

Ayin and Lama Rangdrol

Cherisse & Guest Speaker Lama Rangdrol

Daughter & Father share a warm smile

Sistahs Celebrating

Tina, Sodengi, and Sabrina

Kwanzaa

Adesina teaches about the Kwanzaa Kuaaba Doll

Adesian Ogunelese with Tiona

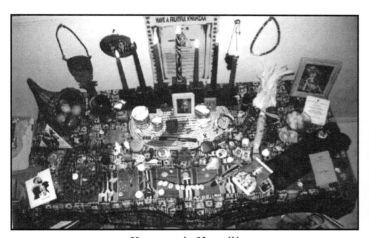

Kwanzaa in Hawai`i

Kwanzaa Table

Sundance, Tiona, and Adesina

Leah Tunkara & Maya Soetoro-NG

Third Sunday Group at Kamehameha III Park

Leah Tunkara

Little Jo Jo

Robin & Daughter

Terri Moore with Juneteenth shirt

Ben, Stan, & Vern

Folks Relaxing

Anthony, Lorraine, & Wanda relaxes at 3rd Sunday in the Park

3rd Sunday @ Kamehameha Park III

Alfred & Tenee'

Group photo

Alethea & Mya

Earl Sundance

Vern

Tenee Amico

George & Terri Rainey

Gloria Purter

Retired Judge Sandra Simms

Alphonso Braggs

Judy Harrison

Deloris Guttman

Jimmy Cathey

Gloria and
Michael Govinda Mixer

Mahealani Uchiyama

Khalil Y. Shaheed

Patricia Henderson

Captain Deborah Taylor
1st Woman Captain
at Maui Community Correctional Center

Clarence and Adrianne

Diana Drake

Lawrence Taylor

African American Cultural Diversity Center Hawai`i

Arid Chappell

Jimmy L French

Alice Adams

Jewel McDonald

Dr. Betty Clayborne

Lama Rangdrol-Afro Buddhism Film Poster

Lama Rangdrol-Teaching on Maui

Lama Rangdrol-Scandanavia

Pampering At Lorraine Beauty Salon 1982

Pema Gilman

Arid Chappell

Lama Rangdrol-American
Yogin Maui Rainforest

Lama Rangdrol-Black
Buddha Book Cover

Lama Rangdrol-South of France

Halloween at the White House Oct. 31, 2009

Island Kwanzaa

Contributors

Kathryn Waddell Takara, born and raised in Tuskegee, Alabama, has recently retired as an Associate Professor from the University of Hawai'i at Manoa's Interdisciplinary Studies Program. She also taught in the Ethnic Studies Department, where she developed courses in African American and African Politics, history, literature, and culture (1971-2003).

She has written three books: Pacific Raven: Hawai'i Poems, New & Collected Poems, and Oral Histories: Blacks in Hawai'i. Her poetry has been published in a variety of publications including Interdisciplinary Studies Humanities Journal, Writing Macao (China), Kudzu, Honolulu Stories, Words Upon the Waters, The African Journal of New Poetry, Arkansas Review, Africa Literary Journal, Julie Mango Press, Poetry Motel, Peace & Policy, From Totems to Hip Hop, Bamboo Ridge, Rainbird, Konch, Kaimana, Hawai'i Review, Chaminade Literary Review, Ramrod, O'ahu Review, Pleiades, All She Wrote: Hawai'i Women's Voices, and World of Poetry, an anthology, Her essays have appeared in the Interdisciplinary Humanities Journal, Du Bois Review: Social Science Research on Race, Social Process In Hawai'i, The Black Scholar, The Encyclopedia of African American Culture and History, and Multi-America: Essays on Cultural Wars and Cultural Peace, The Western Journal of Black Studies, The Honolulu Advertiser, Honolulu Magazine, I Ka Huliau, and Valley Voices.

Takara holds a Ph.D. in Political Science and an M.A. in French and has taught, advised, and mentored innumerable students. Recipient of the Board of Regents Outstanding Teacher Award and a two-time Fulbright Fellow, she has read and performed her poetry and lectured extensively in universities, colleges, schools, and community and military events throughout the Hawaiian Islands, the Continental United States of America and in Beijing and Qingdao, China.

Takara organized, coordinated, and produced several national and international conferences at the University of Hawai'i and in Honolulu. She has also appeared on a variety of television shows, including interviews and documentaries through the years.

Dr. Takara is the daughter of pioneer black veterinarian, author, and world famous Buffalo Soldier, Dr. William H. Waddell, IV, VMD (1908-2007). She enjoys her family, friends, pets, meditation, *qi* gong, garden, raising orchids and interior design.

Helene H. Hale

Hawaii State Legislature

4th Representative District

Hawaii State Capitol, Room 331

415 South Beretania Street

Honolulu, HI 96813

Born

Minneapolis, Minnesota

Personal

Widowed: Former Husband- Richard Kiyota

Children: Indira Hale-Tucker, William Hale, III

Education

B.S., M.A. University of Minnesota

Further Graduate study: Claremont College, U.H. Hilo

Political Office

Board of Supervisors: Member. County of Hawai`i, 1955-1963

Chairman and Executive Officer, County of Hawai`i (forerunner of Mayor), 1963-1965

Hawai`i County Council: Member.1980-1984, 1988-1992, 1992-1994

Hawai`i State Constitutional Convention: Delegate. 1978

Professional

Tennessee A & I State College, San Diego State, Teacher and Lecturer

Konawaena High School, U.H. Hilo, College

Territorial Manager for the BookHouse for Children

Owner: Menehune Bookstore, Kainaliu, Kona; Coffee Farm, South Kona;

Owner: Hawai`i Isle Realty, Ltd.; Hale Consultants, Inc.

Community

President, Board of Directors, YWCA

President, East Hawaii Local Development Corporation

President, Hilo Business and Professional Women's Club

President, Mauna Kea Foundation

President, Hawai`i County League of Women Voters

President, Hawai`i State Federation of Women's Club

President, Hawai`i Island Chapter United Nations Association/USA

President, Hawai`i State Association of Counties

Board of Directors, Member Puna Outdoor Circle, Pahoa Main Street

Hawai`i Island Tourist Guide "Hawai`i Isle Guide" Publisher

Merrie Monarch Festival helped organize and start

Hilo Sewer Treatment Plant helped organize and start (enabled Banyan Drive Hotels to be built)

Big Island Housing Foundation helped organize and start

YWCA Swimming Pool and Multi-Purpose building helped organize and start

Pahoa Swimming Pool helped organize and start

Island of Hawai`i High School Model United Nations Program Helped organize and start

Hale Halawai (Kona) helped organize and start

Kona Sewer Treatment Plant helped organize and start

Naalehu Flood Control Channel helped organize and start

La Serena, Chile & Hawai`i County Sister Cities helped organize and start

Island of Hawai`i High School Model United Nations Conferences helped

organize and start

Member of the Democratic Party.

COMMITTEES:

International Affairs (Chair)

Education

Health

Higher Education

Housing

Human Services

Indira Hale Tucker, daughter of Helene H. Hale, grew up in Hawai`i. She moved to Santa Monica in 1965 and then to Long Beach in 1977. She earned a B.A. in political science from UCLA. She married Marcus O. Tucker. Fascinated by history of all kinds and passionate about life-long learning and dance, Indira Hale Tucker believes that the lessons of history and the lives of black achievers can inspire Americans of all ages and ethnic backgrounds to succeed.

She is the founding member of the Santa Monica Fair Housing Council (1966) and organized its first housing discrimination lawsuit. She served on the Santa Monica YWCA Board of Directors and in 1974 served as first vice president. She is a past member of the Board of Directors of the Law Wives, and the California pool for the handicapped.

PUBLICATIONS:

Helping Your Child In School, A Guide for Parents of 9th-12th Grade Students. Author, Published by the Outreach Office of California State University-Long Beach (1993).

The Heritage of African Americans In Long Beach Over 100 Years. Co-editor with Aaron Day (2007). First book about the local black community ever published in Long Beach.

SELECTED PAST ACTIVITIES:

Political Campaigns in Hawai`i, Santa Monica, and Long Beach;

Organized 3 TOY LOAN Programs in Long Beach (1986-2000);

Jack and Jill of America First Long Beach Chapter (1988) Founding Member,

Black History Program Co-Chair, Corresponding Secretary, Financial Secretary, Group Leader.

COMMUNITY INVOLVENT (current)

Co-founder and retired President of the African American Heritage Society of Long Beach (2009)

Burnett Public Library in Long Beach, organized, promoted and funded in 1997.

SPEAKERS PROGRAM: Lecturer for the USC Emeriti Center Community.

SELECTED AWARDS:

Volunteer of the Year, LA County Dept. of Public Social Services

NAACP Lifetime Achievement Award with husband Marcus O. Tucker, Long Beach Soroptimist Woman of Distinction,

Grand Marshall, Martin Luther King Parade, Long Beach.

SPECIAL PROJECTS:

Burnett Public Library in Long Beach;

1996 **Essie Tucker and Helene Hale Collection** of Black Women's History & Biography.

Hilo Public Library 2005 **Helene Hale Collection: International Women of Courage** Santa Monica Main Library, 2007 Marcus **Tucker Collection: Black Men of Courage** (to honor her husband innovative and judicial career).

Miles M. Jackson is a retired Professor and Dean Emeritus of the University of Hawai`i at Manoa. He served for twenty years in the School of Library and Information Technology and was Dean from 1982 1995. Dr. Jackson is a graduate of Virginia Union University and earned a masters degree from Drexel University's College of Information Studies and a Ph.D. in Communication from Syracuse University. He began his career as a librarian/information specialist with the Free Library of Philadelphia. Following a few years in Philadelphia he held positions as Head Librarian at Hampton University, Territorial Librarian in American Samoa, Chief Librarian at Atlanta University Center, and Associate Professor at State University of New York.

Dr. Jackson has published over 50 articles in various professional journals, and as a freelance writer he is an occasional contributor to the Honolulu *Advertiser*. Among the seven books he has written or edited are: *Pacific Islands Studies* (1986); *Publishing in the Pacific* (1985); *Linkages Over Space and Time* (1986); *And They Came* (2001); and *They Followed the Trade Winds: African Americans in Hawai`i* (2005). He writes a column for Mahogany, a bi-monthly newspaper covering people of color.

Dr. Jackson has served as a consultant to the People's Republic of China, Taiwan, Pakistan, India, Fiji, New Guinea, Australia, New Zealand, and Indonesia. In 1968, 1969 he was a Senior Fulbright Professor at the University of Tehran, Iran and received a Ford Foundation award for travel in East and West Africa. His work in Asia and the Pacific was for the United States Information Agency and U.S. State Department Specialists Program.

Aaron L. Day, was born in Xenia, Ohio in 1939 and is now residing in Long Beach, California. Aaron L. Day has devoted much of his adult life to researching and preserving African American family history. He was the editor of the school newspaper during his junior and senior years. His passion for this venture into African American research was sparked during his senior year in high school, when he was chosen co-editor of his yearbook, the *'Eastonian'* in 1957. He was given the task of researching and documenting the history of Xenia's segregated East High School and the students of its graduating class.

Annual family reunions for his mother's side of the family began in 1981. Following a family reunion in 1998, Day decided to seriously research his father's family history and discovered that the famous cabinet-maker and master craftsman Thomas J. Day, of North Carolina was his 3rd great uncle. Day has traced his ancestry back to 1692 in Northumberland County, Virginia. He has taken DNA tests and discovered that his paternal ancestry traces back to Liberia, and his maternal ancestry traces back to Nigeria. Armed with what he has uncovered, Aaron has challenged African Americans throughout the nation to discover their roots.

As a respected regional author and lecturer (Long Beach, California) Day is a sought-after lecturer on genealogy, has written five books (one a best-seller), and four award-winning articles on researching African American history and heritage. He has lectured at the Afro-American Genealogy Society in Washington, D.C., and the National Archives in Laguna Niguel, California. He frequently lectures and holds genealogy classes for organizations such as the N.A.A.C.P., Long Beach Branch, various genealogy societies, and the African American Heritage Society of Long Beach. Because of his many years of volunteer work with the Long Beach Public Library and the City of Long Beach, Day is affectionately known as Mr. "Library." He has helped establish several book collections on African American genealogy and history at the Long Beach, California Public Library.

Day is one of the contributors to the most recent edition of the historic *African American National Biography'* (AANB). He contributed the biography of Mary Dell Butler. She was the first African American to have a school named for her in the city of Long Beach, California. In 1999, Day became the first and only African American male to ever receive the "Mary Dell Butler Volunteer of the Year Award" from the City of Long Beach.

PUBLICATIONS

The Eastonian School Yearbook. Co-editor Mildred Scott. 1957

Locating Free African American Ancestors: A Beginner's Guide. 2003

History Lessons. 2005

Family Tree. Co-editor Naomi Rainey, President NAACP, Long Beach. 2006

The Heritage of African Americans in Long Beach: Over 100 Years. Co-editor Indira Hale Tucker, Infinity Publishing.com. 2007

Forthcoming: March, 2010 *'DNA To Africa: The Search Continues'*

Forthcoming: June, 2010 *'Preserving Our History'* Co-editor Theodore Day

AWARD-WINNING ARTICLES

Tracing My African American Ancestors. Short story. Southern California Genealogical Society National Writing Contest 2001. *Celebrating Family History* an Anthology of Prize Winning Stories published by the Southern California Genealogical Society. 2005.

The Search for Free African American Ancestors. Essay. Southern California Genealogical Society National Writing Contest. 2002. *Heritage Quest Genealogical Magazine* 2003.

History Lessons. Essay, Iliad Press/Cader Publishing contest 2002.

What's Available For African American Research. Southern California Genealogical Society National Writing Contest. 2004.

adaydec@aol.com, www.day-banks.com

Photo Credit

Alalani Hill, Kahu (Rev.) is the lead professional photographer in this volume. All photos of the Dr. Martin Luther King Jr. March, Holiday, and individual photos are credited to Alalani. Alalani is devoted to learning and perpetuating the ancient Hawaiian ways in Maui. Alalani feels that her mission of love is to continue on her path to serve God and help the children of the earth. She unconditionally accepts all people by offering them truth through love with her wholehearted spirit of aloha. Alalani is known globally for her traditional and ancient Hawaiian weddings and ceremonies, spiritual counseling, and La'au Lapa'au (Hawaiian Healing) www.hawaiianceremonies.com

Z'ma Wyatt is a photographic artist/photojournalist living in Oakland, California and works as a Photojournalist for the Globe Newspapers covering the Bay Area. Z'ma Wyatt is credited with photos of President Barack Obama submitted for this book.

Additional Photo Credit

    Ayin Adams

    Organizing for America

    Barack Obama Campaign

    Aaron L. Day

    Helene H. Hale

    Adesina Ogunelese

    Kathryn Waddell Takara

    Lawrence Taylor

    Indira Hale Tucker

    Patricia Henderson

APPENDIX I
HAWAI'I CENSUS 1900-2000

Table 1

MARRIAGES BY ETHNICITY OF GROOM AND ETHNICITY OF BRIDE, IN 1998

ETHNICITY of Groom	Cauc	Haw	Chin	Fili	Japa	Kore	Samo	Blac	Viet	Othr	Unk	Total	P'cent
Caucasian	1542	325	94	328	296	60	17	47	17	106	19	2851	34.5
Hawaiian	219	777	28	213	175	23	21	1	3	40	6	1506	18.2
Chinese	31	31	147	26	76	13	1	1	7	6	1	340	4.1
Filipino	102	176	15	530	92	12	6	6	3	18	4	964	11.7
Japanese	108	139	49	116	509	79	0	2	6	10	3	1021	12.4
Korean	11	12	1	9	30	105	0	1	0	2	0	171	2.1
Samoan	9	67	2	15	6	1	111	1	0	5	0	217	2.6
Black	76	76	2	53	38	1	9	157	0	17	4	433	5.2
Vietnamese	3	2	8	3	2	0	0	0	33	1	0	52	0.6
Other	46	49	8	33	17	4	11	2	2	124	1	297	3.6
Unknown	14	5	0	7	11	1	0	1	0	1	368	408	4.9
Total	2161	1659	354	1333	1252	299	176	219	71	330	406	8260	100.0

Note:1 "Caucasian" includes Puerto Rican and Portuguese

Source: Vital Statistics Report, Department of Health State Monitoring, 1998, pp. 59-67.

Table 2
ETHNIC OUTMARRIAGES BY ETHNICITY, 1998

ETHNICITY	Resident Groom			Resident Bride		
	Out Marriage	In Marriage	Total	Out Marriage	In Marriage	Total
Caucasian	1,300	1,716	3,016	619	1,542	2,161
Hawaiian	744	774	1518	882	777	1659
Chinese	195	148	343	207	147	354
Filipino	436	529	965	803	530	1333
Japanese	509	522	1031	743	509	1252
Korean	68	105	173	194	105	299
Samoan	104	108	212	65	111	176
Black	296	172	468	62	157	219

APPENDIX II

Hawaii County Population Estimates by Race Alone or in Combination and Hispanic or Latino Origin: July 1, 2002					
County	White alone or in combination	Black or African American alone or in combination	American Indian and Alaska Native alone or in combination	Asian alone or in combination	Native Hawaiian and other Pacific Islander alone or in combination
TOTAL					
HAWAII	497,010	40,329	25,163	726,171	270,710
Hawaii County	82,911	1,954	5,115	73,417	45,860
Honolulu County	317,775	36,769	16,252	556,756	178,854
Kalawao County	48	-	-	25	59
Kauai County	28,464	323	1,148	32,312	13,456
Maui County	67,812	1,283	2,648	63,661	32,481
NOT OF HISPANIC OR LATINO ORIGIN					
HAWAII	435,743	36,016	18,536	686,069	241,385
Hawaii County	72,233	1,572	3,574	65,399	38,599
Honolulu County	277,623	32,973	12,126	531,278	161,997
Kalawao County	42	-	-	25	59
Kauai County	25,248	300	866	29,919	11,723
Maui County	60,597	1,171	1,970	59,448	29,007
OF HISPANIC OR LATINO ORIGIN					
HAWAII	61,267	4,313	6,627	40,102	29,325
Hawaii County	10,678	382	1,541	8,018	7,261
Honolulu County	40,152	3,796	4,126	25,478	16,857
Kalawao County	6	-	-	-	-
Kauai County	3,216	23	282	2,393	1,733
Maui County	7,215	112	678	4,213	3,474

Note: "In combination" means in combination with one or more other races. The sum of the five race groups adds to more than the total population because individuals can report more than one race. Dash (-) represents zero or rounds to zero.

Suggested Citation:

Table CO-EST2002-ASRO-03-15-County Population Estimates by Race Alone or in Combination and Hispanic or Latino Origin: July 1, 2002

Source: Population Division, U.S. Census Bureau

Release Date: September 18, 2003

APPENDIX III

Table 3: Annual Estimates of the Population by Sex, Race and Hispanic or Latino Origin for Hawaii: April 1, 2000 to July 1, 2004							
Sex, Race and Hispanic or Latino Origin	Population estimates					April 1, 2000	
	July 1, 2004	July 1, 2003	July 1, 2002	July 1, 2001	July 1, 2000	Estimates base	Census
BOTH SEXES	**1,262,840**	**1,248,755**	**1,234,514**	**1,222,011**	**1,212,109**	**1,211,537**	**1,211,537**
One race	1,009,048	997,566	986,071	976,133	967,862	967,684	967,684
White	334,752	328,768	322,444	316,831	311,896	313,707	313,707
Black	28,105	27,729	26,664	25,127	23,288	23,334	23,334
AIAN	4,299	4,196	4,063	3,926	3,895	3,835	3,835
Asian	527,546	522,447	518,307	515,207	512,776	510,844	510,844
NHPI	114,346	114,426	114,593	115,042	116,007	115,964	115,964
Two or more races	253,792	251,189	248,443	245,878	244,247	243,853	243,853
Race alone or in combination:(1)							
White	519,269	510,804	501,837	493,739	487,054	488,526	488,526
Black	41,327	40,633	39,078	37,001	34,598	34,293	34,293
AIAN	25,981	25,873	25,523	25,198	25,135	25,022	25,022
Asian	727,650	720,884	715,005	710,396	707,160	704,985	704,985
NHPI	279,651	280,013	280,461	281,289	283,116	283,430	283,430
NOT HISPANIC OR LATINO ORIGIN	**1,163,010**	**1,151,167**	**1,140,118**	**1,131,078**	**1,123,900**	**1,123,838**	**1,123,838**
One race	946,684	936,813	927,588	920,163	914,076	914,174	914,174
White	294,558	290,206	286,084	283,008	280,488	282,442	282,442
Black	25,522	25,243	24,275	22,850	21,057	21,132	21,132
AIAN	3,106	2,993	2,841	2,703	2,630	2,609	2,609
Asian	515,241	510,071	505,914	502,724	500,155	498,258	498,258
NHPI	108,257	108,300	108,474	108,878	109,746	109,733	109,733
Two or more races	216,326	214,354	212,530	210,915	209,824	209,664	209,664
Race alone or in combination:(1)							
White	451,016	444,647	438,587	433,779	429,978	431,753	431,753
Black	36,576	36,023	34,620	32,711	30,374	30,235	30,235
AIAN	19,492	19,240	18,785	18,449	18,191	18,179	18,179
Asian	685,468	679,036	673,850	669,773	666,774	664,740	664,740
NHPI	249,238	249,649	250,336	251,296	253,019	253,385	253,385
HISPANIC OR LATINO ORIGIN	**99,830**	**97,588**	**94,396**	**90,933**	**88,209**	**87,699**	**87,699**
One race	62,364	60,753	58,483	55,970	53,786	53,510	53,510
White	40,194	38,562	36,360	33,823	31,408	31,265	31,265
Black	2,583	2,486	2,389	2,277	2,231	2,202	2,202
AIAN	1,193	1,203	1,222	1,223	1,265	1,226	1,226
Asian	12,305	12,376	12,393	12,483	12,621	12,586	12,586
NHPI	6,089	6,126	6,119	6,164	6,261	6,231	6,231
Two or more races	37,466	36,835	35,913	34,963	34,423	34,189	34,189
Race alone or in combination:(1)							
White	68,253	66,157	63,250	59,960	57,076	56,773	56,773
Black	4,751	4,610	4,458	4,290	4,224	4,058	4,058
AIAN	6,489	6,633	6,738	6,749	6,944	6,843	6,843
Asian	42,182	41,848	41,155	40,623	40,386	40,245	40,245
NHPI	30,413	30,364	30,125	29,993	30,097	30,045	30,045
MALE	**630,025**	**624,122**	**617,656**	**611,854**	**608,714**	**608,671**	**608,671**
One race	502,431	497,847	492,753	488,286	485,869	486,093	486,093
White	178,954	176,079	172,715	169,835	167,672	168,681	168,681
Black	16,477	16,384	15,860	15,110	14,203	14,236	14,236
AIAN	2,280	2,236	2,166	2,076	2,057	2,027	2,027
Asian	247,443	245,769	244,517	243,497	243,533	242,753	242,753
NHPI	57,277	57,379	57,495	57,768	58,404	58,396	58,396
Two or more races	127,594	126,275	124,903	123,568	122,845	122,578	122,578
Race alone or in combination:(1)							
White	271,385	267,267	262,594	258,412	255,423	256,231	256,231
Black	23,308	23,059	22,265	21,264	20,043	19,911	19,911
AIAN	13,169	13,145	12,958	12,745	12,686	12,621	12,621
Asian	348,130	345,569	343,418	341,606	341,320	340,349	340,349
NHPI	140,037	140,291	140,604	141,032	142,224	142,322	142,322
NOT HISPANIC OR LATINO ORIGIN	**578,230**	**573,563**	**569,045**	**565,469**	**564,131**	**564,373**	**564,373**
One race	469,133	465,431	461,752	458,941	457,993	458,368	458,368
White	156,665	154,730	152,743	151,477	150,828	151,922	151,922
Black	15,108	15,056	14,567	13,892	13,027	13,077	13,077
AIAN	1,615	1,567	1,493	1,410	1,374	1,363	1,363
Asian	241,507	239,777	238,509	237,461	237,459	236,694	236,694
NHPI	54,238	54,301	54,440	54,701	55,305	55,312	55,312
Two or more races	109,097	108,132	107,293	106,528	106,138	106,005	106,005
Race alone or in combination:(1)							
White	235,241	232,319	229,410	227,307	226,124	227,095	227,095
Black	20,821	20,627	19,937	19,022	17,878	17,822	17,822
AIAN	9,941	9,832	9,624	9,447	9,286	9,279	9,279
Asian	327,496	325,126	323,366	321,902	321,815	320,926	320,926
NHPI	125,046	125,315	125,788	126,354	127,512	127,665	127,665
HISPANIC OR LATINO ORIGIN	**51,795**	**50,559**	**48,611**	**46,385**	**44,583**	**44,298**	**44,298**

One race	33,298	32,416	31,001	29,345	27,876	27,725	27,725
White	22,289	21,349	19,972	18,358	16,844	16,759	16,759
Black	1,369	1,328	1,293	1,218	1,176	1,159	1,159
AIAN	665	669	673	666	683	664	664
Asian	5,936	5,992	6,008	6,036	6,074	6,059	6,059
NHPI	3,039	3,078	3,055	3,067	3,099	3,084	3,084
Two or more races	18,497	18,143	17,610	17,040	16,707	16,573	16,573
Race alone or in combination:(1)							
White	36,144	34,948	33,184	31,105	29,299	29,136	29,136
Black	2,487	2,432	2,328	2,242	2,165	2,089	2,089
AIAN	3,228	3,313	3,334	3,298	3,400	3,342	3,342
Asian	20,634	20,443	20,052	19,704	19,505	19,423	19,423
NHPI	14,991	14,976	14,816	14,678	14,712	14,657	14,657
FEMALE	**632,815**	**624,633**	**616,858**	**610,157**	**603,395**	**602,866**	**602,866**
One race	506,617	499,719	493,318	487,847	481,993	481,591	481,591
White	155,798	152,689	149,729	146,996	144,224	145,026	145,026
Black	11,628	11,345	10,804	10,017	9,085	9,098	9,098
AIAN	2,019	1,960	1,897	1,850	1,838	1,808	1,808
Asian	280,103	276,678	273,790	271,710	269,243	268,091	268,091
NHPI	57,069	57,047	57,098	57,274	57,603	57,568	57,568
Two or more races	126,198	124,914	123,540	122,310	121,402	121,275	121,275
Race alone or in combination:(1)							
White	247,884	243,537	239,243	235,327	231,631	232,295	232,295
Black	18,019	17,574	16,813	15,737	14,555	14,382	14,382
AIAN	12,812	12,728	12,565	12,453	12,449	12,401	12,401
Asian	379,520	375,315	371,587	368,790	365,840	364,636	364,636
NHPI	139,614	139,722	139,857	140,257	140,892	141,108	141,108
NOT HISPANIC OR LATINO ORIGIN	**584,780**	**577,604**	**571,073**	**565,609**	**559,769**	**559,465**	**559,465**
One race	477,551	471,382	465,836	461,222	456,083	455,806	455,806
White	137,893	135,476	133,341	131,531	129,660	130,520	130,520
Black	10,414	10,187	9,708	8,958	8,030	8,055	8,055
AIAN	1,491	1,426	1,348	1,293	1,256	1,246	1,246
Asian	273,734	270,294	267,405	265,263	262,696	261,564	261,564
NHPI	54,019	53,999	54,034	54,177	54,441	54,421	54,421
Two or more races	107,229	106,222	105,237	104,387	103,686	103,659	103,659
Race alone or in combination:(1)							
White	215,775	212,328	209,177	206,472	203,854	204,658	204,658
Black	15,755	15,396	14,683	13,689	12,496	12,413	12,413
AIAN	9,551	9,408	9,161	9,002	8,905	8,900	8,900
Asian	357,972	353,910	350,484	347,871	344,959	343,814	343,814
NHPI	124,192	124,334	124,548	124,942	125,507	125,720	125,720
HISPANIC OR LATINO ORIGIN	**48,035**	**47,029**	**45,785**	**44,548**	**43,626**	**43,401**	**43,401**
One race	29,066	28,337	27,482	26,625	25,910	25,785	25,785
White	17,905	17,213	16,388	15,465	14,564	14,506	14,506
Black	1,214	1,158	1,096	1,059	1,055	1,043	1,043
AIAN	528	534	549	557	582	562	562
Asian	6,369	6,384	6,385	6,447	6,547	6,527	6,527
NHPI	3,050	3,048	3,064	3,097	3,162	3,147	3,147
Two or more races	18,969	18,692	18,303	17,923	17,716	17,616	17,616
Race alone or in combination:(1)							
White	32,109	31,209	30,066	28,855	27,777	27,637	27,637
Black	2,264	2,178	2,130	2,048	2,059	1,969	1,969
AIAN	3,261	3,320	3,404	3,451	3,544	3,501	3,501
Asian	21,548	21,405	21,103	20,919	20,881	20,822	20,822
NHPI	15,422	15,388	15,309	15,315	15,385	15,388	15,388

(1) 'In combination' means in combination with one or more other races. The sum of the five race groups adds to more than the total population because individuals may report more than one race.

Note: The April 1, 2000 Population Estimates base reflects changes to the Census 2000 population from the Count Question Resolution program and geographic program revisions. Dash (-) represents zero or rounds to zero. (X) Not applicable

Abbreviations: Black = Black or African American; AIAN = American Indian and Alaska Native; NHPI = Native Hawaiian and Other Pacific Islander

Suggested Citation:

Table 3: Annual Estimates of the Population by Sex, Race and Hispanic or Latino Origin for Hawaii: April 1, 2000 to July 1, 2004 (SC-EST2004-03-15)

Source: Population Division, U.S. Census Bureau

Release Date: August 11, 2005

This brief Bibliography is a partial listing. Taken from the book, "And They Came" A brief history and annotated Bibliography of Blackls in Hawai`i. (2001) Permission to use research has been granted by the copyright holder and publisher, Miles M. Jackson, PhD, and Kathyrn Waddell Takara, PhD, and editor Ayin M. Adams, PhD.

ARTICLES
(Journals and Magazines)

1. Barbee-Wooten, Daphne. "*The Campbells.*" **The Hawai`i Bar Journal**, October 1999, pp. 99-100.

   A brief article on the late Senator Charles Campbell. Campbell was a successful high school teacher in Honolulu before entering politics full time. For additional information, see **Men and Women of Hawai`i,** 1972.

2. Barbee-Wooten, Daphne E., Valerie Vaz and Andrea Pinkney. "Aloha, Essence Vol. 24, 1994, pp. 11;8.

   Fairly objective and positive article on vacationing in Hawai`i and about African American residents.

3. **Beacon.** "*The Negro in Hawai`i.*" November 1967, pp.49-50.

   An interesting article about long time African Americans residents who lived in Islands for many years. Among those included are Solly Ward Jr., Patt Patterson, And Senator Charles Campbell.

4. *Blacks in Hawai`i: A bibliography.*" (Honolulu: Hawai`i State Library, Hawai`i-Pacific, 1991) 5 p.

   Although this is a brief selection of materials on African Americans in Hawai`i, it is significant and proved to be helpful.

5. Broussard, Albert S. "*Carlotta Stewart Lai, A Black Teacher in the Territory of Hawai`i.*" **The Hawaiian Journal of History**, Vol. 24, 1990, pp. 129-154.

   Carlotta Stewart Lai was a teacher in Hawai`i from 1902 to 1944. Her papers are Deposited with the "Stewart-Flipping Papers" at the Moorland-Spingarn Research Center, Howard University. The above source has photographs of Mrs. Lai on Pages 132,135,141, and 143.

7. Nankivell, Hohn M. **Twenty Fifth Infantry**. (Ft. Collins: The Old Army Press, 1927, 1972), 212 p. This history of the 25th Infantry Regiment covers the period, 1869-1926.

8. Nellist, George, **"William F. Crockett." The Story of Hawai`I and Its Builders**. (Honolulu: Honolulu Star Bulletin, 1925) p. 284.

   Crockett was a successful lawyer before coming to Hawai`i, practicing in Birmingham and Nashville. He was born in Wyeth, Virginia in 1860. His descendants still reside on Maui.

9. Oukrap, Carol. "*Frank Marshall Davis: A Diplomat in Black.*" **Honolulu Record**, Vol.34, March/April, No. 5, 1986, pp. 8-9

   A Tribute to the talents of Davis and his contributions to improve race relations through his work as a journalist.

10. **Paradise of the Pacific**. "*Negroes as Laborers.*" Vol. 10, No.9, 1897, p. 132.

    A proposal by the manager of Ewa plantation to bring 25 African American Families to work on his plantation.

11. Scruggs, Marc. *"Anthony D. Allen: A Prosperous American of African Descent In Early 19ᵗʰ Century Hawai`i."* **The Hawaiian Journal of History**, Vol. 26, 1992, pp. 55-81.

A thoroughly done research study of Anthony Allen, a former slave who settled in Hawai`i in the early 1800s. The work is heavily documented with primary source materials from letters and journals found at the Mission Houses Museum Library, The Hawaiian Historical Society and other historical collections in Boston and New York.

12. Takara, Kathryn W. *"Frank Marshall Davis in Hawai`i. Outsider Journalist Looking In.* **" Social Process in Hawai`i**, Vol. 39, 1999, p. 127-144.

Another perspective of Davis' more than 40 years living in Hawai`i as an African American. See also Professor Takara's dissertation, fire and the Phoenix.

13. _____ *"Rage and Passion in the Poetry of Frank Marshall Davis."*

The Black Scholar, Vol. 26, No. 2, Summer, 1996, pp. 17-26.

An analysis of Davis' poetry and Hawaii's impact on his creativity.

14. _____ (Kay Brundage) *"To Be Black in Paradise."* **Honolulu**,   July 1970, pp. 30-31; 48-50.

15. Gugliotta, Bobette. Nolle **Smith: Cowboy, Engineer, Statesman. (**New York: Dodd, Mead, 1971), 210p.

Nolle Smith and his family came to the new Territory in the early 1900s. Smith Was well respected in business and political circles in Hawai`i. He was one of the few African Americans who played a significant role in the Republican Party of Hawai`i.

16. Vital Statistics Report. (Honolulu: Department of Health State Monitoring, 1998) pp. 59-67. This report g ives recent data on intermarriage. For Blacks it includes intermarriage by ethnicity, age, residence of bride/groom, nationality, etc. Also, included is information on divorce.

17. Takara, Kathryn. Fire and the Phoenix: Frank Marshall Davis. (An American B i o g r a p h y)   H o n o l u l u : University of Hawai`i, 1993( 410 p. PhD. Dissertation. Professor Takara devotes chapters eight and nine (pp. 340-392) to Davis' Hawai`i years and analyzes his creative work during that time.

18. _____ (It Happens All The Time or Does It?**" In Multi-America: Essays on Cultural Wars and Cultural Peace.** (New York: Penguin Books, 1998) pp. 54-65. A sensitive essay on discovering Hawai`i and its Multi-ethnic communities.

19. Siddal, Hohn William, ed. "Maples, William Lineas." In **Men of Hawai`i.** (Honolulu Star Bulletin, 1917) p. 119.

A brief biography of Dr. Maples, a 1892 graduate of Howard University Medical School. He came to Hawai`I in 1901 and was employed in the hospital of the HC&S plantation in Puunene, Maui. Maples passed in 1943 at the age of 73 in Wailuku. (See obituary in Maui Sun, 1/23/43. p.3.)

20. Stephens, Michael J. "The Function of Music" in **Black Churches on O`ahu, Hawai`i as Illustrated at Trinity Baptist Missionary Church.** (Honolulu: University of Hawai`i, 1990) Thesis for M.A. degree. Stephens provides background history of spirituals and gospel music in Black Churches in general and on O`ahu specifically. Trinity is located at Hickam Air Force Base and is attended primarily by Black military families.

21.   African American Organizations in Hawai`i, Final Report (Honolulu: Hawai`i State Foundation on Culture and the Arts, 1990) 3 p.

A survey of African American organizations in Hawai`i and their archives. The survey was conducted by Lorna Peck.

VIDEOS

22.   "Frank Marshall Davis, Writer" Video (30 min.) VHS format, 1987.

A production from the University of Hawaii's Center for Labor Education and Research, Rice and Roses Series.

23.   "Hawaii's African Americans Video (30 min.) KHET, 1993.

24.   "Racism and the Law" Video (50 min.) January 1991. Attorney Daphne Barbee-Wooten discusses discrimination against African Americans in Hawai`i.

25.   "Racist Speech and the First Amendment Rights" Video (60 min.) Discussants are Haunani-Kay Trask, Chuck Lawrernce, and Rustam Barbee of the Afro American Lawyers Association of Hawai`i.

26.   Takara, Kathryn W. "Amazing Grace: An Interview with Maya Angelou." November 16, 1994. KHET (30 min.). Dr. Angelou discusses the meaning of Hawai`i to her and recalls her visits to Hawai`i as an entertainer in the 1950s.

Further Research and other Sources

For further research and other sources about African Americans in Hawai`i, researchers Can review Robert Langdon's Whaling Logbooks and Journal, 1613-1927. Langdon's work provides an index to the Hawaiian ports and names of whalers and ships that were located in more than 40 libraries and private collections outside of Hawai`i. The University of Hawaii'sHawaiian/Pacific Collection holds most of the logbooks on microfilm.

27.   MISSION HOUSES MUSEUM LIBRARY

The Museum and Library are part of the Hawaiian Mission Children's Society. The library has an extensive collection from missionaries who came to the Hawaiian Islands for the Board of Commissioners for Foreign Missions. Unpublished materials include letters, diaries, journals, and special reports by missionaries.

28.   HAWAIIAN HISTORICAL SOCIETY, Honolulu

The Society was organized in 1892 and is dedicated to collecting and preserving historical materials related to Hawai`i. It sponsors scholarly research pertaining to Hawaiian history. The Society publishes *Hawaiian Journal of History* and has sponsored some monographs. The manuscript collection includes letters, journals, diaries, unpublished manuscripts and research notes. *The Journal* encouraged the research on Anthony Allen and Carlotta Stewart Lai and published both manuscripts.

29.   HAWAI`I STATE ARCHIVES, Honolulu

The Hawai`i State Archives are potentially a rich resource for pre-annexation Hawai`i. Researchers should consult the Archive's own publications, especially Hawai`i State Archives. Government Records Inventory, Vital Statistics, Vols. 17 and 28. This important guide includes the years 1826-1950. Other volumes cover name index, tax records, voting records, naturalization and ship records.

30.   THE U.S. ARMY MUSEUM OF HAWAI`I, Honolulu

Museum's library is small, but has a rich collection of photographs of African Americans serving in the U.S. Army as early as 1910. There are rare photographs of the 25th Infantry Regiment at Schofield Barracks. A few books and newspaper clippings help document African American soldiers in Hawai`i.

31.   BISHOP MUSEUM, Honolulu, Hawai`i

The Museum's archives cover Hawai`i and the Pacific and consists of a wide variety of resources for research. The collections include: (1) art, (2) audio, (3) manuscripts, (4) maps, (5) films, (6) museum archives of archeological reports and field notes, and (7) photographs from 1840 to date, including the outstanding On Char Collection…There are published diaries, narratives and memoirs relation to the 18th and 19th century Hawai`i. The online catalog and indexes can be reached at: www.bishopmuseum.org.

INDEX

A

Adams, Alice – 191,
Adams, Ayin M. – i, ii, iii-v, vii, viii, ix, x, xii, xiii, 27, 28, 41, 139, 157, 168, 169, 172, 173, 174, 175, 176, 177, 178, 185, 186, 199, 204, 208,
Adisa, Opal Palmer – 167,
Adrianne, – 191,
African American Heritage Foundation of Maui – 184,
African American National Biography – vii, 198,
African American Society of Long Beach – 196,
African American Organizations in Hawai'i, – 170,
Agrawal, Karunesh Kumar – xii,
Alethea, – 189,
Alexander, Archie – 24,
Alfred, – 189,
Alima, – 180,
Allen, Anthony D. – 4, 205,
Allen, Lorenzo – 176,
Allen, Toni – 176,
Alolo, Luther – 64,
Amico, Alfred – 189,
Amico, Amazon – 178,
Amico, Sofia – 178,
Amico, Tenee – 178, 189,
Amina, – 180,
Amos, Wally, (Famous) – 76,
Anderson, Audrey Fox – 73,
Angelou, Maya – 167, 206,
Anthony, – 189,
Arakawa, Alan – 172,
Araki-Regan, Lynn – 172,
Ariyoshi, Koji – 47,
Ashley, Baia – 97,
Axelrod, David – 107,

B

Bailey, Devery – 182,
Ball, Alice – 28, 29, 64,
Ball, James P., Jr. – 28,
Ball, James P., Sr. – 28,
Banks, Sir Joseph – 10,

Barack Obama Campaign – 199,
Barbee-Wooten, Daphne – 204, 206,
Barbee, Rustam – 206,
Beach Boys, (The) – 155,
Bedford, Joseph, (Joe Dollar) – 4,
Beechert, - 56,
Ben, – 188,
Berger, Henry – 5,
Berry, Halle – 155, 160,
Biden, Joe – 99, 107,
Bingham, Hiram – 19,
Binns, Frederick E. – 4,
Black Jack, (Keaka'ele'ele) – 4,
Blaine, (U.S. Sec. of State) – 5,
Boki, (Gov.) – 4,
Bonk-Abramson, Keiko – 34,
Boone, Ben Isaiah – 179,
Boone, Julian Marcus – 179,
Boone, Nara – 152, 179,
Boyce, Denise – 75,
Braggs, Alphonso – 76, 163, 190,
Brennan, – 180, 181,
Bridges, Harry – 48, 56,
Broussard, Albert S. – 204,
Brundage, Kay – 205,
Brundage, Karla – 69,
Buffalo Soldiers – 66, 67, 68, 69,
Burnett, Cassandra – 72,
Bush, George W. – 99, 100, 103, 160,
Butler, (Mr.) – 19,
Butler, Mary Dell – 198,

C

Campbell, Charles – 204,
Carmichael, Stokely, (Kwame Ture) – 167,
Carver, George Washington – 68,
Cathey, Jimmy – 190,
Cevallos, Dean – 37,
Chamberlain, Levi – 20,
Chappell, Arid – xii, 155, 158, 191, 192,
Chaucer – 33,
Cheney, Dick – 99,
Christian, Barbars – 167,
Clarence, – 191,
Clasby, Reuben – 18,

Clayborne, Betty, (Bala) – 164, 191,
Clegg, Legrand H. – iv,
Clinton, Bill – 99, 100,
Clinton, Hillary Rodham – 96, 99,
Connor, Ed – 179,
Cook, (Captain) – 10, 54,
Cook, James – v,
Cooper, Ann Nixon – 109,
Corley, Brian – 180,
Cottrill, Charles – 15, 29,
Coulombe, Maggie – 155, 158,
Courier, Roberta – 161,
Covington, Kelly – 151,
Crockett, Annie V. – 12, 70, 71,
Crockett, Wendell Frank – 6, 12,
Crockett, William F. – 7, 8, 12, 204,
Curtis, David – 5,

D
Daggett, John – 35,
Danks, Bill – 167,
Davenport, Calvin Jerome – 158, 183,
Davenport, Shirley Jean – xii, 158, 183,
David, - 93,
Davis, Angela – 167,
Davis, Frank Marshall – vii, xiii, 44, 45, 46, 47, 48, 49, 50, 51, 52, 53, 54, 55, 56, 57, 58, 59, 60, 167, 168, 204, 205, 206,
Davis, Jefferson – 142,
Day, Aaron L. – i, vii, viii, xii, xiii, 196, 197, 198, 199,
Day, Theodore A. – 198,
Day, Thomas J. – 197,
Dean, Howard – 99,
Deliasantos, Lesley – 164,
Devine, Loretta – 155,
Digman, Robert – 176,
Drake, Diana L. (Dee) – 154, 191,
Dunham, Madelyn Lee Payne – 124, 132,
Dunham, Stanley Armour – 121, 124, 132,
Durbin, Dick – 81, 99,
E
Eaglin, Chadd – 146,
Edwards, John – 84,

Epstein, Henry – 45,
Evarts, Jeremiah – 18,
Ezekiel, - 93,

F
Faulkner, William – 94,
Farrakhan, Louis T. – 65,
Fitzpatrick, Colleen – 94
Fong, Hiram Leong – 26,
French, L. Jimmy – 164, 165, 191,

G
G, Kenny – 162,
Garrett, Marva Chaney – 71,
Gates, Henry Louis, Jr. – vii,
Gibo, Claire – xii,
Gilliam, Arthur – 171,
Gilman, Hokuoka'ale – 153,
Gilman, Kenyavani (Pema Wangmo) – 153, 154, 192,
Gilman, Robert – 153, 154,
Gilman, Matthew – 153,
Golden, Ernest – 76,
Goliath, - 93,
Gooding, Cuba, Jr. – 16,
Govinda, Gloria – 190,
Govinda, Michael – 190,
Green, Ashbel – 18,
Green, Dwight – 176,
Green, (Rev.) – 19
Griffin, Devin – 183,
Griffin, Richard – 183,
Groffey, Frieda – xii
Guglietta, Bobette – 28, 205,
Guttman, Delores – 170, 190,
Gyaltsen, Lama – 162,

H
Hale, Helene Hilyer – xii, xiii, 32, 33, 34, 35, 36, 38, 39, 40, 41, 42, 43, 65, 71, 194, 195, 197, 199,
Hale, William, Jr. – 32,
Hale, William, III – 194,
Hall, Jack – 47,
Hall, Melissa B. – 165,
Hanohano, Faye – 37, 42,

Harrison, Judy D. – 159, 190,
Hass, (Admiral) – 142,
Hatcher, Terri – 155,
Hayashi, Yoshimi – 165,
Hekes, Bob – 36,
Henderson, Patricia – 155, 156, 190, 199,
Hennessey, Martin Charles, (Marty Dread) – 152,
Henry of the Congo – 9,
Higginbotham, Evelyn Brooks – vii,
Hill, Alalani – xii, 174, 199,
Hill, Joe – 145,
Hilton, Paris – 155,
Hilyer, Andrew – 32,
Hilyer, Ellen – 32,
Hilyer, Gale – 32,
Ho, Jack – 37,
Hodges, Harold – 181,
Hodges, Sheries – 181,
Hoggard, John T. – 163,
Hood, Ernest – 144,
Hood, Marshall Kelvin – 142, 144,
Horton, Eric – 37,
Hose, Peter – 143,
Hostos, Eugene – 165,
Houston, Whitney – 162,
Hurston, Zora Neale – 169, 208,

I

Ingram, Bobby – 177, 178,
Isis – x,

J

Jackson, Michael – 162,
Jackson, Miles M. – iii, xii, xiii, 29, 74, 197, 204,
Jagger, Thomas Augustus – 67,
Jaime, – 179,
Jefferson, Thomas – 49,
Jesus – 54,
Jones, John Coffin – 19,
Johnson, Andrea – 176,
Johnson, Charles – 5,
Johnson, George Marion – 150,
Johnson, Gwen – 75,

Johnson, James Weldon – 2,
Johnson, John Rosamond – 2,
Johnson, William – 4,
Joyner, MarshaRose – 142, 143, 144, 145, 146,
Jose' de Sucre, Jose – 25,

K

Kalanimoku, (Prime Minister) –
Kamo'oula, William – 19,
Keaka'ele'ele – 4,
Keakana, (family) – 50,
Kendall, Kyra-Denise – 176,
Kennedy, Faye – 75,
Kennedy, John F. – 103,
Kennedy, Ted – 99,
Kenoi, Billy – 37,
Kerry, John – 82, 83, 84,
King, Donnie – 183,
King Kamehameha, I – v, 4, 20,
King Kamehameha, II – 4,
King Kamehameha, III – 5,
King Liholiho – 18,
King, Martin Luther, Jr. – viii, xiv, 28, 65, 97, 145, 146, 152, 157, 158, 161, 162, 164, 166, 172, 174, 175, 176, 178, 181, 182, 199,
King, Martin Luther, III – 65,
King, SaEeda – 173,
Kitt, Eartha – 155,
Kiyota, Richard – 194,
Kokubu n, Russell – 37,
Kristofferson, Kris – 152,
Krout, Mary H. – v,

L

Lacey, Glen – 180, 181,
Laden, Osama bin, - 103,
Lai , Carlotta Stewart – 12, 204,
Lai, Yum Kim – 12,
Lama, Dalai – 161,
Landon, Allan R. – 29,
Langdon, Robert – 206,
Lau, Myrtle – 12,
Lawrence, Chuck – 206,
Lincoln, Abraham – 87,

Little Jo Jo – 188,
Lohan, Lindsay – 155,
Loomis, Elisha – 19,
Lorde, Audre – 167, 169, 208,
Lorraine, – 189,
Love, Earl, Sr. – 176, 177, 178,
Lowery, Joseph E. – 2,
Lugar, Dick – 88,

M
MacAllister, John – 146,
Mackey, Charles T. – 171,
Mahesh, Maharishi – 164,
Mango, Judy – 194,
Maples, Edward – 12,
Maples, Elizabeth – 13,
Maples, Gladys – 13,
Maples, Sadie Williams – 13,
Maples, Samuel – 12,
Maples, William Lineas – 6, 12, 13, 205,
Margaret, Ann – 155,
Marin, Carlos Andre – 25,
Marley, Bob – 66, 152, 157,
McCain, John – 96, 100, 101, 102, 103, 104, 107,
McDonald, Jewel – 158, 191,
McElrath, Ah Quon – 47, 50,
McFadden, Marsha – 75,
Mengesha, Carol – 71,
Miller, Doris, (Dorie) – 16, 17,
Mills, Lionel – 155,
Mills, Sodengi Camille Orimaladi – xii, 154, 155, 173, 177, 185, 186,
Mills, Wahkimba – 155,
Mink, Patsy –
Mitchell, James Oliver – 13,
Molina, (Mr.) – 150,
Montalvo, Elder Juan, (Windcloud) – 180,
Moore, Bobbie – 176,
Moore, Terri – 153, 188,
Moses, - 93,
Mottl, Iwalani Smith (Sneidman) – xiii, 22, 23, 26, 27, 28, 72,
Mrantz, Maxine – v,
Muktananda, Swami – 154,

Mya, – 189,

N
NAACP – 171,
Naeole, Emily – 37, 42,
Na'ope, George –36,
Namkhar, Lama – 162,
Nankivell, Hohn M. – 204,
Naranjo, Manuel – 25,
Nawang, Lama – 162,
Neal, Bryant – xii, 17, 156, 157, 175, 177, 180, 184,
Neal, Debbie – 157,
Neal, James – 171,
Neal, Lucille – 171,
Neal, Olivia – 157,
Nefertiti – x,
Nellist, George – 204,
Nelson, - 171,
Nelson, Rick – 155,
Nicholson, Charles – 4,
Nicole, Cherisse – 158,
Nimitz, Chester W. – 16,
Nixon, Pat – 24
Nixon, Richard – 24, 36,
Noll, Esterene – 173,
Norbu, Thinley – 162,

O
Obama, Barack, H. – i, vii, ix, x, xiii, 42, 44, 75, 79, 80, 81, 82, 83, 84, 85, 86, 87, 89, 90, 91, 92, 93, 94, 95, 96, 97, 98-105, 106-110, 111-115, 116-139, 169, 181, 182,
Obama, Barack, Sr. – 79, 81, 119, 129, 131,
Obama, Malia – 80, 99, 107, 126, 134, 136,
Obama, Michelle – 79, 99, 102, 107, 125, 126, 127, 133, 134, 135, 136, 137, 138, 139, 193,
Obama, Sasha – 80, 99, 107, 126, 134, 136,
Ogunelese, Adesina – 27, 28, 157, 174, 184, 185, 187, 199,
Oliver, Elizabeth Murphy – 142,

Oliver, Jacob B. – 142, 143,
Oliver, John – 142,
Oliver, Stephanie Stokes – 146,
Omar, Adisa – 174, 178,
Organizing for America – 199,
Osborn, Michael – 18,
Osiris – x,
Oukrap, Carol – 204,

P
Paige, Gina - viii, 89,
Palin, Sarah – 107,
Parker, Pat – 208,
Patterson, Patt – 204,
Patton, George – 91, 101,
Pharaoh, - 93,
Pinkney, Andrea – 204,
Plouffe, David – 107,
Poindexter, Joseph – 143,
Potter, Rodney – 156,
Prentice, Cassandra – 176,
Purdy, - 23,
Purter, Gloria – 164, 190,

Q
Queen Ka'ahumanu – 4,
Queen Kamamalu – 19,
Queen Keopuolani – 19,
Queen of Sheeba – x,
Queen Lili' uokalani – v, vi, 28, 68, 174,
178, 181,

R
Ra, Chaka – 160,
Rainey, George – 151, 152, 190,
Rainey, Naomi – 198,
Rainey, Terry – 151, 190,
Rangdrol, Cherisse – 186,
Rangdrol, Lama Choyin – 161, 162, 163,
186, 192,
Ray, Doris I. – 72,
Reagan, Ronald – 95,
Reed, Ishmael – 167,
Reddy, Helen – 155,
Richards, William – 19,
Richardson, William S. – 165,

Richie, Lionel – 162,
Richmond, Thomas – 10,
Rider, Alalani Le'ohu – 172,
Rinpoche, Jamgon Konetrul – 154,
Rinpoche, Kalu – 154,
Rinpoche, Khenpo Orgyen Tinly
(Khenpo Chozod) – 162,
Rinpoche, Lama Tharchin – 162,
Rippy, John Stan – xii, 150, 180, 182,
Rippy, Loraine Noll – 150, 173, 182,
Roberts, Patricia – 180, 181,
Robeson, Paul – 46, 48,
Robin & daughter – 188,
Robinson, Abigail – 176,
Robinson, Konjit – 176,
Robo, Ed – 47,
Roosevelt, Theodore – 67,
Runions, Martha Jane – 12,

S
Sabrina, – 186,
Schofield, George Wheeler – 67,
Schofield, John McCallister – 67,
Schuler, George – 67,
Scott, Mildred – 198,
Scruggs, Marc – 205,
Shaheed, Khalil Yeamie Toure, Jr. –
165, 190,
Shakespeare – 33, 161,
Shamus, - 82,
Shattuck, America – 5,
Shawhan, Sandra – xii, 160, 173,
Shepperd, Earl (Sundance) – 153,
Short, Walter – 143,
Siddal, Hohn William – 205,
Silvera, Frank – 168,
Simpson, O. J. – 96,
Simmons, Winifred – 73,
Simms, Sandra A. – 165, 166, 190,
Sisson, J'aime Martinique Ka'iminaniloa
Kawaioneokekai -
157,
Small, David – 185,
Small, Mariah – 185,
Smith, Eva Beatrice Jones – 24, 25, 26,
28,

Smith, Leinani Patricia – 23, 26,
Smith, Marie – 76, 173,
Smith, Melissa Boulware – 26,
Smith, Nolle, Jr. – 26,
Smith, Nolle R., Sr. – xiii, 22 , 23, 24, 25, 26, 28, 29, 205,
Smith, Silas Peter – 26
Smith, Sookie Kim – 23
Smith, Tsulan – 23,
Soetoro, Alma – 107,
Soetoro, Ann Dunham–Obama – 79, 81, 119, 130, 131,
Soetoro, Lolo – 79, 130,
Soetoro, Maya – 107, 130, 148, 187,
Soussa, John Phillips – 161,
Spraggins, Linda – 180,
St. Francis of Assisi – 153,
St. John, Kedar – 174,
Stafford, E. I. – 171,
Stan, – 188,
Steinback, (Gov.) – 50,
Stephens, Michael J. – 205,
Stewart, Carlotta – 5, 6,
Stewart, Charles Samuel – 5, 6, 18, 19, 20, 21,
Stewart, T. McCants – 6, 12,
Stockton, Betsey – vii, xiii, 5, 18, 19, 21, 70,
Stockton, Robert – 18
Stokes, Charles M. – 146, 149,
Stone, W. Clements – 150,
Sundance, Earl – 173, 174, 175, 180, 181, 185, 187, 189,
Sundance, Tiona – 174, 181, 187,

T
Taft, William – 15,
Takara, Kathryn Waddell – i iii, ix, xi, xii, xiii, 4, 15, 18, 29, 49, 61, 62, 63, 64, 65, 66, 67, 68, 69, 70, 71, 72, 73, 74, 75, 76, 167, 168, 170, 194, 199, 204, 205, 206,
Taylor, Deborah – 154, 190,
Taylor, Charles – 153,
Taylor, Lawrence – 153, 191, 199,
Taylor, LeClaire – 153,

Taylor, Terence – 154,
Teabo, Shirlee – xii,
Thubten, Tulku, (Anam Thubten) – 154, 162,
Thurston, Lorrin A. – 67,
Tina, – 186,
Tinley, Khenpo Yurmed – 162,
Torres, Rosaria Regina – 185,
Trask, Haunani-Kay – 206,
Tshombe, Fulton – 178,
Tucker, Angelique – 40, 42,
Tucker, Essie – 197,
Tucker, Marcus O. – 40, 42,
Tucker, Indira Hale – i, vii, viii, xii, xiii, 32, 33, 34, 35, 40, 42, 194, 196, 198, 199,
Tunkara, Leah – 160, 178, 187, 188,

U
Uchiyama, Mahealani – 158, 190,

V
Valentine, Andrew – 173,
Vaz, Valerie – 204,
Vegas, Roland – 173,
Vern, – 188, 189,

W
Waddell, William H. – 68, 69, 194,
Wagner, Mary – 173,
Walker, Alice – 167,
Walker, Rebecca – 162,
Waller, Fleming R – 171,
Wanda, – 189,
Wangmo, Kama Yeshe – 162,
Ward, Solly, Jr. – 204
Ware, Caroline – 173,
Washington, Booker T. – 5, 8,
Washington, George – 49,
Watu, Marie – 173,
Alexander, White – 176,
White, Brandon – 178,
White, Naimu – 178,
White, Elisa Joy – 75,
Wildy, Clarissa – 64,
Wilheim, Gene – 36,

William the Baker – 4,
Winn, Jim – 181,
Wilson, Woodrow – 15, 142,
Winfrey, Oprah – ix,
Williams, Vannessa – 155,
Wolper, David – 161,
Wooten, Daphne-Barbee – 146, 147,
148, 149, 150, 204,
Wooten, Andre' – 145, 146, 147, 148,
149,
Wright, Jeremiah – 92, 93, 94, 96,
Wright, Richard – 169, 208,
Wyatt, George W. – 5,
Wyatt , Z'ma – xii, 199,

X

Y
Yager, Bret – 36,
Yarratt, Wm. – 72
Yates, Wanda – 159, 186,
Yuhudah, Yoellah

About the Author

Ayin Adams is a performance artist, inspirational teacher and spiritual healer.

Author of more than 5 volumes of poetry books, Ayin is published by *"Women in the Moon"* Publishing, *Bum Rush, The Page, In The Family*, and *Quiet Mountain Essays*. Ayin is the winner of numerous awards and grants, including the *Pat Parker Poetry Prize, The Audre Lorde Memorial Prose Prize*, and *the Zora Neal Hurston/Richard Wright Award*.

Ayin's writing is dynamic, stimulating, and thought provoking. Ayin believes writing emotionally weave the bonds of sisterhood/brotherhood in a world that would kill her if she did not fight with her words, dreams, and her spiritual position. Ayin believes that everyone has the wherewithal to surpass oneself by suiting up, showing up and following through. She makes her home on Maui where she writes daily, teaches, counsels and enjoys nature.

I live beyond that which the world tells me is probable and most likely to happen. With a positive attitude of gratitude, nothing can get in the way of my forward movement. My life is one of growth, expansion, and creative possibilities". ~ Ayin Adams